Big Flavours & Rough Edges

Recipes from the Eagle

David Eyre and the Eagle cooks

**With photographs by Jason Lowe
and illustrations by Chloe Cheese**

HEADLINE

First published in 2001
by HEADLINE BOOK PUBLISHING

10 9 8 7 6 5 4 3 2 1

British Library Cataloguing in Publication Data
Eyre, David
Big flavours, rough edges
1. Cookery
I. Title
641.5
ISBN 0 7472 7229 8

Printed and bound by
Canale & C. Spa, Italy

Copy-edited by Jane Middleton
Designed by Jon Kennedy
Compiled by Ruth Quinlan
Edited by Lindsay Symons

HEADLINE BOOK PUBLISHING
A division of Hodder Headline
338 Euston Road
London NW1 3BH

www.headline.co.uk
www.hodderheadline.com

Thank you to Mike for holding it all together!

Contents

Foreword by Kathryn Flett   6

Introduction   8

Biographies   10

Soups   12

Light Dishes   33

Pasta and Rice   65

Fish   93

Meat   109

Side Dishes   141

Index   157

6

I don't like pubs, but I love the Eagle.

When I first came to work in London EC1 in the early 1990s the area wasn't exactly the gastrohub and oasis of grooviness it is now – though it certainly seemed to have its own microclimate. Before the designer loft explosion, back in the days when Exmouth Market was scented by Special Brew rather than Calvin Klein, my memory of life in and around the Farringdon Road is of a relentlessly dour raininess, with lunchtimes posing a considerable challenge to those of us for whom a sad sandwich or pie didn't exactly hit the spot.

I cannot imagine what life must have been like for the hungry worker with pernickety tastebuds in Farringdon pre-Eagle, but my generation got very lucky when, in 1991, the local pub evolved into a kind of London 'Cheers' with knobs on. At the Eagle not only did everybody know your name, they also knew that you were very particular about consuming your luncheon sausage and mash or steak sandwich with a dollop of Dijon mustard. And, in no uncertain terms, they'd roll their eyes and tell you to bring your own. If you *must*.

Situated on a glamour-lite corner site opposite a fine example of NCP car park vernacular architecture, the Eagle boasted charm in abundance. Admittedly this was a bull****-free rough-edged sort of urban charm, but it was a charm to be cherished. And now, a decade down the line, the Eagle has changed barely at all, which is a compliment because, I think, one of the things that makes a great pub is a sense of continuity. While time might have been expected to erase all traces of previous staff, menus and punters, at the Eagle this just isn't the case – the walls may get a paint job every year, but it's always the same comfy shade of clotted cream. And it may be that hundreds of wooden chairs have died and been replaced (indeed I may even have despatched one or two of them myself in moments of extreme exhaustion and emotion), but new furniture for the sake of new furniture? Fashion for the hell of it? Not at the Eagle – and thank God for that.

And the food. At the Eagle I have eaten something approaching tons of very fine, no-fuss modern food: zingy salt cod, delicately aromatic pastas, robust and (literally) heartwarming soups, not to mention countless steaks, chickens, salads and sausages... meals characterised by David Eyre's original culinary blueprint: top quality ingredients prepared with exemplary ease and simplicity and served in satisfyingly old-fashioned portions. It seems extraordinary, but just a decade ago these were rare and elusive qualities in London dining and completely unheard of within the context of pub dining. In the early 1990s, of course, London was in a recession and it is no exaggeration to say that the Eagle pioneered a welcome move away from the excesses of the previous decade.

It was goodbye to the sort of foodie fads which saw £100 per head meals of midget portions, au revoir to nouvelle cuisine and a very big hello to modern comfort food.

On a personal note, while I was editing *Arena* magazine between 1992 and 1995, the Eagle was the staff canteen of our dreams – here meetings were conducted, copy written and edited, arguments raged, staff departures mourned, staff arrivals celebrated... The Eagle was so much a part of the fabric of our working lives that it seemed entirely logical to ask David Eyre to write the magazine's food column. At that time the idea of a regular cookery slot in a men's glossy magazine was still pretty left-field. We were soon vindicated, however, because suddenly everybody was at it – cooking was the new sex (if not actually the new rock'n'roll) and sometimes David even met his deadlines. Happy days! Then, in 1995, I left *Arena* and moved all the way across the Farringdon Road to the *Observer*. At the time a friend of mine suggested that a prime motivation in taking the job was 'so you can still have lunch at the Eagle'. Well, *obviously*.

In the last ten years I have quenched numerous cruel thirsts with a glass of Chilean Chardonnay and sated innumerable yawning hungers with the most satisfying Eagle meals. For me, the Eagle has provided many of the finest flavours, tastes and smells during a decade of working and playing, loving and losing, crying and laughing and, it must be said, occasionally falling over. Particularly on the way downstairs to the lavatory. Thanks, then, to David and Michael and the ever-evolving Eagle team spirit. Believe me, it really can't be beat – and now, with the arrival of *Big Flavours and Rough Edges*, we can all take it home and eat it too.

Kathryn Flett, August 2000

Introduction

I've always been more than a little bemused about

why the Eagle was regarded as such a radical notion when it opened, and then how it became so influential in changing what we all now expect from a pub. To my partner, Mike Belben, and me, it was always obvious that simple, intelligent food was what London pubs lacked. 1990 was not a happy time for many London restaurants: the recession was hurting badly and, notwithstanding our desperation to have our own restaurant, we just couldn't see how a medium-sized, medium-priced operation could make any money. Rents and premiums were ridiculous, the costs of providing all the expected trappings of service couldn't be justified, and it was illegal to sell alcohol to anyone not eating a full meal. Besides, we didn't have the minimum of £250,000 needed to open a simple restaurant. Fortunately, in the wake of the Monopolies and Mergers Commission's ruling on the major breweries' tenanting practices, there was for the first time a number of pubs available with new-style leases.

The Eagle was the first and cheapest dead pub we found. The lack of trade was such that we had to stand on tables outside peering over dark curtains at the gloom within. But beneath the sad grime we could see an attractive, if small, room with huge windows and a maple floor. It also had the fine brick facade of an early Truman corner-sited pub. Three weeks later we had our cheeky offer accepted by the outgoing lessees, had taken out a small bank loan and borrowed a further £5,000 from each of our families. My brother became the only employee, and after three weeks of scrubbing and throwing out standard brewery pub kit we had our opening night.

There was a major constraint on our aim of providing my idea of pub food. The existing kitchen behind the bar measured 8 feet by 5 feet. There was a kitchen in the flat – well, it had an oven – but on the ground floor all we had was a small domestic fridge, a small microwave, a small eye-level grill of sorts, a domestic sink and a two-burner hob. It was early January and it would be Easter before we could afford to stretch the bar to make the kind of kitchen we needed. No matter, the menu would have a soup; sausages bought twice daily from the established Italian grocer's, Gazzano & Son, next door; crostini from the grill, loaded with vegetables patiently cooked under the same grill all morning; a steak sandwich from my Mozambique childhood cooked on one of the burners (the other was needed for our Vesuvian coffee pots); a salad of some kind; and from the flat at 12.30 would come a casserole and an oven dish.

Into this came our first chef, Pedro, via the River Café, and together we would somehow cook up to 80 lunches before having to shop for the evening. But the Eagle's food really took off after that Easter, with a kitchen that now had a chargrill, a cooker and a proper fridge. Shortly after, we gained a prep room downstairs, but the kitchen still had space for only two cooks. The menu's key feature has thus remained one-plate eating – the argument being that if two cooks were required to cook 120 lunches in 120 minutes, then this would preclude starters and desserts; besides it was to remain a pub, and not become a restaurant.

As the reviews started coming in (we made excellent copy), we were approached by some brilliant suppliers. We were now able to access fantastic Spanish, Italian and Portuguese products, and fish came in from several small outfits, but I am most thankful for the arrival of Greg Wallace and Terry Bailey of George Allans Greengrocers. Remember that as recently as 1991, chefs just couldn't get the stuff they use today. These guys eschewed the carrots and baking potatoes mentality of New Covent Garden. Herbs arrived in vast bunches, tomatoes and peppers were ripened on a vine in some sunny land and not in a Dutch hothouse, tiny purple artichokes and fat wet garlic were seen for the first time. And then the quality of the chefs that came to me for a job: some had had years of professional experience but were anxious to leave the hierarchies and tedium of the then-mainstream kitchens; others had never worked in a kitchen but were desperate to. Most (like myself) were 'self-taught', but all had that essential passion for eating real food and, regardless of their ability, all of them were necessarily dropped into the thick of it – the kitchen had space for only two cooks, remember. Nearly all the cooks that have passed through the Eagle's kitchen are still cooking and an awful lot of them have their own establishments. It is their influences that have shaped the kitchen's repertoire. The maxim, 'Big Flavours and Rough Edges', is paraphrased from an early review in the *Sunday Times*. Jonathan Meades was, I suspect, qualifying an otherwise favourable column but I've always taken the description to be flattering and perfectly apt. The kitchen still has space for only two, the menu still changes every day, and the Eagle is still a pub that happens to serve grilled scallops instead of microwaved scampi.

I'd like to dedicate this book to all who have worked at the Eagle P.H.; to the customers who have been keen but unwitting guinea pigs whilst we were learning lots; and to my mother, who taught me what good food should be in the middle of nowhere in colonial Mozambique.

David Eyre, July 2000

Biographies

AMANDA PRITCHETT worked at the Eagle from mid 1991 until she left to open the Lansdowne, in north London, the following year. She'd often stay in the spare bedroom when working back-to-back shifts, which generally meant that by the time I had dragged myself out of bed Amanda would have already knocked up several tarts and a pissaladière and a casserole would be well on its way. She remains one of the finest cooks I know, which is reflected in the style and quality of the Lansdowne.

PEDRO CHAVES was our first employee, having arrived from the River Café in Hammersmith. From him we learnt pasta lore, and his method for cooking dried haricots is the standard. He has a legendary sweet tooth, and real puddings have never really featured on our menus since he left to live in Germany (*the* place for cream cakes). He now lives in Washington.

TRISH HILFERTY came from Australia via the Brackenbury restaurant in west London, where she learnt to scratch cook properly, butchering whole animals. She loves using offal and was occasionally seen dismembering pigs' heads, which caused excitement amongst punters and staff alike. She's immensely capable, down to earth and popular.

POLA WICKHAM worked at the Eagle during 1992 before leaving for art school in New York, where she supported herself by catering for private dinners. She then worked at the very influential Chez Panisse restaurant in Berkeley, California.

JEMIMA BURRILL came to us with Pola, they being long-time buddies. It was a memorable time when the two of them decorously controlled the salads and pastas. She is currently at Chelsea College of Art and Design.

BRAD FOXWELL is our newest recruit and makes delicious stews with great gusto and loads of booze.

PHIL PICKERING was for some time our longest-serving cook. Between 1992 and 1995 he brought his Kiwi good nature and graft – the type always ready to pick up a shift – becoming the soup and stew specialist. He has now returned to New Zealand.

CARLOS VARGAS arrived in 1994 via Venezuela and Andalucia, speaking barely a dozen words of English. Spanish and Gaditano classics taught to him by his grandmother quickly found their way on to the Eagle's blackboards. Easily the sexiest cook to work behind our counter, he headed the kitchen after I left at the end of 1997 and now runs the Commissary at Holborn Studios, London. If ever you need a paella cooked in a field or after a fashion show, he's your man.

JAKE HODGES worked with us in 1995 and 1996, between leaving the River Café and opening the award-winning Moro restaurant in Clerkenwell. One of the best cooks to work in the Eagle kitchen, he taught us a lot. He now has the terrific Cígala in Bloomsbury.

PAULO SANTOS comes from Bahia, Brazil. Between 1995 and 1996 he combined his serious and accurate approach to simple cooking with the laidback charm that a tropical upbringing provides. Capoeira flip-flaps performed in the bar at closing time had to be seen to be believed. He returned to the pub in 2000 and now works with Jake at Cígala.

It would be hard to imagine the Eagle without **RUTH QUINLAN**. Some days she can be found in the bar, the kitchen and even the office, where she both masterminded and compiled this book. She is as keen a traveller as cook, and always returns from trips abroad with new and exciting dishes to try.

KATE LEWIS previously worked at Baker & Spice in Knightsbridge. She has a great eye for colour and contrasts in food, particularly vegetable dishes – it was Kate who introduced *escalivada* to our repertoire. She now runs a freelance catering business.

FULVIA MARCONI learnt her cooking from her grandmother in Italy and brought some excellent ideas with her. She now manages Studio 6 bar, near Waterloo.

TOM NORRINGTON-DAVIES has run the Eagle's kitchen since 1998. A protégé of the indomitable Carla Tomasi, he's a bit of a north Italian specialist. He elevates vegetarian cooking from the prissy to the hardcore. I will always be grateful that the stance of the kitchen has remained intact in his hands.

JORGE CARDOSO is from Lisbon. He reinforced the Portugueseness of our menu, gently chiding when the authenticity of our *feijoadas* and *caldeiradas* fell short. The pub is never too busy for him – his cool remains unruffled, especially when the joint is jumping and the grill is chokka.

GEORGE MANNERS was at the Eagle in 1996 and 1997, having toured every front-of-house job in restaurants from London to Paris, San Francisco to Sydney. Charming to work with and amazingly quick to learn the repertoire, he left with a much improved taste in (Italian) motorcycles to open his pub, the acclaimed Atlas, near Earls Court, with his brother.

JOHN HUMPHRIES supplied us with Catalan food products in the early days and still sells the pub the very wonderful Raventos i Blanc cava. He was there to relieve us during a brief period in early 1994 when we were severely short staffed. From him comes the Catalan spinach recipe – seen on the menu at least weekly ever since. He is the author of *The Essential Catalan Companion*.

DAVID EYRE: I opened the Eagle with **MIKE BELBEN** on 15 January 1991. I'm really meant to be a mechanical engineer but failed miserably at that. Born and raised on sugar plantations in Mozambique and Malawi, I have my mother to thank for teaching me how to eat by bringing us up in the kind of house that baked bread every day and made its own bacon and hams. It was Mike who gave me my first restaurant job as a busboy at Smith's restaurant, Covent Garden, in 1984, and the mad-but-lovely Freddie who gave me my first cooking job at Mélange (R.I.P.) in 1986. I've since opened Eyre Bros in Shoreditch with my brother Rob (the original Eagle barman) and we're launching an as yet unnamed restaurant, also in Shoreditch, in spring 2001.

soups

Red Onion & Red Wine Soup with Parmesan Bruschetta

Northern Italian in origin, this is a satisfying and warming winter soup
– thick and juicy, with a tangy sweetness.

Ingredients (serves 6)

- **1 bottle of red wine**
- **4 cloves**
- **4 bay leaves**
- **a few sprigs of thyme, plus extra to garnish**
- **50g / 2oz butter**
- **4 tablespoons olive oil**
- **12 red onions, sliced**
- **4 garlic cloves, chopped**
- **2 teaspoons tomato purée**
- **500ml / 18fl oz vegetable stock**
- **2 tablespoons balsamic vinegar**
- **1 teaspoon ground cinnamon**

For the Parmesan bruschetta:

- **6 slices of country-style bread**
- **2 garlic cloves, peeled and halved**
- **extra virgin olive oil for drizzling**
- **freshly grated Parmesan cheese**

Method

Pour the wine into a casserole, add the cloves, bay leaves and half the thyme and boil over a high heat until reduced by half. Strain, reserving the liquid. In the same casserole, melt the butter in the olive oil, then add the red onions and garlic. Cook gently over a medium heat until sweet and tender, stirring from time to time – this will take at least half an hour. Add the reduced wine, tomato purée, vegetable stock and the remaining thyme and cook at a gentle simmer for half an hour. Stir in the balsamic vinegar and cinnamon and leave the mixture to simmer for a further 15 minutes. Check the seasoning.

To make the bruschetta, toast the bread on a griddle or in a dry heavy-based frying pan, then rub with the garlic and drizzle over some extra virgin olive oil. Sprinkle with a liberal layer of grated Parmesan.

Put a piece of Parmesan bruschetta in each soup bowl and pour over the soup. Serve garnished with a couple of sprigs of thyme.

Peas with Chouriço & Poached Egg

14

A simple Portuguese recipe that could be considered a soup, though when served with a poached egg it is elevated to a cosy supper dish. I nearly always use frozen tiny petits pois, unless very fresh young peas are available. Similarly, Spanish chorizo is often more readily available than my preferred Portuguese chouriço, which is generally drier, coarser and fattier.

Ingredients (serves 4)

- 1 large white onion, chopped

- 3 tablespoons olive oil or
  2 tablespoons good-quality lard

- 2 garlic cloves, finely chopped

- 3 tablespoons chopped flat-leaf parsley

- 150g / 5oz chouriço, sliced

- 800g / 1¾ lb small peas,
  very fresh or good-quality frozen

- 1 litre / 1¾ pints light meat stock or water

- 4 very fresh 'real' (i.e. organic) eggs

- salt and freshly ground black pepper

Method

Gently fry the onion in the olive oil or lard until transparent, then add the garlic and parsley.
At the same time cook the sliced chouriço in a dry pan over a very low flame to melt some of the fat.
Drain the chouriço and add to the onion with the peas and stock or water. Cook for about 10 minutes,
then purée a cupful of the peas in a blender to thicken the soup. Season generously with black pepper
– you may not need any salt, depending on the saltiness of the sausage.

When ready to serve, poach an egg for each person in a saucepan with a teaspoon of vinegar
in the normal manner. Ladle the soup into bowls and place an egg on each portion.

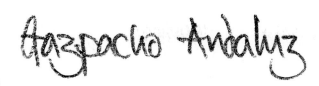

Gazpacho, meaning cold soup, comes from Andalucia. This refreshing soup was historically made for agricultural workers during the hot summer months. Traditionally it was prepared using a pestle and mortar but these days you can save a lot of time with a food processor. There are as many gazpacho recipes as there are people who make it. They all have their own secrets.

To skin tomatoes, pour boiling water over them and drain them after 30 seconds. The skin should then come off easily.

Ingredients (serves 6–8)

- **3 garlic cloves, chopped**
- **500g / 1lb 2oz ripe tomatoes, skinned and seeded**
- **2 green peppers, chopped**
- **2 small cucumbers, peeled and chopped**

- **250g / 9oz stale white country-style bread, torn into small chunks**
- **250ml / 8fl oz olive oil**
- **3 tablespoons sherry vinegar**
- **1.5 litres / 2½ pints water and ice, mixed**
- **salt**

Method

Pulse the garlic, tomatoes, peppers and cucumbers in a food processor until well mixed. Strain the mixture through a sieve to remove the pepper skins. Stir in the bread, olive oil, vinegar, iced water and salt to taste; the bread will soften and dissolve in the liquid. Chill before serving.

Sopa al Ajillio
– Andalucian Garlic Soup with Soft-boiled Egg

This is one of the many recipes I was taught by Adam Robinson

while working at the Brackenbury restaurant in west London. Like much of his food, it is simple and really tasty. Serve with chilled dry sherry.

Ingredients (serves 6)

- a day-old loaf of heavy white bread (Italian, sourdough or even ciabatta)
- 2 heads of garlic, separated into cloves, unpeeled
- 150ml / ¼ pint olive oil

- 2.5 litres / 4½ pints good chicken stock
- a big pinch of saffron
- 6 free-range eggs, soft-boiled and shelled
- sea salt and freshly ground black pepper

Method

Trim the hard crusts off the loaf and separate the bread into chunks. Put the bread and garlic cloves on a baking tray and douse with the olive oil, then season with sea salt and a grinding of black pepper. Cover with a lid or foil and bake slowly in an oven preheated to 150°C/Gas Mark 2 until the bread is golden and has soaked up the oil and the garlic is soft. This may take about 30–40 minutes. Leave to cool, then squeeze the garlic from its skin and purée in a blender or food processor with the bread to make crumbs.

Bring the stock to the boil with the saffron. Add the crumbs and bring the mixture back to a simmer. Adjust the seasoning. Place a soft-boiled egg in each warm serving bowl and pour the soup over.

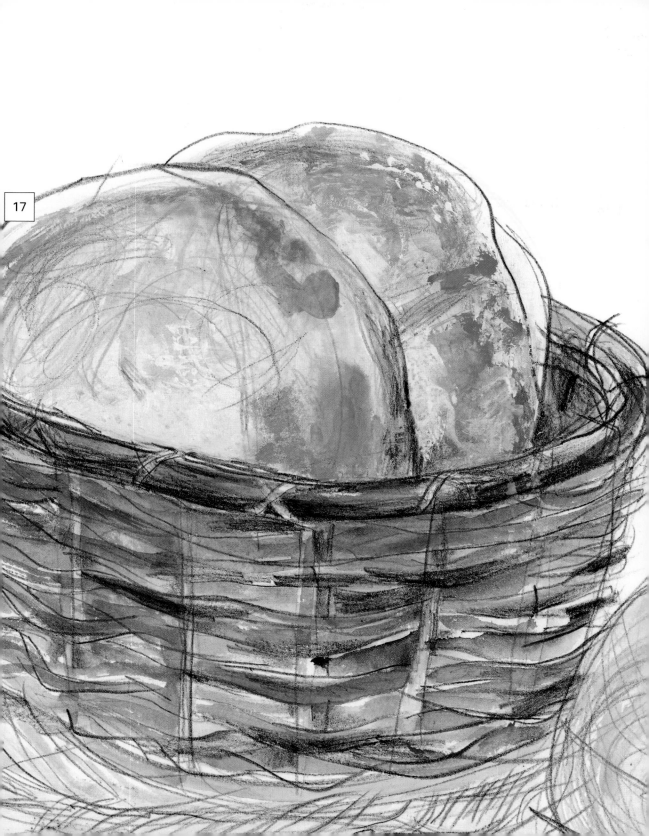

Canja – Portuguese Chicken Broth with Rice, Mint & Lemon

This is almost Portugal's national dish, at least in the down-home section.
It's a kind of always-available-even-if-too-late-for-lunch restaurant dish. Anyway, this is not an apology; it's the best of all chicken soups, with proven restorative qualities.

Ingredients (serves 4–6)

- 2 large chicken breasts, washed
- rind of 1 lemon (use a potato peeler)
- a dozen mint leaves, chopped
- 200g / 7oz rice (or rice-shaped pasta)
- juice of 1 lemon
- salt and freshly ground black pepper

For the stock:

- 1 boiling chicken or 1kg / 2¼ lb chicken wings or drumsticks, washed
- a carrot, an onion, 2 celery sticks – all roughly chopped
- some bay leaves and peppercorns
- some parsley and mint stalks

Method

For the stock, put all the ingredients in a large pan, cover with about 3 litres / 5 pints cold water and bring to a gentle simmer. Simmer for an hour but don't let it boil, even for a minute, or the fat will emulsify and the stock will become cloudy – the aim is an infusion of the chicken and aromatics. Strain the stock and skim the fat from the surface. If you are making it in advance, you can chill the stock and then simply lift off the solidified fat.

Return the stock to the clean pan and reheat it, then poach the chicken breasts in it with the lemon rind and chopped mint. Remove the chicken breasts when they are cooked and slice into thin strips. Return them to the pan with the rice (or tiny pasta) and the lemon juice. When the rice is cooked, season the soup – you may need more lemon juice – and serve immediately.

Black Mushroom Soup

David Eyre

19

This has the appearance of a broth or consommé. The addition of tiny soup pasta makes it more substantial but I sometimes prefer to serve it over a large slice of grilled bread.

Ingredients (serves 6)

- 25g / 1oz dried ceps (or more if you want deeper notes to the end result)
- 1 large onion, finely chopped
- 1 large leek, finely chopped
- 1 celery stick, finely chopped
- 2 garlic cloves, sliced
- 800g / 1¾ lb field mushrooms, finely sliced

- about 20 sage leaves, chopped
- 100ml / 3½ fl oz olive oil
- 1 litre / 1¾ pints water or chicken stock
- 200g / 7oz small soup pasta, such as ditalini, mezzi tubetti or conchigliette
- a couple of mint sprigs, chopped just before you add them to the pan
- juice of 1 or more lemons, to taste
- salt and freshly ground black pepper

Method

To serve: freshly grated Parmesan cheese / grilled country-style bread rubbed with garlic (optional)

Soak the dried ceps in 1 litre / 1¾ pints hot water for 30 minutes. In a covered pan, gently cook the onion, leek, celery, garlic, field mushrooms and sage in the olive oil with some salt. When the mushrooms have steamed themselves to an almost black colour, add the ceps, together with their strained soaking liquor and the water or chicken stock. Simmer gently for 30 minutes. Meanwhile, cook the soup pasta separately until *al dente*, then drain.

Check the seasoning of the soup, stir in the mint and add lemon juice to taste. Divide the pasta between individual bowls, pour the soup on top and serve with Parmesan and grilled garlic-rubbed bread, if using.

Root Vegetable Soup with Greens

Simple broths thickened with potato and stale bread are known in Italy

as *pancotto*. The more root vegetables you add the better, but potatoes and onions alone will do the trick. The greens, too, are open to interpretation. In the winter months choose hardy brassica, like Savoy cabbage or Brussels sprout tops. In the summer use young spinach, rocket or even herbs. Chervil and flat-leaf parsley work best.

You do not need stock for this soup – sweating several vegetables together with oil and a little water will give you all the flavour you need. But feel free to use chicken or vegetable stock if you want to.

Ingredients (serves 6)

- **3 tablespoons olive oil**
- **3 onions, chopped**
- **2 garlic cloves, peeled and slightly crushed**
- **2 large floury potatoes (baking potatoes or 'whites'), peeled and roughly diced**
- **about 500g / 1lb 2oz vegetables, such as turnips, parsnips, celeriac, fennel and leeks (the more anaemic looking the better, so avoid pumpkin, beetroot and carrots), peeled and diced**

- **a mugful of water**
- **about 100g / 4oz stale, rustic-style bread, such as sourdough or ciabatta, with the crusts removed**
- **3 generous handfuls of chopped greens**
- **salt and freshly ground black pepper**
- **extra virgin olive oil, to serve**

Method

Gently heat the oil in a large, heavy-bottomed pan, add the onions and garlic and fry until soft, without browning. Add the potatoes and other vegetables, plus a couple of pinches of salt and about half the mug of water. Stir thoroughly and cover. Leave to simmer gently for about 20 minutes or until all the vegetables are tender. Add the stale bread and a little more water. When the bread has gone soft, gently mash everything together and start to add more water until you have the consistency you want. Remember it should be broth-like enough to be able to cook the greens in it. Season to taste with salt and pepper.

Bring the soup to a simmer again and add the greens. If using cabbage, the soup will need another 5 minutes' simmering. If using herbs or rocket, serve immediately. Garnish each bowlful with a drizzle of extra virgin olive oil.

Variations

1   Meat eaters can include bacon in the soup. It should be added to the pot with the onions and garlic.

2   If there is Parmesan or pecorino in the fridge, grate some and put it in a bowl on the table when you serve the soup.

3   Pancotto made with rocket is traditionally garnished with crushed dried chillies as well as with the extra virgin olive oil.

Sopa de Pedra – Portuguese "Stone" Soup

David Eyre

22

There is absolutely nothing subtle about northern Portugal's answer to

minestrone or the neighbouring Spanish *caldo gallego*. The perplexing translation of its name is 'stone soup', the story being that a penniless and hungry traveller arrives in a village and announces that he is able to conjure the tastiest soup for the whole village from nothing more than a large pan of water and a stone. These are provided and, whilst solemnly stirring the pot, he suggests that though the soup will be quite delicious it would be improved with a cabbage and a little chouriço sausage. These are eagerly fetched and a little later he repeats the suggestion that perhaps an onion and some beans would be a small improvement – and so on until he has a fine catch-all dish.

Thus, within reason, sopa de pedra can include any cured pork and vegetables, so the recipe below may be modified as you wish. However, it should always include chouriço, cabbage and beans. Really another variation on the pork and beans theme, it's the kind of dish that makes damp winters seem not so very bad. It is also one of those composite dishes that benefit from being made the previous day, but be sure to cool it down as rapidly as you can; warm beans love to ferment, given the chance.

Ingredients (serves 6–8)

- 250g / 9oz red beans, such as kidney beans, soaked overnight in cold water

- 200g / 7oz piece of smoked bacon or pancetta

- a gammon hock or a raw ham end (most delicatessens are happy to sell these cheaply)

- 2 chouriço sausages

- 1 black pudding – if you can find the Portuguese *morçela* or the Spanish *morcilla*, all the better

- 2 onions, chopped

- 2 small turnips, chopped

- 2 carrots, chopped

- 400g / 14oz waxy potatoes, cut into spoon-sized pieces

- 3 garlic cloves, sliced

- 2 tablespoons tomato purée

- 2 tablespoons *massa de pimentão* (red pepper purée – not essential but a good thing to have; Turkish grocers stock a similar product, or use puréed roasted red pepper)

- 100ml / 3½ fl oz olive oil

- the darker leaves from a smallish Savoy cabbage, shredded

- a bay leaf or two and some thyme and parsley

- salt and freshly ground black pepper

Method

Drain the red beans, put them in a large pan and cover with water. Bring to the boil and cook vigorously for 10 minutes. Drain and rinse off any scum from the beans. Return to the pan with 2 litres / 3½ pints water, the smoked bacon, gammon hock, chouriço sausages and black pudding. Simmer steadily until the beans are nearly cooked. Remove the meat and cut it into pieces.

In a separate pan, fry the chopped vegetables, garlic, tomato purée and red pepper purée in the olive oil for a few minutes, until softened a little. While they are still bright, add the vegetables to the beans with the meat, cabbage and herbs. Cook for a further 20 minutes or until the beans are soft, then correct the seasoning. Eat with bread.

Cooking Dried Beans and Lentils

Dried beans and lentils are, I think, looked upon with deep suspicion by many, who imagine that they must be soaked for days, then cooked for hours to render them safe. This is simply not true. The important thing is to buy quality beans that are not years old from a reputable source. The older they are, the tougher they will be and the longer they will take to soak and cook. The Eagle buys its beans from northern Spain, the source of the world's finest dried beans, especially butter beans and tiny white haricots. Tinned beans are okay in some dishes but they must be washed before use.

Dried white, red and black haricots, butter and broad beans, flageolets and chickpeas all require soaking overnight (or during the working day). Drain the soaked beans and bring them to the boil in fresh water. When scum appears on the surface, drain again, then cover by 2.5cm / 1 inch with cold water and bring back to a simmer. If the beans are red or black they must be boiled hard for 10 minutes; otherwise just simmer them steadily in a covered pan to achieve evenly cooked beans. Expect them to take at least 1½ hours, and add more water if the level drops below the surface of the beans. Don't add any salt until the beans are cooked, as it hardens the skin. When cooked, keep them covered in the cooking liquid with a good glug of olive oil. If you are using them in a soup, purée a cupful or two to give a creamy texture. If you are not using the beans immediately, refrigerate them as soon as they are cool.

Italian and Spanish brown lentils and the famous French, purple-tinged *lentilles du Puy* require no soaking and will take under an hour to cook. Cover them by 5cm / 2 inches with cold water, bring to a simmer with a couple of cloves of garlic and a stick of celery and cook until tender. Partially drain the lentils and, whilst they are still warm, season and dress with olive oil and lemon juice. Any left over make a good basis for a salad if dressed with more lemon and olive oil, and would go very well with smoked fish.

Potaje de Garbanzos – Chickpea Stew, or is it a soup?

A *potaje* is one of the most popular poor foods in Spain. By 'poor', I mean that
it is made from cheap, storecupboard ingredients. *Potaje* is a word used mainly by Andalucians. If you go further north, a similar
dish would be called *cocido* or even *olla*, which means simply a pot. *Potaje* contains stock with meat or fish and either dried beans
or chickpeas. It doesn't need to be carefully watched and tended, making it popular with busy housewives. The final point about
potaje is that it tastes even better the day after it is made. The meat can be left out if you prefer.

Ingredients (serves 6–8)

- 150ml / ¼ pint olive oil
- 2 bay leaves
- 500g / 1lb 2oz chickpeas, soaked overnight in plenty of cold water
- a piece of Serrano ham fat and trimmings, or similar
- 2 fresh chorizos, sliced
- 50g / 2oz pancetta, chopped

- 50g / 2oz white country-style bread, cut or torn into small pieces
- 4 tablespoons chopped flat-leaf parsley
- 6 garlic cloves, unpeeled
- 1 egg, hard-boiled and chopped
- 300g / 11oz potatoes, peeled and chopped
- 300g / 11oz spinach or Swiss chard, roughly chopped
- salt

Method

In a large pan, bring 2 litres / 3½ pints of water to the boil with 3 tablespoons of the olive oil and the
bay leaves. Drain the soaked chickpeas and add them to the boiling water with the ham fat and trimmings,
chorizo and pancetta. Simmer for about half an hour.

In another pan, gently fry the bread, parsley and garlic in the remaining olive oil until lightly coloured.
Add this to the chickpeas with the hard-boiled egg, potatoes and spinach or Swiss chard. Cook for about
40 minutes – 1 hour, until the chickpeas are soft. Take out the ham and roughly mash the stew to break
up some of the chickpeas and the garlic. Taste and adjust the seasoning. You might be surprised at how
much salt you need to add. Add a little, stir, leave to rest for a few minutes and then taste again.

Caldo Verde — Greens & Potato Soup with Chouriço

You'll find this on every Portuguese menu and, like all potato-based soups, it is really easy to make, needing only an onion or so as the aromatic element. If the potatoes are flavourful, stock is unnecessary. Be sure to use floury rather than waxy varieties of potato otherwise the result will be glutinous; those labelled as baking potatoes are ideal.

Ingredients (serves 6–8)

- 1 large onion, finely chopped
- 2 large garlic cloves, finely chopped
- 100ml / 3½ fl oz good olive oil, plus extra to serve
- 4 or 5 large baking potatoes, peeled and diced

- 200g / 7oz spicy Portuguese chouriço sausage (the dried ones are best)
- 800g / 1¾ lb dark spring greens (weight after the stalks have been removed)
- salt and freshly ground black pepper

Method

Gently cook the onion and garlic in the olive oil for a few minutes until softened. Add the potatoes and pour over enough water to cover. Bring to the boil and simmer until the potatoes begin to collapse. Mash the potatoes in the pot and then thin the soup with 1 litre / 1¾ pints water.

Meanwhile thinly slice the chouriço and put it into a cold, greased heavy frying pan. Fry over a low heat until the chouriço is crisp and most of the fat has melted. Drain on kitchen paper and add to the soup. Season with salt and pepper to taste and keep warm.

Shred the greens into fine filaments. The best way to do this is to take 6 or so de-stalked leaves, roll them into a tight 'cigar' and then cut it into thin strips with a large, sharp knife. A julienne disc on a food processor may work if the cigar fills the feed tube tightly. In any case, aim for the slices to be 1–2mm / ¹⁄₁₂ inch wide.

When almost ready to serve, throw the cabbage into the soup and simmer until it is bright green. Garnish each bowl with a drizzle of olive oil.

Cold Roast Aubergine Soup with Yoghurt

The flavour of this soup will vary slightly according to how you roast the aubergines. Charring them over a gas flame or grill gives a smoky edge, whereas roasting them in a hot oven results in a rich, slightly buttery taste.

Ingredients (serves 8)

- **4 large aubergines, pricked all over**
- **2 red peppers**
- **2 tablespoons olive oil**
- **3 onions, finely chopped**

- **3 garlic cloves, finely chopped**
- **1 teaspoon paprika**
- **500ml / 18fl oz Greek-style yoghurt**
- **about 1 litre / 1¾ pints vegetable stock or water**
- **salt and freshly ground black pepper**

Method

Char the aubergines over a gas flame for 10–15 minutes, turning them occasionally, until they are blackened and 'collapsed' and feel very soft. Alternatively brush them with a little olive oil, sprinkle with salt and put them in the oven at full blast for about 30 minutes, until very soft. Roast the red peppers at the same time, until charred all over. Put the aubergines and peppers in a large bowl and cover with a plate – this creates steam which helps to loosen the skin. Leave for at least half an hour.

Meanwhile, gently heat the olive oil in a large pan and add the onions and garlic. Cover and sweat very gently, without letting them brown, for about 30 minutes, until soft and translucent. Half way through this time, stir in the paprika.

Now remove the skin from the aubergines – they may well fall apart on you as you do this, which is a good thing. It is tempting to skin them under a tap but try not to, as you will lose some flavour. Don't worry if there are little bits of charred skin on the flesh; they will disappear when you purée them. Strip the skin off the roasted peppers too, discard the seeds, then finely chop the flesh and toss with a little olive oil and salt. Set aside.

Remove the onions and garlic from the heat and stir in the aubergine flesh, then purée to a smooth paste in a blender. Transfer to a bowl. Once the paste has cooled down (it doesn't need to be stone cold), add the yoghurt and stir until it is fully incorporated. Now dilute the mixture by adding cold stock or water; keep it nice and thick, so that the roasted peppers will float on top. Season to taste with salt and pepper. To serve, pour into individual bowls and garnish with the roasted peppers.

27

Minestra
Pasta e Fagioli – Pasta & Bean Soup

Here are two classic examples of Italian *minestra* **– generous thick soups that** usually have a piece of pancetta or fat bacon with aromatic vegetables and herbs as the starting point. They may include pasta and / or pulses as the starchy element and do not always require a stock. Minestrone is literally a 'big soup', which uses lots of different ingredients and epitomises earthy, meal-in-a-bowl eating. Note that both these soups include pasta; if you don't intend to eat the soup straight away, or if you are making enough for more than one meal, don't cook the pasta in the soup or it will eventually become soggy. Instead, cook it separately just before you eat and add it to the soup as you serve it.

Ingredients (serves 8)

- **500g / 1lb 2oz dried beans, such as borlotti or cannellini, soaked overnight in cold water**

- **4 tablespooons olive oil**

- **250g / 9oz pancetta, chopped**

- **2 medium onions, chopped**

- **2 carrots, chopped**

- **2 garlic cloves, finely chopped**

- **3 celery sticks, chopped**

- **2 branches of flat-leaf parsley**

- **a sprig of rosemary**

- **2 sprigs of oregano**

- **400g / 14oz tinned tomatoes, drained and chopped**

- **250g / 9oz pasta, such as ditali or macaroni, or noodles snapped into short lengths**

- **100ml / 3½ fl oz extra virgin olive oil, warmed**

- **salt and freshly ground black pepper**

- **freshly grated Parmesan cheese, to serve**

Method

Drain the soaked beans, put them in a large pot and cover with fresh water. Bring to the boil and boil for 10 minutes (don't add any salt or the beans will become tough). Drain the beans and wash any scum from them.

Heat the olive oil in a large pan, add the pancetta, onions, carrots, garlic, celery, parsley, rosemary and oregano and cook gently until the vegetables are softened. Add the tomatoes and the drained beans, then pour in enough water to cover the pot contents by 5cm / 2 inches. Cook steadily with the lid on for 1–2 hours, depending on how fresh the beans are, until they are soft but still whole. Remove a couple of ladlefuls of beans and purée them; stir this back into the pot to thicken it. Now add salt and pepper to taste and fish out the herb branches. Add the pasta to the soup and cook until tender, then turn off the heat and stir in the warm olive oil. Serve with Parmesan cheese and bread.

Minestra Minestrone

Use any combination of vegetables from the groups below – for example, if you haven't got any fennel, increase the quantities of the other aromatic vegetables accordingly. Don't chop them too finely, and it is a good idea to have everything ready before you start cooking.

Ingredients (serves 8)

For the aromatic base (soffritto):

- 1 large onion
- 1 large leek
- 2 garlic cloves
- 3 celery sticks
- 1 fennel bulb
- 2 carrots
- 200g / 7oz smoked streaky bacon
- 6 tablespoons olive oil

For the root vegetables:

- 2 medium waxy potatoes
- ½ medium turnip
- ½ celeriac

For the 'tender' vegetables (total weight 700g / 1lb 9oz):

- tomatoes, deseeded and chopped
- green beans
- peas
- broad beans
- courgettes, chopped
- cooked or tinned beans or chickpeas
- Savoy cabbage, turnip greens etc, shredded

Plus:

- a piece of Parmesan rind
- 2 tablespoons chopped parsley, basil, oregano or sage
- 150g / 5oz pasta (cartwheel shapes are traditional)
- 4 tablespoons chopped parsley, grated Parmesan cheese or pesto
- salt and freshly ground black pepper

Method

Chop the vegetables and bacon for the aromatic base, then fry them in the olive oil in a large pot until they begin to colour. Chop the potatoes, turnip and celeriac and add them to the pot, stirring well to coat them in the oil. Cook for a few minutes, then add the tender vegetables, cheese rind (which adds flavour to the soup and can be fished out later) and herbs. Cover with water, bring to the boil and simmer for 15 minutes, until all the vegetables are just tender. Check the seasoning, then add the pasta and simmer until it is done. Don't overcook – the soup should look bright and alive. Serve straight away, garnished with the parsley, Parmesan or pesto.

Carabaccia - Florentine Pea Soup

David Eyre

30

This is an absolute favourite springtime soup, making the best use of the starchiness of fresh peas (although I confess that I'm happy to make an ersatz version at any time of year using frozen peas). Considered by the Tuscans to be primarily an onion soup, Carabaccia dates from the Renaissance, when it was sweetened with cinnamon and almonds. It is sometimes served with a poached egg on top.

Ingredients (serves 6)

- 100ml / 3½ fl oz olive oil, plus extra for the bread

- 3 large onions, chopped

- 3 celery sticks, chopped

- 1 carrot, finely chopped

- 1 garlic clove, finely chopped

- 500g / 1lb 2oz freshly podded peas (about 1.2kg / 2¾ lb unpodded weight)

- 1 litre / 1¾ pints light chicken or vegetable stock

- 6 slices of day-old white, country-style bread, such as pugliese or pain de campagne

- salt and freshly ground black pepper

- freshly grated Parmesan cheese, to serve

Method

Heat the oil in a large pan, add the onions, celery, carrot, garlic and some salt and pepper, then cover and cook over a very low heat for about an hour, until the vegetables become a very soft mush. Add the peas and a little of the stock and simmer for 10 minutes or until the peas are tender. Purée half of the soup in a blender. Return it to the pan with the rest of the stock and reheat.

Toast the bread and oil it generously. Place a slice in each soup bowl, pour over the soup and serve with grated Parmesan.

Black Bean Soup

32

This was adapted from the black beans that are so prevalent in San Francisco's *taquerias*, where some of the best Mexican food is to be found. They are the mainstay of any burritos worth their salt. The soup is as nourishing as it is simple to make, and hearty sustenance when faced, as I regularly am, with an empty fridge at home.

Ingredients (serves 4–6)

- **250g / 9oz black beans or Spanish *frijoles negras*, soaked overnight in cold water**

- **about 1.5 litres / 2½ pints light vegetable stock or water**

- **2 white onions, chopped**

- **2 garlic cloves, chopped**

- **1 red chilli, seeded and finely chopped**

- **1 celery stick, chopped**

- **3 tablespoons sunflower oil**

- **1 tablespoon cumin seeds, lightly toasted in a dry frying pan**

- **400g / 14oz tin of tomatoes, drained and squeezed**

- **a fairly big bunch of coriander, coarsely chopped**

- **a pinch of sugar**

- **150ml / ¼ pint soured cream (or double cream whipped with a squeeze of lemon juice)**

- **salt and freshly ground black pepper**

Method

Drain the black beans, cover with fresh water, then bring to the boil and drain again. Return to the pan, cover with the stock or water and bring to a simmer. Make sure there is plenty of liquid as the beans will swell and eventually release their starch into the soup, thus thickening the liquid.

In a separate pan, fry the onions, garlic, chilli and celery in the oil until translucent. Add the toasted cumin seeds and cook for a few minutes to blend the flavours. Then add the tomatoes and most of the coriander. Cook down and then stir all the vegetables into the beans as they begin to soften. Leave to simmer for half an hour or so, to allow all the flavours to blend. Season with the sugar and some salt. You may not need any pepper because of the chilli. Serve garnished with a dollop of soured cream and the remaining coriander.

Note

This recipe may be served as an accompaniment to cooked meat if you use much less stock and allow the mixture to thicken.

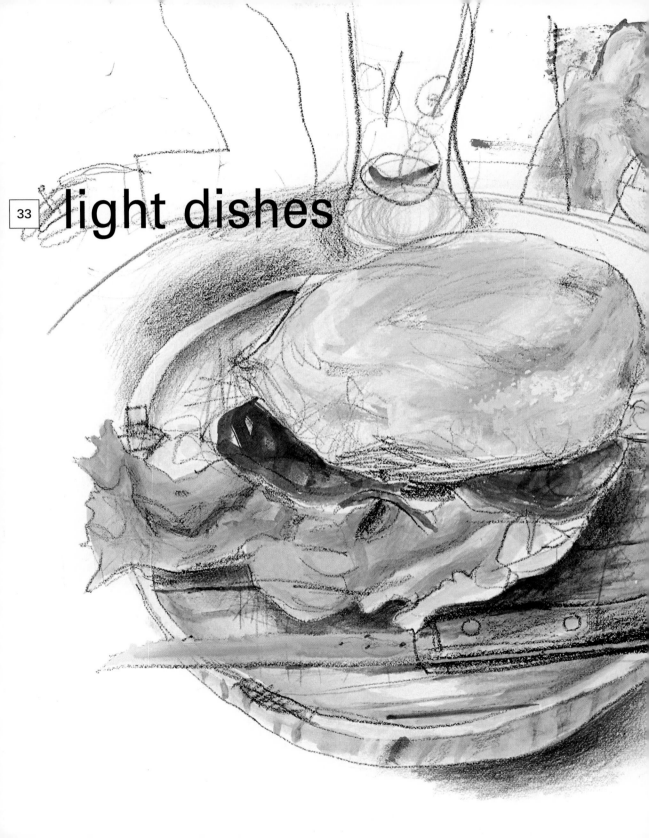

light dishes

Grilled Chicken Salad with Truffle Oil

34

You will need four long wooden skewers for this recipe.

Soak them in water for half an hour or so before use, to prevent them burning on the grill.

Ingredients (serves 4)

- **4 skinless, boneless free-range chicken breasts, each cut into 4**

- **5 tablespoons olive oil**

- **2 large red peppers**

- **450g / 1lb new potatoes**

- **125g / 4½ oz finely sliced coppa di Parma (or pancetta coppata or pancetta stesa)**

- **about 200g / 7oz rocket**

- **5 teaspoons capers, soaked in cold water for 30 minutes and then squeezed**

- **2 tablespoons black kalamata or Niçoise olives, pitted**

- **1 tablespoon lemon juice**

- **4–5 tablespoons white truffle oil**

- **salt and freshly ground black pepper**

- **lemon wedges, to serve**

Method

Thread the chicken pieces on to the soaked skewers, rub with 3 tablespoons of the olive oil and season with salt and pepper.

Put the red peppers under a hot grill, turning them occasionally, so that the skin starts to blister and blacken all over. When they are charred, put them into a bowl and leave to cool for about half an hour. Remove the skin, which should now come off easily, and cut the peppers into strips.

Put the potatoes in a pan and cover with cold water. Add a decent pinch of salt, bring to the boil and cook for about 20 minutes or until they are tender. Drain them, cut each in half and season with a little salt while they are still hot.

Grill the chicken skewers on a chargrill pan or under an overhead grill for about 15 minutes, until cooked through. Meanwhile, take the rind off the coppa if necessary and cut each slice in half. Tear the rocket into pieces and put it in a large mixing bowl with the capers, olives, red peppers, lemon juice, remaining olive oil and some salt and pepper to taste. Toss all this together.

Put the potatoes on a large, flat serving plate. Scatter the salad on top and then arrange the coppa over this. Finally place the chicken (with or without skewers) on top and drizzle with the truffle oil. Serve straight away, with lemon wedges and good, fresh bread.

Seafood Salad with Cooked Lemon & Coriander

Jemima Burrill

35

This version of a seafood salad is best served on top of thinly sliced raw fennel, or bruschetta rubbed with a little garlic and drizzled with olive oil (see page 53). Use any combination of scallops, prawns, squid or a firm, white fish – whatever looks best at the fishmonger's.

Ingredients (serves 4)

- 1 lemon

- 3 tablespoons olive oil

- 2 bay leaves

- 1 tablespoon fennel seeds

- 400g / 14oz piece of halibut or similar, cut into slices 2cm / ¾ inch thick

- 8 small cleaned squid, cut into rings 2cm / ¾ inch thick, tentacles detached

- 4 large raw tiger prawns, peeled, de-veined and decapitated

- 8 fresh scallops

- a handful of coriander leaves

- salt and freshly ground black pepper

Method

Put the lemon in a pan with water to cover and boil for half an hour or until soft. When it has cooled, cut it up into small pieces, discarding the pips, and place in a large serving bowl, being sure not to lose any of the zesty juice. Add the olive oil and some freshly ground pepper.

Steam all the seafood, one sort at a time, either in a steamer or in a colander with a lid set over a pan of boiling water. Add the bay and fennel seeds and a little salt to the water. First steam the halibut, which will take about 7 minutes; it's better to take it out a little underdone as it will continue to cook in its own heat. Add to the lemon in the serving bowl. Then steam the squid rings and tentacles for about 5 minutes or until they are tender and lose their translucency. Plunge them into cold water to stop the cooking and drain well. Add to the serving bowl.

Steam the prawns for about 5 minutes or until·they have turned pink. Plunge into cold water, then drain and add to the serving bowl. Finally slice the scallops in half horizontally, trying to keep the orange corals attached. Steam them as briefly as possible, just until they become opaque. Add them to the bowl and stir well. Add the coriander leaves, then taste and season with salt and add more olive oil if necessary.

Greek Salad

Unlike the bottle of Metaxa brought home from your holiday on the islands,

a Greek salad travels well if reserved for the hottest of summer days. I make a variation for balmier days that uses green beans, fresh broad beans and peas in place of the cucumber, and fresh coriander or mint in place of the oregano and caper berries.

Ingredients (serves 4)

- 12 ripe tomatoes, quartered
- 2 cucumbers, partially peeled, halved down their length and then sliced
- 1 large red onion, very finely sliced
- 250–300g / 9–11oz ewe's milk feta cheese, broken into large pieces

- 150ml/1/4 pint fruity olive oil
- juice of 2 lemons
- 1 tablespoon dried or fresh oregano
- a handful of kalamata olives
- a dozen caper berries, washed of their brine or vinegar

Method

Divide the tomatoes, cucumbers and onion between 4 plates and place the feta on top. Whisk the olive oil, lemon juice and oregano together and use to dress the salad. Garnish with the olives and caper berries.

About Grilled Meat

The centre of the Eagle's very small and open kitchen is the well-used chargrill. At times, more than half the menu's dishes include at least one component that has been cooked on the grill and consequently much of our reputation for big flavours and rough edges should be attributed to it. Now in an ideal world, the grill would be fired by charcoal and not by gas and lava rocks, for the reason that food cooked over glowing coals just tastes better. So we should all be happy that the barbecues we have at home are really the best thing on which to grill food (even if it may not be everyone's desire to fire up the barbecue for a couple of veal chops for their tea). That said, a barbecue should have a much larger surface area than the food being grilled is likely to occupy; the perimeter, where the heat is less intense, is useful for slowing things down or for resting them after cooking. The next best thing to using a barbecue is a large, rectangular, ridged cast iron grill pan – the type that uses two adjacent burners on your stove.

When grilling cuts of meat that have an element of fat – chops and most steaks – a medium heat is best. Salt the fat only and lightly oil the meat (not the grill bars, which serves no purpose), then start with the fat and any bone nearer to the hotter parts (salt helps to draw out water and lets the more volatile fats melt quickly, leaving the more robust fat to crisp up). Turn the meat 90 degrees half way through cooking the first side and salt when turning it. Half way through cooking the second side, turn again and move the meat to where the heat is lowest to complete the grilling. This will prevent it inadvertently overcooking and, as with roasts, will allow it to relax a little. Any bones will have warmed up and the meat near them will have cooked.

Lean cuts – chicken breasts, fillet steak, goat, venison and the like – require steady cooking on a higher heat but only until done to a degree before you want them. Then rest them for 5–10 minutes in a warm spot to finish. If you don't rest the meat, the result will be unevenly cooked and probably tough. Thin slices such as calf's liver can be cooked all the way on the hottest part of the grill without resting.

Duck breasts are an extreme example. On one side there is very lean meat with no fat at all and on the other a thick layer of fat that needs to be rendered crisp. So start with the salted and scored fatty side on the lowest heat available and cook until the fat is toasty brown. Turn the breast and now cook fiercely and briefly to rare, then leave to rest in a warm spot until pink throughout.

You may have noticed that chefs are forever prodding grilling meat with their forefinger. This is simply to ascertain the degree of 'doneness' and it is the only really practical method; thermometers are fine when testing roasts but not much good for smaller cuts. In general, a rare cut such as a steak will feel much like the edge of your palm below the little finger; medium rare like the fleshy part of your palm at the base of the thumb, and medium like the centre of your palm. It takes some practice, but that is the way I test for doneness.

Broccoli & Treviso with Anchovy Dressing

This recipe creates a big batch of dressing. It keeps for ages in the fridge and makes a great Caesar-type salad with Cos lettuce and Parmesan, a dip for raw vegetables, or a spread for hot toast. It can also be served with fish such as sea bass, bream or hake.

Ingredients (serves 4–6)

- **3 heads of broccoli**
- **2 heads of radicchio di Treviso**

For the dressing:

- **150g / 5oz cured anchovies in olive oil**
- **2 garlic cloves, chopped**
- **2 teaspoons Dijon mustard**
- **1 tablespoon sherry vinegar**
- **350ml / 12fl oz olive oil**
- **1 teaspoon freshly ground black pepper**
- **1 small red chilli, chopped**
- **a handful of basil, chopped**

Method

Purée the anchovies, garlic, mustard and vinegar in a food processor until smooth. With the machine running, add the oil very slowly, as if making mayonnaise. Season with the black pepper, then pulse in the chilli and basil.

Divide the broccoli into florets, then peel the stems and slice them into chunks. Separate the Treviso into leaves. Bring a large pot of salted water to the boil. Blanch the broccoli florets in it briefly (perhaps 1 minute) because they have to be crunchy, then remove with a slotted spoon and shake off excess water. Repeat with the stalks, cooking them for longer if necessary. Toss the broccoli with the Treviso and enough of the dressing to coat it lightly.

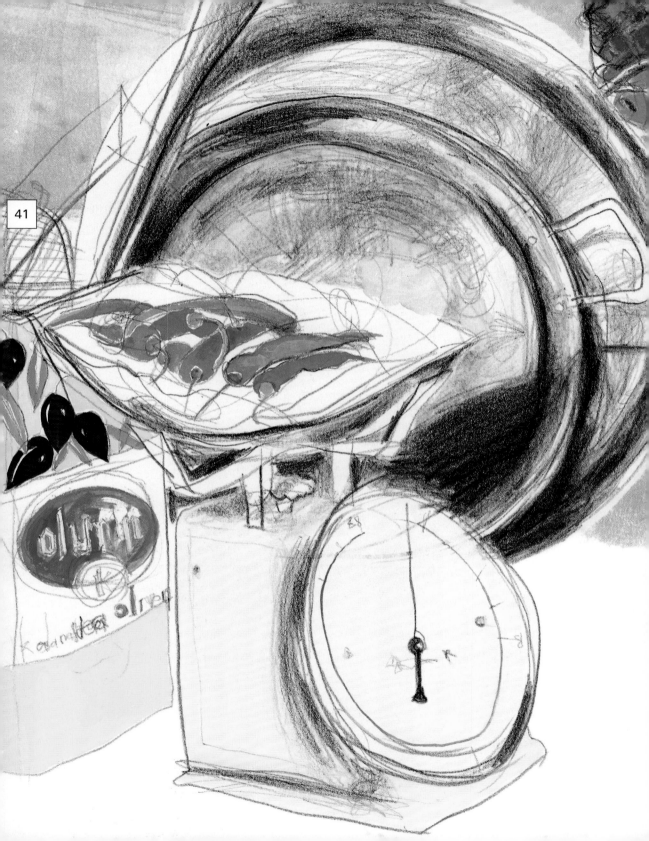

42

Tagliata – Cut Seared Beef Salad

David Eyre

I have modified the original Italian dish with the addition of fresh tarragon
– tarragon and beef being a favourite combo of mine. I also prefer to cut the steak after, not before, cooking.

Ingredients (serves 2)

- **100g / 4oz waxy new potatoes, such as Charlotte, La Ratte (Belle de Fontenay), Jersey Royals or Pink Fir Apple**

- **2 x 225g / 8oz steaks – forerib fillet (ribeye), sirloin or fillet**

- **100g / 4oz rocket**

- **1 tablespoon good Modena balsamic vinegar, but don't spend silly amounts**

- **3 tablespoons really good olive oil**

- **1 tablespoon chopped tarragon**

- **coarse sea salt or Maldon salt and freshly ground black pepper**

Method

Boil the potatoes in salted water until tender, then drain. Grill or fry the steaks rare (see About Grilled Meat, page 38) and then leave to rest on a warm plate. Cut the potatoes into pieces. Divide the rocket and potatoes between 2 serving plates. Make a dressing with the vinegar, oil, tarragon, and some salt and pepper. Cut the steaks into thin strips, mix with the dressing and then scatter them over the salad.

Roast Pumpkin & Red Onion Salad

This dish has fabulous colours. The salty Parmesan makes a great contrast to the sweet vegetables. These quantities are enough for a first course or light meal. It also goes well with grilled fish. The salad is served at room temperature, so you need to allow a couple of hours for the roasted vegetables to cool.

Ingredients (serves 4)

- 6 tablespoons olive oil
- 6 red onions, peeled and halved
- 100ml / 3½ fl oz red wine
- 2 tablespoons balsamic vinegar
- 3 sprigs of thyme
- ½–1 small pumpkin (or you could use 2 butternut squash)
- 2 handfuls of rocket (about 200g / 7oz)
- a block of Parmesan cheese (at least 50g / 2oz)
- salt and freshly ground black pepper

Method

Put half the oil into a deep heatproof baking dish or heavy-duty roasting tin on a high heat. Add the onions, stirring them to distribute the oil. Add the red wine, balsamic vinegar and some salt and pepper. The balsamic vinegar intensifies the colour of the onions and caramelises them. Strip the leaves from the thyme and throw them in. When the mixture is bubbling away, cover tightly with foil, transfer to an oven preheated to 200°C/Gas Mark 6 and bake for 30 minutes. Remove the foil and bake for a further 10 minutes, until tender.

Cut the pumpkin into segments, following its natural creases, peel, and scrape out the seeds. Place the segments on a baking tray, drizzle with the remaining olive oil and season with salt and pepper. Roast at 200°C/Gas Mark 6 for 20–30 minutes or until brown at the edges and soft to the point of a sharp knife.

Leave the vegetables to cool to room temperature, then toss them with the rocket, using the juices from the red onion as a dressing. Top with shavings of the Parmesan.

Salade Niçoise

David Eyre

So much has been said about how to make the true salade niçoise

that I know I'm courting complaint just by providing a recipe. Some say no tuna, some no anchovies, some say nothing cooked, and so on. Still, there is no finer lunch or more perfectly balanced plate of food. This, then, is my *vrai salade niçoise*. I prefer to use Spanish yellowfin or bonito tuna in olive oil – skipjack and albacore are best left for the cat. Tinned tuna in brine is horrid.

Ingredients (serves 4, generously, at lunch)

- 75g / 3oz green beans (any type)
- 250g / 9oz new potatoes
- 4 eggs
- 100ml / 3½ fl oz olive oil
- 1 tablespoon lemon juice
- 1 smallish Cos lettuce
- 75g / 3oz fresh or dried butter beans, broad beans, white haricots or whatever is around, cooked

- 6 ripe tomatoes, cut into eighths
- 250g / 9oz tinned tuna in oil, drained
- 2 tablespoons salted capers, rinsed several times and then left to soak until no longer salty
- 100g / 4oz small, tasty olives
- 8 cured anchovy fillets (see page 58)
- freshly ground black pepper

Method

Cook the green beans, uncovered, in boiling salted water until just tender, then drain and immediately plunge them into cold water to set their colour. Drain again. Cook the potatoes until tender, then drain. Boil the eggs for just 5 minutes so that the yolks are still slightly 'greasy'. Cool in cold water, then shell and halve them.

Whisk the oil and lemon together with some black pepper. Toss the lettuce leaves with a little of this dressing. Mix the green beans, potatoes, cooked fresh or dried beans, tomatoes and a third of the tuna with more dressing. Divide the lettuce between 4 large plates or shallow bowls and then pile the vegetables on top. Toss the remaining tuna and the capers, olives and anchovy fillets with the remaining dressing and divide them, with the halved eggs, between the plates.

Baked Chicory Wrapped in Prosciutto

This is a very Italianate gratin. It is easy to make, so do not be put off by
a number of must-dos ahead of cooking. Must-do number one is to ask in your local deli for the prosciutto to be sliced
a little thicker than normal (tell them what you need it for, as they should be familiar with prosciutto used this way).

Must-do number two is to be diligent when buying chicory. It should be firm and white. Avoid any that has started
to go brown or that has green sprouting from the top.

Must-do number three is to bully your chicory into behaving the way you want it to once you get it home. What it
wants to do when you cook it is go a horrible grey colour and produce a ton of watery juice. So pre-cooking is essential.
Some cooks advise blanching it in acidulated water but this is by no means foolproof. We find that roasting works best.

Ingredients (serves 6)

- 6 heads of chicory
- 2 garlic cloves, peeled and partly crushed
- 2 lemons
- a glass of white wine
- olive oil
- 1 tablespoon sugar

- 18 slices of prosciutto,
  cut a little thicker than usual
- a bunch of sage
- 500ml / 18fl oz double cream
- 100g / 4oz Parmesan cheese, freshly grated
- salt and freshly ground black pepper

Method

Preheat the oven to its highest temperature. Place the chicory in a roasting tin and throw in the garlic.
Squeeze the lemons over the chicory and add the wine. Drizzle with olive oil and scatter the sugar over
everything. Cover with foil and bake for about half an hour or until the chicory is tender right through.

Leave the chicory to cool, then pick it up and squeeze it very gently to get rid of all the watery juice.
Discard this liquid, and the garlic. Now wrap the chicory in the ham. Three slices should cover each head.
Line each slice of ham with a whole sage leaf as you wrap. Return the chicory to the roasting tin. Pour the
cream over it and scatter the Parmesan on top, then season with salt and a generous amount of pepper.

Place the tin back in the hot oven and bake for about 15 minutes or until the top has browned and the
cream is bubbling. Serve with good bread for mopping up. Our favourite side dish for this is watercress
or lamb's lettuce dressed with plenty of olive oil and balsamic vinegar.

Caponata – Sicilian Aubergine Relish

Caponata was originally made in summer and bottled for winter use.

It is delicious on bruschetta (see page 53) or as a sweet and sour relish with cold meats or cheese.
Use good-quality tinned tomatoes unless you find fabulous fresh ones.

Ingredients (serves 4)

- 2 onions, chopped
- 150ml / ¼ pint extra virgin olive oil
- 2 celery sticks,
  cut into 1–2cm / ½–¾ inch pieces
- 400g / 14oz tin of plum tomatoes
  (squash them thoroughly in a colander
  and discard the juice)
- 75g / 3oz green olives
- 2 tablespoons salted capers, soaked in cold
  water for 30 minutes and then squeezed
- 20g / ¾ oz caster sugar
- 3 tablespoons white wine vinegar
- 2 aubergines,
  cut into 1–2 cm / ½–¾ inch cubes
- salt and freshly ground black pepper

Method

Season the onions and fry them gently in 3 tablespoons of the olive oil until soft. Add the celery and
cook for 3 minutes. Increase the heat, add the tomatoes and simmer until reduced to a thick consistency.
Add the olives, capers, sugar and vinegar and simmer gently for 20 minutes, stirring from time to time.

Heat the remaining olive oil in a large frying pan. Season the aubergines and sauté in the oil over
a medium heat until lightly browned and cooked through. Lift out with a slotted spoon and add to
the other vegetables. Taste and adjust the seasoning.

Serve at room temperature. Caponata will keep for weeks in the fridge if covered with oil.

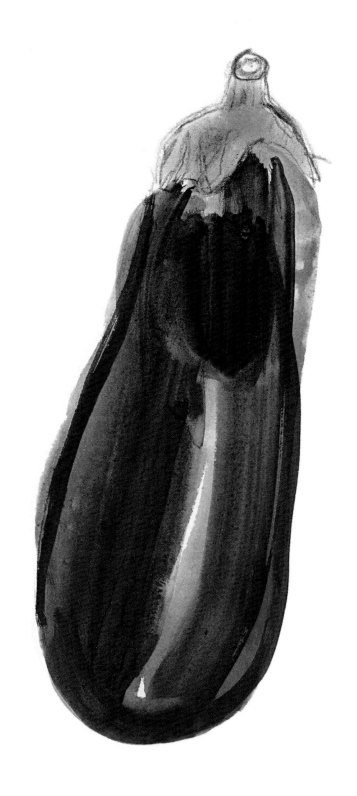

Imam Bayeldi
– Baked Aubergines Stuffed with Tomatoes

This is a classic Turkish dish. The name means 'the Imam fainted', the story being that the Imam, or clergyman, swooned with joy when his wife presented it to him. Serve with a green salad dressed with tahini and lemon.

Ingredients (serves 6)

- 6 aubergines, halved lengthways
- 4 red onions, sliced
- 2 garlic cloves, sliced
- 150ml / ¼ pint olive oil, plus a little extra for drizzling
- 1 teaspoon cumin seeds

- 1 teaspoon dried mint
- 400g / 14oz tomatoes, diced
- 2 bay leaves
- a small bunch of coriander, stems chopped, leaves reserved
- 1 lemon
- salt and freshly ground black pepper

Method

Score the flesh of the aubergines, then scoop it out with a spoon, being careful not to tear the skin. Dice the flesh, salt it lightly and set aside in a colander to drain. Salt the shells and leave them upside down to drain for 30 minutes. Wash and pat dry.

Sweat the onions and garlic in 100ml / 3½ fl oz of the olive oil until they are soft. Stir in the cumin seeds and mint and cook for 1 minute. Add the tomatoes and bay and cook for 5 minutes, then transfer the mixture to a bowl.

Rinse and dry the aubergine flesh. Heat the remaining olive oil and sauté the aubergine until soft and light brown, then add to the tomato mixture. Adjust the seasoning and mix in the chopped coriander stems.

Spoon the filling into the aubergine shells and fit them into an oiled baking dish in a single layer. Squeeze over the lemon juice and pour in enough water to come half way up the side of the aubergines. Drizzle over a little more oil, then bake in an oven preheated to 180°C/Gas Mark 4 for 30–40 minutes, until the shells are soft. Leave to cool. Serve at room temperature, strewn with coriander leaves.

Tortilla de Bacalao – Salt Cod Tortilla

The name of this famous Spanish omelette comes from the word torta, or tart.

The main difference between Spanish and French omelettes is that Spanish ones are flat whereas French ones are rolled. The former usually contain potatoes, too. Tortilla is eaten widely and often in Spain because of its versatility. It can be served hot or cold, in a sandwich or *bocadillo*, or as a quick *tapa*. There are countless variations on the basic tortilla but one of the tastiest ones is made with salt cod. You could also use roasted red peppers, chopped spinach or, for a spring vegetable tortilla, peas and broad beans.

Ingredients (serves 4–6)

- 300g / 11oz salt cod, soaked (see page 101)
- 4 tablespoons olive oil
- 4 large potatoes, peeled and sliced

- 1 medium onion, sliced
- 8 eggs, beaten
- a few sprigs of flat-leaf parsley, chopped
- salt

Method

Put the soaked salt cod in a large saucepan of simmering water and cook gently for 15–20 minutes, until the flesh is beginning to flake. Drain and leave to cool, discarding the skin and bones while it is still warm. Heat the oil in a large frying pan until smoking hot, add the potatoes and fry for a few minutes, until golden. Then add the onion and cook for 3 minutes, covering the pan. The resulting condensation softens the potatoes and onion. Once the vegetables are cooked, take them out of the pan with a slotted spoon and mix with the beaten eggs and flaked salt cod. Add the parsley, and some salt if required.

Pour out all but 3 tablespoons of the oil from the frying pan and tip in the tortilla mixture, cooking it over a very low heat until it is set underneath and coming away from the sides of the pan. You may need to cover the pan to help cook the middle. To turn the tortilla, remove the pan from the heat, place a plate over it and turn the pan over so the tortilla is on the plate. Then slide the tortilla back into the pan and cook for 3 more minutes, uncovered.

51

Ratatouille – Braised Provençal Vegetables

This classic Provençal dish is often made badly. The main point to note is that the vegetables should be cut into largish pieces and fried separately. It makes a great lunch with crusty bread or goat's cheese. Alternatively serve it as an accompaniment to grilled or roast meat or fish.

The Catalan equivalent of ratatouille is *samfaina*, which is identical except that the vegetables are cut into thin slices. *Samfaina* is only ever served as an accompaniment.

Ingredients (serves 6)

- 4–5 tablespoons olive oil
- 2 courgettes, roughly chopped
- 2 onions, roughly chopped
- 2 garlic cloves, sliced
- 2 red or green peppers, roughly chopped
- 2 aubergines, roughly chopped

- 400g / 14oz tin of tomatoes (preferably organic)
- a small bunch of oregano or marjoram
- 2 sprigs of thyme or rosemary
- 1 bay leaf
- a small bunch of flat-leaf parsley
- salt and freshly ground black pepper

Method

Heat 2 tablespoons of the oil in a casserole or thick-bottomed pan, add the courgettes and season with salt and pepper. Fry until lightly coloured, then remove from the pan and set aside. Heat another tablespoon of the oil in the pan, add the onions and garlic, then season and cook gently for 5–10 minutes, until soft. Add the remaining oil to the pan, then stir in the peppers and aubergines, season, and cook over a medium heat until lightly coloured. Add the courgettes, tomatoes, the leaves from the oregano or marjoram, the rosemary or thyme and the bay. Stew gently for 30 minutes. Taste for seasoning and then stir in the whole parsley leaves. Serve hot or at room temperature.

Bruschetta with warm Ricotta Salad

David Eyre

Try to buy ricotta loose rather than in tubs, from a deli that has a good turnover, as it has a much better flavour when very fresh. Warming it is a good way of improving the flavour of bland commercial brands. If you can find authentic ewe's milk ricotta, then buy it straight away – ricotta should be the by-product of pecorino cheese.

Ingredients (serves 4)

- **1 garlic clove, finely chopped**
- **3 spring onions, finely chopped**
- **finely chopped mint, basil and flat-leaf parsley – about 4 tablespoons in total**
- **400g / 14oz ricotta cheese**

- **3 tablespoons olive oil**
- **juice of 1 lemon**
- **4 slices of bruschetta (see below)**
- **a few fat black olives, pitted**
- **a few fresh broad beans (optional)**
- **freshly ground black pepper**

Method

Mix together the garlic, spring onions, herbs, ricotta, oil, lemon juice and black pepper and warm gently in a pan or low oven. Pile on to the bruschetta and scatter over some olives and, if in season, some raw, shelled and peeled broad beans.

About Bruschetta

Bruschetta is nothing more than grilled bread, rubbed with garlic, then salted and drenched in olive oil. Yet it is incredible how this can be ruined. The bread should be long slices cut from the centre of a day-old round Italian country loaf. These are normally sourdough. Don't attempt to make bruschetta from soft, bleached white bread. It must be grilled on a barbecue or, at a pinch, on a ridged chargrill pan; don't even think about using a toaster. Rub the grilled bread with a peeled clove of garlic, then sprinkle with crunchy coarse sea salt or Maldon salt and drizzle with your best extra virgin olive oil. The oil is the whole point of bruschetta, so don't be thrifty with either the quality or the quantity.

A really ripe tomato can be rubbed crudely on to the bread before the olive oil to make the Catalan *pa amb tomàquet*.

Bruschetta with Roast Tomatoes and Grilled Sardines

Sardines on toast, my way, and just the thing for the garden on a hot day.

To make a starter for an informal lunch, use any form of anchovies (see page 58) in place of the sardines.

Ingredients per person:

- **3 fresh sardines, scaled and gutted**
- **4 roast tomatoes (see page 145)**
- **1 slice of bruschetta (see page 53)**
- **½ lemon**
- **salt**

Method

Salt the sardines all over, especially the head and tail. Grill on a barbecue (or on a chargrill pan or under a grill) for 2–3 minutes per side (it is easier to roll sardines over their back when trying to turn them). Press the tomatoes on to the bruschetta and then lay the sardines on top. Squeeze the lemon all over. Eat the sardines using the bruschetta as a sort of plate or trencher, and then eat the now sardine-flavoured bread.

Bruschetta with Mozzarella, Treviso & Balsamic Vinegar

Treviso is a type of radicchio, or red chicory. It has a deep burgundy colour and, unlike the more common round radicchio di Verona, long, slender leaves. You could use round radicchio or white chicory for this recipe, but if you can hunt it out Treviso really is a find. It is very bitter, which is why I always bake it with a little sugar, but you can omit this if you prefer.

Another variation of this recipe, perhaps for a warm day, is to leave everything uncooked except for the bruschetta. The crunchy, bitter leaves of the Treviso are a great foil for the silky, bland mozzarella.

Ingredients (serves 4)

- **2 heads of radicchio di Treviso**
- **extra virgin olive oil**
- **balsamic vinegar**
- **1 teaspoon sugar**

- **4 slices of bruschetta (see page 53)**
- **3 tablespoons roughly chopped fresh oregano or 1 tablespoon dried oregano**
- **3 x 125g balls of mozzarella, each cut into 4 slices**
- **sea salt and freshly ground black pepper**

Method

Heat the oven to its highest setting. Cut the Treviso into quarters lengthways and place them on a baking tray. Drizzle with some olive oil and a little balsamic vinegar, then sprinkle the sugar over everything and season with a little salt and pepper. Cover with foil and bake for about 15 minutes, until the leaves have wilted and the heart has softened.

Lay 2 Treviso quarters on each bruschetta and then put 3 slices of mozzarella on top of that. Scatter the oregano over the whole thing and place the bruschetta in the tray in which you baked the Treviso. Hopefully there will be a little debris and juice left behind, which the bruschetta will mop up.

Bake briefly until the mozzarella has melted. This will only take a couple of minutes. Season with a little more balsamic vinegar and sea salt, then serve.

Escalivada - Spanish Roast Vegetable Salad

This dish isn't sure if it's a salad or a stew but it is lovely both as an
accompaniment to meat or fish and as a dish on its own. If you can cook the vegetables on an open fire or barbecue,
so much the better, as the flavour will be much improved. Otherwise, roast them in a hot oven.

Ingredients (serves 4–6)

- **2 large baking potatoes**
- **3 aubergines**
- **3 red peppers**
- **2 red onions**

- **extra virgin olive oil**
- **10 basil leaves, torn**
- **2 courgettes, cut into 2cm / ¾ inch pieces**
- **sea salt and freshly ground black pepper**

Method

Pierce the skin of each potato and aubergine 3 or 4 times with a fork or sharp knife. Place all the vegetables except the courgettes on a baking sheet and roast on the top shelf of an oven preheated to 220°C/Gas Mark 7, until they are cooked through and the skins are evenly coloured (or roast them over a hot fire or barbecue). The peppers and aubergines will need 20–30 minutes and the potatoes and onions up to an hour.

When the vegetables are cool enough to handle, peel them and roughly break them into large chunks. Dress the aubergines and potatoes generously with olive oil, salt, pepper and some of the torn basil and mix together in a serving dish.

Season the courgettes and then fry them in olive oil until lightly coloured and tender. Lay them on top of the aubergine and potatoes with the peppers and onions. Season well, add the remaining basil and dress with more olive oil. Serve hot or at room temperature.

57

About Anchovies

Anchovies come in four forms:

Fresh: when they are filleted, floured and fried, these are the definitive fried fish. If, after frying, you marinate them in garlic-infused olive oil, vinegar, coriander and pepper, they can be served as a salad or tapa of anchovies *en escabeche*.

Marinated or soused in vinegar and oil: these are marinated raw, as in the Spanish *boquerones* or the Italian *alici*. Don't use them for cooking but they are great with herbs or tomatoes on grilled bread (see page 53).

Salted and packed whole: my preferred form of larder anchovies. The flavour is unique, without any of the rank pungency many people associate with anchovies. They need to be desalted and filleted before use, which is easily done. Soak the fish in cold water for half an hour or so, then carefully rub them between your fingers to remove the skin – this divests them of overt saltiness. Use your thumb to remove the fillets, discarding the tail and tiny dorsal fin. If you don't intend to use the fillets immediately, pat them dry, layer them in a dish and cover with olive oil. They will keep like this in the fridge for a week but the flavour will diminish.

Cured tinned fillets in oil: bear in mind that the best tinned anchovies are always going to be a little expensive, as they will have been filleted and packed by hand. They should be fat and pink, without hairy little bones, taste somewhat sweet and not at all oversalty.

When you are cooking salted or cured anchovies for, say, pasta, their flavour will more easily merge with other ingredients if they are chopped finely and then dissolved in oil. Do this double-boiler fashion – i.e. stir them into olive oil in a small pot set within a larger one of simmering water until creamy. Never fry chopped anchovies in oil. They will quickly harden and become bitter.

Fried Fillets of Fresh Anchovies

David Eyre

I've seen fresh anchovies recently in a couple of good London fishmonger's and they are generally available in the fish market, so your fishmonger should be able to get hold of them for you. If you have no joy with your tame 'monger, then use very fresh sardines and follow the instructions for filleting them on page 78. Filleting anchovies is not as ridiculous a pastime as you might imagine, I promise; they can be done in under 30 seconds. Fresh anchovies can grow up to 20cm / 8 inches in length but are normally around 10cm / 4 inches long – much larger than one would think – and since they are delicate, no knife is required.

Ingredients (serves 4, but you'll want more)

- **16 firm fresh anchovies**
- **1 egg, beaten**
- **2 tablespoons white wine**
- **2 tablespoons finely chopped flat-leaf parsley**

- **4 tablespoons plain flour, seasoned with salt and pepper**
- **2 tablespoons polenta or cornmeal**
- **vegetable oil for frying**
- **2 lemons**
- **salt and freshly ground black pepper**

Method

Wash the anchovies in a bowl of water, then fillet them: hold a fish in one hand and run the edge of your thumb gently from the body cavity along one side of the spine towards the tail. Do this a couple of times until the fillet starts to fall away from the spine. Repeat on the other side and then, pinching the head, lift the spine from the fillets and break it off just in front of the tail. You should now have a 'butterfly', or double fillet.

Mix the beaten egg, wine and chopped parsley together in one bowl and the seasoned flour and polenta in another. Pour 3cm / 1¼ inches vegetable oil into a wide pan and heat until hot but not smoking. Holding 2 opened fish together by the tail in a sort of fan arrangement, dip first in the egg and then in the flour and fry immediately. Adjust the heat so that they take around 2 minutes to brown. Drain and eat promptly with a squeeze of lemon. Repeat with the remaining fish.

Vitello o Capone Tonnato – Veal or Chicken with Tuna Dressing

There are as many recipes for vitello tonnato as there are Italian chefs.
This one offers a nod to cookery writer Marcella Hazan. It is the perfect party dish, as all the preparation can be done well in advance.

Capons are castrated male chickens – a process that was practised for centuries to obtain a heavier, plumper bird. When Paris welcomed Catherine de Medici in 1549, the sumptuous banquet given in her honour included 43 capons. However, castrating chickens is now illegal, so just use the biggest free-range chicken you can find.

Ingredients (serves 6)

- **1 large chicken, or 1 topside of veal weighing 1.5kg / 3¼ lb, trimmed of fat and tied**
- **1 head of garlic, cloves separated and chopped**
- **3 celery sticks, chopped**
- **2 small onions, chopped**
- **2 carrots, chopped**
- **2 bay leaves**
- **a sprig of thyme**
- **4 black peppercorns**
- **a pinch of salt**

For the dressing:

- **2 egg yolks**
- **2 teaspoons Dijon mustard**
- **300ml / ½ pint olive oil**
- **125g / 4½ oz good-quality tuna in oil**
- **8 anchovies, chopped, plus a few extra to decorate**
- **1 tablespoon capers, plus a few extra to decorate, soaked in cold water for 30 minutes and then squeezed**
- **juice of ½ lemon**
- **salt and freshly ground black pepper**

Method

If using chicken, put it in a large pot with the garlic, vegetables and herbs and pour in just enough water to cover. Add the peppercorns and salt and bring slowly to a simmer. Cook gently for 20 minutes, then take off the heat and cover loosely. Leave the chicken to cool completely in the stock; it will finish cooking as it cools.

If you are using veal, put it in a large pot with the garlic, vegetables and herbs and pour in enough water to cover. Remove the veal, bring the water to the boil, then return the veal to the pot, adding the peppercorns and salt. Bring to a simmer and cook gently for 1¼ hours. Take off the heat and leave the meat to cool completely in the liquid.

Make the dressing as for mayonnaise: put the egg yolks, mustard, a pinch of salt and a good grinding of pepper in a food processor or blender and mix well. With the machine running, add the oil slowly at first, gradually adding it faster as the mayonnaise becomes emulsified. Beat in the tuna along with its oil, the chopped anchovies and capers. Add the lemon juice and adjust the seasoning. The finished mayonnaise should have a coating consistency. If it is too thick, add a little stock.

To assemble the dish, remove the meat from the cooking liquid. With the chicken, pull all the flesh from the carcass – this isn't a neatly carved affair. Slice the veal fairly thinly. Spread half the dressing on a large plate. Arrange the meat in a single layer on top, then coat with the remaining dressing. If possible, leave it for an hour to allow the flavours to mingle.

Strew the extra capers and anchovies over your finished dish. Eat it with a big green salad, crusty bread and a bottle of rosé.

Bife Ana – The Eagle Steak Sandwich

This has to be in this book; it's the only dish to have been on the menu at the Eagle every single day since we opened. When notions of having a pub first arose, a steak sandwich was just about the first item to appear on the business plan's menu. Not just any steak sandwich, but the one I remembered eating almost daily whilst a teenager home on school holidays in Mozambique.

Not to be confused with the Portuguese fried pork escalope of the same name, this (beef) steak sandwich is named after Dona Ana, a larger-than-life *mafiosa* who owned a cattle ranch, bakery and bar. The bakery and ranch provided the primary ingredients for the huge *pregos* – the real (Portuguese) name – served in the bar.

Ingredients (serves 2)

- **500g / 1lb 2oz rump steak, thinly sliced (the original would have used fillet)**
- **2 large crusty rolls – we use stone-baked Portuguese rolls called carcaças**
- **2 tablespoons olive oil**
- **Cos lettuce leaves**
- **salt**

For the marinade:

- **1 onion, thinly sliced**
- **1 garlic clove, chopped**
- **1 small dried chilli, crushed**
- **1 bay leaf, broken up**
- **1 tablespoon chopped parsley**
- **1 teaspoon dried oregano**
- **2 tablespoons red wine**
- **3 tablespoons olive oil**
- **freshly ground black pepper**

Method

Mix together all the ingredients for the marinade, add the steak and leave to marinate for a few hours (but no longer than 8 hours). Remove the steaks from the marinade, then strain the marinade and set aside.

Warm the rolls in a medium oven. Heat a heavy-based frying pan until very, very hot, then add the olive oil and fry the steaks very quickly. If your pan was hot enough, they will need to be turned within a minute. Remove the steaks and keep warm, then add the dry ingredients from the marinade to the pan with some salt.

Cut the rolls in half and arrange the Cos lettuce and then the steaks on the lower halves. Add the strained marinade liquid to the pan and let this bubble and reduce a little, then pour into the top halves of the rolls. Close the sandwiches and eat immediately, with both hands.

The Eagle kitchen cooks about 8,000 bife Anas a year.

Huevos a la Flamenca— Gypsy Eggs

David Eyre

63

A robust down-home Andalucian supper dish.

Ingredients (serves 4)

- 100g / 4oz serrano ham, chopped
- 100g / 4oz Spanish chorizo, chopped
- olive oil
- 1 onion, finely chopped
- 2 garlic cloves, finely chopped
- 1 teaspoon paprika (preferably Spanish *pimentón*, which is smoked)

- 2 x 400g / 14oz tins of chopped tomatoes
- 100g / 4oz shelled peas or broad beans
- 10 new potatoes, sliced (leftovers are fine)
- 100ml / 3½ fl oz chicken stock or water
- 8 eggs
- salt and freshly ground black pepper

Method

Slowly cook the ham and chorizo in a little olive oil for 5 minutes. Remove the meat from the pan, add a little more oil, plus the onion, garlic and paprika and cook until the onion is soft. Add the tomatoes, peas or beans and potatoes with the chicken stock or water and some salt and pepper. Cover and cook for 10 minutes – or until the potatoes are done if you are using uncooked ones.

Divide the sauce between 4 individual ovenproof bowls, break 2 eggs into each and scatter the ham and chorizo over them. Then bake in a hot oven for 5–10 minutes, until the egg whites have set.

Chorizo a la Llama – Fried Choricitos with Pimientos, Aguadiente & Garlic

The Spanish name for this dish is a bit of a mystery – no one seems to know of its origins. Choricitos are diminutive cooking chorizos sold linked together.

Serves 4

Cut 8 soft choricitos on the bias into slices 2cm / ¾ inch thick. Heat a heavy frying pan and gently fry them in a little olive oil until cooked through and well coloured. Turn the heat up, add a splash of *aguadiente* or brandy and ignite it (standing well back), then let the alcohol burn off. As the flames die, add 2 sliced cloves of garlic and 4 or more roasted pimientos (preferably wood-roasted red *piquillo* peppers, which are sold oil-packed in tins, or you could roast and peel some small red peppers). Turn off the heat when the garlic slices start to colour. Add some chopped flat-leaf parsley and serve immediately, with bread. The whole operation should take no longer than 10 minutes.

pasta & rice

Cooking Dried Pasta

First of all, which dried pasta? Ignoring the artisan-made and sexily packaged Christmas gift type that costs silly money, there are some brands that are worth the extra. I am devoted to the De Cecco brand, but La Molisana is another favourite. Dried pasta is firmer and chewier than fresh or home-made pasta, which is, I think, its appeal.

When it comes to cooking it, lots and lots of boiling salted water is what's needed – around 5 litres / 9 pints of furiously boiling water and at least 1 tablespoon of salt per 500g / 1lb 2oz packet. Don't put oil in the water in the belief that it will stop the pasta sticking, as it tends to 'wrap' the pasta while it swells, causing it to remain undercooked in the centre. By all means add oil to the water for fresh pasta (which only requires a couple of minutes to cook) but the only way to prevent gummy pasta is to cook it in lots of water and stir often. You also need a decent-sized colander to drain it in once it has reached *al dente*, but don't drain it too much – a little moisture helps the sauce join the pasta. After draining is the time to oil the pasta.

Cooking to the *al dente* stage means that it should give some resistance to the bite – the cooking times printed on the packets of De Cecco are precise. My per-person statistics are 75g / 3oz for a starter and 100g / 4oz for a main course.

Bucatini with Cauliflower, Anchovies, Pinenuts & Raisins

Use the wonderful, light green Romanesco cauliflowers (known as broccoli in Italy), if you can find them. A good variation is to add a pinch of saffron to the frying pan with the cauliflower.

Ingredients (serves 6)

- **2 heads of cauliflower, cut into small florets (keep any leaves)**
- **500g / 1lb 2oz bucatini (or spaghetti)**
- **5 tablespoons olive oil**
- **1 large onion, thinly sliced**
- **a pinch of dried chilli flakes**
- **4 garlic cloves, finely chopped**
- **75g / 3oz pine nuts, toasted lightly in a dry frying pan**

- **75g / 3oz raisins, soaked in a little hot water for 15 minutes**
- **50g / 2oz tin of good-quality anchovies, drained and chopped**
- **extra virgin olive oil**
- **about 3 handfuls of flat-leaf parsley, roughly chopped**
- **100g / 4oz Parmesan cheese, freshly grated**
- **salt and freshly ground black pepper**

Method

Boil the cauliflower florets in a large pan of salted water until not quite tender, then remove with a slotted spoon. Blanch any leaves in the same water, then remove. Add some more salt to the water and cook the pasta in it while making the sauce.

Heat the olive oil in a large frying pan, add the onion and chilli flakes and fry over a medium to high heat until the onion is tender and slightly browned. Add the cauliflower and continue cooking until it begins to soften but is still slightly crunchy. Now add the garlic, pine nuts and raisins. The garlic should brown a little but be careful not to let it burn. Reduce the heat to low, add the anchovies and stir until they disintegrate – about 5 minutes. Taste and season if necessary.

When the pasta is *al dente*, drain and add to the cauliflower mixture with a little water, adding enough extra virgin olive oil to coat the pasta thoroughly. Toss together with the parsley and half the Parmesan. Serve with the remaining Parmesan.

Penne with Sausage, Tomato & Sage

This recipe was brought to the Eagle by Paulo Santos. It was one of the first dishes I cooked here. I like it for its simplicity most of all, but also for its rough and readiness. It's very 'Eagle' – boisterous and filling.

Ingredients (serves 4)

- 3 tablespoons olive oil
- 6 good-quality pork and herb sausages
- 1 redonion, finely chopped
- 2 garlic cloves, finely chopped
- 400g / 14oz tin of plum tomatoes, drained

- 400g / 14oz penne pasta
- 10 sage leaves, finely chopped
- 4 tablespoons double cream
- 40g / 11 / 2oz Parmesan cheese, freshly grated
- salt and freshly ground black pepper

Method

Heat the oil in a frying pan. Peel the skins from the sausages and crumble the sausage meat into the oil, frying it gently until cooked. Add the onion and garlic and cook until soft and translucent. Then add the drained tomatoes and cook gently, covered, for 20 minutes or longer, until you have a thick sauce. Add the sage to the sauce 5 minutes before the end and season to taste.

Meanwhile, bring a large saucepan of salted water to the boil and cook the pasta until *al dente*. Drain and mix with the sauce. Add the cream and half the Parmesan and mix well. Serve immediately, sprinkling the rest of the Parmesan over the top.

Penne with Artichoke Hearts & Greens

We like to use cavolo nero, or Italian black cabbage, at the Eagle for this pasta
dish, because of its strong flavour and handsome colour. It is strictly a winter vegetable, not to be used before the first frosts, but other greens such as sprouting broccoli and kale make great substitutes in the spring.

For this dish to taste at its best you need the preserved artichokes sold in jars as antipasti. You will find them swimming in nasty polyunsaturated oil and this needs to be got rid of. It will be replaced by your own olive oil, of course, chock full of chilli and garlic.

Ingredients (serves 5)

- **2 or 3 garlic cloves**

- **2 red chillies, seeded if you don't want too much heat**

- **6 tablespoons extra virgin olive oil**

- **500g / 1lb 2oz penne pasta**

- **2 or 3 heads of cavolo nero (about 250g / 9oz), stripped from the thick stalk and finely sliced**

- **450g / 1lb jar of artichoke hearts, drained and roughly chopped**

- **100g / 4oz Parmesan cheese, freshly grated**

- **salt**

Method

Chop the garlic and chillies finely together. Stop chopping just short of ending up with a paste and combine them with the oil. Let this sit for about 10 minutes. That is just enough time to put on a large pot of water for the pasta and prepare the cabbage and artichokes.

Add the pasta to the boiling water, then heat a large frying pan (or a wok) until it is smoking. Add the chilli oil and, very shortly afterwards, the cabbage. This will make a fierce popping sound. Fry for about 5 minutes, stirring all the time, then add the artichoke hearts. If the cabbage is frying too fiercely, add a tablespoon of water to the pan but don't reduce the heat. When the cabbage is tender and the contents of the pan are well and truly coated in the chilli oil, transfer to a large, warmed bowl.

Drain the cooked pasta and quickly combine it with the sauce. Stir in the Parmesan just before serving. Season with salt and maybe a little more olive oil.

Orecchiette with Butter, Sage, Garlic & Parmesan

This is exactly the thing to cook after you come home from work; the sauce takes
the same time to make as the pasta takes to cook. I think that you must use orecchiette – it is a chewy type of pasta that looks, as the name suggests, like little ears.

Ingredients (serves 4)

- **75g / 3oz unsalted butter**
- **450g / 1lb orecchiette pasta**

- **2 garlic cloves, crushed but left whole**
- **20 or so sage leaves, finely chopped**
- **4 tablespoons freshly grated Parmesan cheese**

Method

Clarify the butter by melting it over the lowest possible heat and then skimming off the bits that float on top. Gently pour the clarified butter into a clean pan, discarding the curds (or is it the whey?) that will have collected at the bottom. Meanwhile, cook the pasta in a large pan of boiling salted water until *al dente*, then drain.

Heat the butter with the garlic cloves and sage. When the garlic just begins to brown, remove it and throw it away. Mix the butter and sage with the orecchiette and Parmesan.

Spaghettini with Walnut Sauce

A classic dish that requires the freshest of walnuts.

Ingredients (serves 6)

- **150g / 5oz shelled walnuts**
- **2 garlic cloves, crushed**
- **20 sage leaves, chopped**
- **135ml / 4½ fl oz olive oil**

- **50g / 2oz Parmesan cheese, freshly grated, plus extra to serve**
- **2 tablespoons crème fraîche**
- **500g / 1lb 2oz good Italian spaghettini**
- **salt and freshly ground black pepper**

Method

Spread the walnuts out on a baking tray and roast them under a hot grill or in a moderate oven for a few minutes. Then skin them – this is best done by rubbing them vigorously in a tea towel while they are still hot, then tipping them into a colander and shaking until the skins fall to the bottom and out of the holes. Don't worry if you can't remove much of the skin.

Purée the garlic and sage with the olive oil in a food processor, then pulse in the nuts, keeping a rough texture. Fold in the Parmesan, crème fraîche and some pepper. Cook the spaghettini in a large pan of boiling salted water until *al dente*. Drain quickly and toss with the sauce, adding a little of the pasta cooking water.

Fettuccine alla Ciociaria
Egg Fettuccine with Porcini, Sausage & Peas

This is a strong winter dish which comes from my grandmother.

She's from Ciociaria, a hilly area in the Lazio region of Italy, where the main ingredients (also my favourites) are commonly found.

Ingredients (serves 2)

- 20g / ¾ oz dried porcini mushrooms
- 1 tablespoon olive oil
- ½ small onion, finely sliced
- 1 small garlic clove, finely sliced
- 1 Italian fresh pork sausage, skinned and chopped

- 125g / 4½ oz peas
- 200g / 7oz egg fettuccine
- a knob of butter
- 2 tablespoons freshly grated Parmesan cheese
- salt and freshly ground black pepper

Method

Soak the porcini in 500ml / 18fl oz warm water for 15 minutes, then drain, reserving the liquid. Heat the olive oil in a pan, add the onion and cook until lightly browned. Add the garlic and sausage and cook on a gentle heat for 5 minutes. Stir in the porcini and cook for 15 minutes. Now add the peas and stir in the water from the porcini bit by bit. Cover and cook for about 30 minutes, until the liquid has reduced to about half its volume. Season to taste.

Meanwhile, bring a large pan of water to the boil and cook the pasta until al dente. Drain, add the sauce, butter and Parmesan and mix everything together very well.

David Eyre

Egg Fettuccine with Radicchio, Borlotti Beans & Pancetta

In the UK most shoppers seem to regard radicchio as nothing more than a colourful addition to a leaf salad, whereas in its home territory of Italy it is valued much more as a vegetable – and is generally never far away from a bit of bacon. By radicchio, I mean radicchio di Verona, the ball of tightly formed magenta and white-veined leaves.

This is a pasta to eat in autumn or winter, when radicchio is at its best and used to embellish some simple beans-and-bacon.

Ingredients (serves 4)

- 1 small onion, sliced
- 5 sage leaves
- a thick slice of smoked pancetta or smoked streaky bacon, diced
- 3 tablespoons olive oil
- 1 head of radicchio (or chicory), cored and thinly sliced
- ½ glass of white wine
- 400g / 14oz tin of borlotti beans, drained and rinsed
- 400g / 14oz egg fettuccine or tagliatelle
- 4 tablespoons freshly grated Parmesan cheese

Method

Fry the onion, sage leaves and pancetta in the olive oil until they begin to brown. Add the radicchio and cook for a minute or two until it begins to wilt. Add the wine and let it bubble and reduce a little before following with the beans. Keep warm.

Cook the pasta in a large pan of boiling salted water until *al dente*. Drain very briefly and then mix with the sauce and Parmesan.

Egg Fettuccine with Ricotta, Peas & Smoked Pancetta

An elegant and lightweight pasta that uses half a dozen ingredients but relies on the quality of all of them. The peas must be young and fresh, the ricotta not very long ago milked from the sheep, and the bacon dry cured, solid and sweet.

Ingredients (serves 4)

- **200g / 7oz shelled young peas (about 500g / 1lb 2oz unshelled weight)**

- **150g / 5oz smoked pancetta or dry-cured smoked streaky bacon, cut into strips**

- **50g / 2oz butter**

- **400g / 14oz egg fettuccine or tagliatelle**

- **150g / 5oz ricotta cheese**

- **2 tablespoons freshly grated Parmesan cheese**

- **a dozen basil leaves, torn as you use them**

Method

Boil the peas in salted water until just cooked, then drain. Gently melt the pancetta with the butter for 10 minutes or until the fat has run and the pancetta has become crisp. Add the peas to the pan and cook gently for a few minutes. Meanwhile, cook the pasta in a large pan of boiling salted water until *al dente*. Drain and mix in a warmed serving bowl with the ricotta, Parmesan and torn basil leaves. Reheat the peas and bacon and pour over the pasta.

Spaghetti with Roasted Fennel, Lemon & Chilli

I think that fennel bulbs are at their best in winter but this pasta dish
is full of the promise of summer. It is very simple and addictive. If you are making it in warmer weather, replace the
parsley with basil or oregano. Choose the fat female bulbs of fennel – they are much tastier than the flatter male bulbs.

Ingredients (serves 2)

- 1 fennel bulb
- about 100ml / 3½ fl oz extra virgin olive oil
- juice and ½ the zest of 1 unwaxed lemon
- ½ red chilli, finely chopped
- 1 tablespoon capers, soaked in cold water for 30 minutes, then squeezed and chopped
- 1 garlic clove, finely chopped
- 200g / 7oz spaghetti
- 75g / 3oz Parmesan cheese, freshly grated
- 1 tablespoon chopped flat-leaf parsley
- salt and freshly ground black pepper

Method

Remove the little stalks and the tough outer layer from the fennel bulb. If there is a little of the herb (it looks like dill) poking out of the stalks, keep it and chop it with the parsley. Cut the fennel in half down its length, then lay it cut-side down on a board and slice very finely, much as you would an onion.

Pour half the oil into a small roasting tray and add the fennel, lemon zest and half the juice, chilli, capers and garlic. Mix all the ingredients thoroughly with your hands. Season with salt and pepper and cover with foil. Place the tray on the top shelf of an oven heated to its highest setting and roast for about 20 minutes. Remove the foil and leave for another 10 minutes, until the fennel is slightly coloured and very tender.

This is now your pasta sauce. Simply leave it to one side in a large bowl. In the time it takes to boil the spaghetti, it will not cool enough to need reheating. The pasta will do that for you. So cook the pasta until *al dente*, drain it and toss it around the bowl with the fennel mixture. Throw in two-thirds of the Parmesan and all the parsley, then check the seasoning. You may wish to use a little more of the oil and the remaining lemon juice.

Serve with the remaining Parmesan and some good bread for mopping up whatever's lurking at the bottom of the bowl when you've finished.

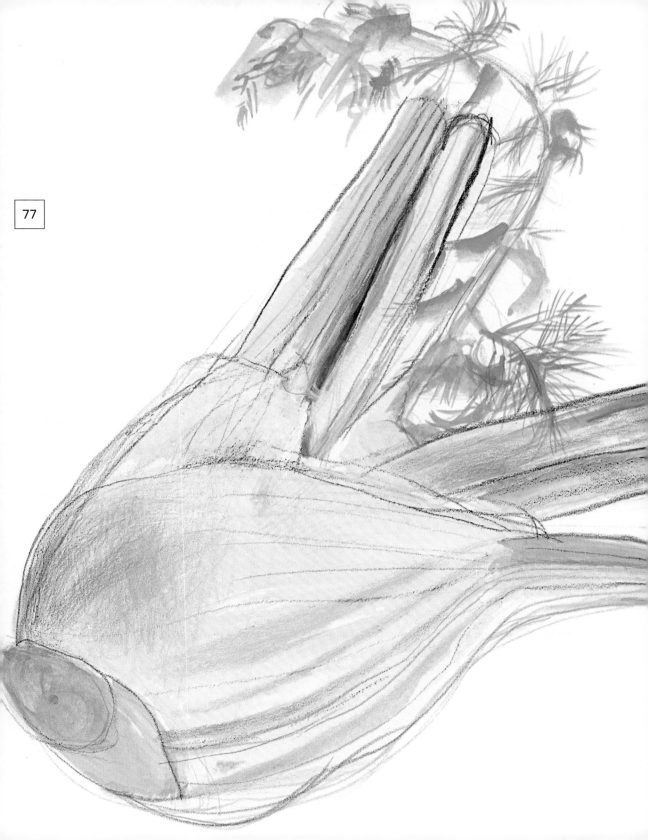

Wholewheat Spaghetti with Sardines

David Eyre

78

An elemental dish from the Deep South of Italy that requires a handful
of the freshest ingredients. Sardines, fennel, parsley and lemon are a terrific bright combo that makes a good
foil to the earthy wholewheat pasta.

Ingredients (serves 4)

- **8 large fresh sardines**
- **4 tablespoons extra virgin olive oil**
- **2 garlic cloves, chopped**
- **½ fennel bulb, finely chopped**
- **400g / 14oz wholewheat spaghetti (sometimes known as bigoli)**
- **2–3 tablespoons chopped flat-leaf parsley**
- **2 lemons**
- **black pepper**

Method

To clean and fillet the sardines, gently rub the scales off each fish under a running tap, then run your thumb down its back to loosen the flesh from the spine. Cut off the head and slice open the belly down to the tail with a small, sharp knife. Pull out the innards and then open out the fish by running your thumb down one side of the spine. Lift the spine away, starting at the head end, then break it off at the tail, so that you end up with a 'butterfly'. Wash the fillets, pat them dry and salt both sides lightly.

Heat half the oil in a pan large enough to fry 4 fillets at the same time. Fry half the garlic and fennel in the oil for 30 seconds or until the aroma rises. Slip 4 sardine fillets into the pan skin side down and then flip them over after a minute. Fry for another minute or so, until they are *just* cooked. Transfer the fillets to a plate and repeat with the remaining oil, garlic, fennel and sardines.

While the sardines are being fried, cook the pasta in a large pan of boiling salted water until *al dente*, then drain it and oil it a little. Add the parsley and pasta to the sardine pan and stir to coat with the flavoured oil. Lay the sardines on the pasta, season with black pepper and squeeze over the lemon juice.

Pizzoccheri – Baked Buckwheat Pasta with Sage, Fontina & Cabbage

This baked pasta dish is a speciality of the Milanese. The name refers to both the type of pasta used – a buckwheat noodle roughly the shape of fettuccine – and to this recipe, which as far as I know is pretty much the only way the noodle is served. I have had a hard time finding pizzoccheri in London. Some Italian delicatessens have it. If they don't, you can get away with wholewheat spaghetti (my sincere apologies to any Milanese up in arms at that last remark).

This is quite a bulky meal – pasta, potatoes, cheese and cabbages! But it is very easy to prepare once you have exhausted yourself looking for the buckwheat pasta.

Ingredients (serves 6)

- about 5 tablespoons extra virgin olive oil
- a bunch of sage finely chopped
- 2 garlic cloves, finely chopped
- 250g / 9oz (usually one box) pizzoccheri pasta, broken up roughly into 5cm / 2 inch pieces
- 1 Savoy cabbage, without the heart, roughly chopped (include as many of the dark outer leaves as you can; their flavour is a little more intense)
- 2 large waxy potatoes, peeled and diced
- 100g / 4oz fontina cheese, cut into small cubes
- 100g / 4oz unsalted butter, cut into small cubes
- 100g / 4oz Parmesan cheese, freshly grated
- salt and freshly ground black pepper

Method

Gently heat about 3 tablespoons of the olive oil and infuse it with the sage and garlic over a very low heat for a few minutes. Be careful not to burn the sage.

Cook all the bulky ingredients – the pasta, cabbage and potatoes – separately in boiling salted water until just tender, then drain. Put them in a large mixing bowl and cover with the infused olive oil. Add the rest of the oil if you need it to stop the mixture sticking together. Mix together thoroughly and season with salt and pepper. Now transfer the mixture to a large shallow dish (a lasagne dish or gratin dish is ideal) and cover with the fontina and butter, followed by the Parmesan. Bake in an oven preheated to 180°C/Gas Mark 4 for about 30 minutes, until the mixture has warmed through and the Parmesan has browned slightly. Eat immediately, then lie down and sleep.

Lasagna with Rabbit

One of the joys of the casual style we have at the pub is that we can serve some dishes in a rather un-restaurantlike way. On busy weekdays we might cook a huge lasagne in one of our terracotta baking trays. If we place it strategically on the bar as everyone rushes in for lunch, it can be demolished in minutes.

As far as I know there is nothing authentic about game and lasagne but I can tell you that it is a very good thing. If possible, ask the butcher to chop the rabbits up for you, as it's a messy job. You want the legs, shoulders and the meaty part of the body (the saddle). Throw away the rib cage.

We tend to serve this dish in winter. Our favourite accompaniment is a watercress salad dressed simply with olive oil and lemon juice.

Ingredients (serves 6)

- 3 tablespoons olive oil
- 2 wild rabbits (about 2kg in total), jointed (see above)
- 3 garlic cloves, roughly chopped
- 2 onions, roughly chopped
- a small bunch (about 30 leaves) of sage, roughly chopped
- about ½ bottle of red wine
- 2 tablespoons tomato purée
- 1 teaspoon sugar
- 1 tablespoon butter
- 1 packet of lasagne pasta (how much you use will depend on the size of the baking dish)
- salt and freshly ground black pepper

For the béchamel sauce:

- 100g / 4oz butter
- 50g / 2oz plain flour
- 750ml / 1¼ pints whole milk
- a pinch of grated nutmeg
- 100g / 4oz Parmesan cheese, freshly grated

Method

First, prepare the meat sauce. This can easily be done the day before you intend to eat this dish, and in some ways it is all the better for that as the meat rests in the boozy gravy. If you do this, refrigerate it as soon as it reaches room temperature.

Heat the olive oil in a large frying pan. Brown the rabbit pieces all over and then place to one side in a casserole. Lower the heat under the pan, add the garlic, onions and sage and fry until soft and translucent – don't worry if they catch a little. Pour in the wine and stir thoroughly so that it deglazes the pan a little. Add the tomato purée, sugar and some salt and pepper and pour all this over the rabbit pieces. If it does not quite cover the rabbit, top it up with some boiling water from the kettle. Add the butter, then cover the casserole, place it over a high heat and bring to simmering point. Lower the heat and cook for about 1½ hours or until the rabbit is very tender. It should be literally falling off the bone. If it begins to look a little short on juice while cooking, do add a bit more water. You will have plenty of opportunity to correct the seasoning later on.

When the rabbit is cooked, leave it to cool and drain off all the gravy. Keep this to one side. Pick all the rabbit meat off the bones and put it back into the gravy, then check the seasoning.

To make the béchamel sauce, gently melt the butter in a small pan and stir in the flour. Let it eat up all the butter; at this point things will look pretty unpromising. Cook over a low heat for 3–4 minutes, then slowly add the milk, stirring continuously, and bring to the boil. When you have a creamy white sauce, about the consistency of single cream, remove from the heat and season with nutmeg, salt and pepper. Stir in two-thirds of the grated Parmesan.

Now you are ready to build the lasagne. Grease a baking dish well. Start with a layer of the rabbit mixture and top this with pasta. Top the pasta with a thin coating of the white sauce. Now start again with the rabbit, finishing with pasta and white sauce. Cover the top with the remaining Parmesan – this can all be done well ahead of the meal.

Bake for approximately 35 minutes at 180°C/Gas Mark 4. I always start a lasagne on a low shelf or covered with foil. This stops the Parmesan browning too fast. About 10 minutes before the cooking time is up, test the pasta for softness with a fork and transfer the dish to the top shelf until the cheese is as browned as you fancy it.

Arroz con Conejo – Spanish Rice with Rabbit

This dish is juicier than paella because it is cooked in a deeper pot, a *cazuela*, allowing less water to evaporate during cooking. It's a very useful dish because it can be made with a wide variety of vegetables and bits of leftover chorizo. The main ingredients, apart from the rabbit, are broad beans and peas.

If possible, ask your butcher to chop up the rabbit for you. You need the legs, shoulders and the meaty part of the body (the saddle). Throw away the rib cage or use it to make the stock.

Ingredients (serves 6 generously)

- **150ml / ¼ pint olive oil**
- **1.5kg / 3¼ lb rabbit, jointed**
- **1 onion, chopped**
- **5 garlic cloves, chopped**
- **1 red and 1 green pepper, sliced**
- **2 large tomatoes, chopped**
- **2 carrots, finely chopped**
- **2 sprigs of thyme**
- **2 cured chorizos, sliced**

- **500g / 1lb 2oz calasparra or arborio rice**
- **1 bay leaf**
- **150g / 5oz broad beans (podded weight)**
- **100g / 4oz peas (podded weight)**
- **1 litre / 1¾ pints hot rabbit, chicken or vegetable stock**
- **1 tablespoon hot paprika**
- **2 lemons**
- **a handful of flat-leaf parsley, chopped**
- **salt and freshly ground black pepper**

Method

Heat the olive oil in a casserole dish and fry the rabbit until it is browned on all sides. Add the onion, garlic, peppers, tomatoes, carrots and thyme and fry for 10 minutes over a medium heat. Then add the chorizo and fry until it releases its fatty juice. Add the rice and stir well so that it absorbs the fat. Now add the bay, beans and peas. After 2 minutes, stir in the hot stock and the paprika. When the mixture starts to boil, reduce the heat and simmer for about 15 minutes or until the rice is almost cooked. Then take the pot off the heat and leave to rest for 10 minutes. Squeeze on the lemon juice, then season to taste, sprinkle with the parsley and serve.

Paella Valenciana

Paella originated in Valencia and its name derives from *paellera*, **the wide,**
shallow, two-handled pan in which it is cooked. Contrary to what most people think, it was originally made with meat but these days shellfish is more popular. There are so many different theories about the right way to make paella that it's difficult to know which, if any, to accept. I will explain the main points here and leave the rest to your own interpretation.

Traditionally calasparra rice is used. This is difficult to find unless you know of a Spanish shop, but it is similar to the Italian arborio rice, which is stocked by most supermarkets. Like arborio, calasparra is a round-grain rice which takes longer to cook than long-grain rice such as basmati. It absorbs liquid very slowly and then when the grains have swelled they release their starch all at once. Unlike a risotto, all the liquid is added to a paella in one go rather than in stages. You need a large flame, so if you don't have a big burner on your cooker it is probably best done on a barbecue.

Ingredients (serves 4–6)

- 2 *ñoras* (Spanish sweet dried peppers, also known as romescos), or 1 red pepper, chopped

- 150ml / ¼ pint olive oil

- 500g / 1lb 2oz boneless chicken, cut into small pieces

- 100g / 4oz boneless pork (leg or loin), cut into small pieces

- 1 small onion, finely chopped

- 1 small carrot, finely chopped

- 2 green peppers, chopped

- 150g / 5oz fresh butter beans (or use drained and rinsed tinned ones)

- 50g / 2oz peas

- 4 garlic cloves, finely chopped

- 3 or 4 tomatoes, skinned and finely chopped

- 100g / 4oz live snails (or use scrubbed cockles or clams if you can't get live, purged snails)

- 100g / 4oz cooked ham, diced

- 500g / 1lb 2oz calasparra or arborio rice

- 2 tablespoons paprika

- a pinch of saffron strands

- 1 litre / 1¾ pints hot chicken stock

- juice of 1 lemon

- salt

- lemon wedges, to serve

Method

If using *ñoras*, soak them in hot water for an hour, then drain and tear them into pieces.

Heat the olive oil in a paellera at least 40cm / 16 inches in diameter. Add the chicken and pork and fry until browned all over, then remove from the pan with a slotted spoon. Stir in the onion, carrot, green peppers, butter beans, peas, garlic and *ñoras* and cook until softened. Then add the tomatoes and wait until the juice runs, stirring several times. Add the snails (or cockles or clams) and ham. The heat will make the snails come out of their shells; at that moment add the rice. Stir well, return the chicken and pork to the pan and add the paprika and about 2 teaspoons of salt. Fry the mixture for 2 or 3 minutes so that the rice starts to catch, then add the saffron to the hot stock and pour it into the pan. When the paella starts to boil, add the lemon juice and turn the heat to low (the lemon juice prevents the rice becoming too sticky). It's best not to stir the paella now. Instead, move the pan occasionally so the heat is evenly distributed. When the rice is cooked (after about 15 minutes), cover with foil and leave to rest for 5 minutes. Adjust the seasoning if necessary and then serve with lemon wedges.

Risotto Law

I used to be terrified of attempting to cook a risotto. I imagined that it was best left to Italian mothers, since it required years of practice, and anyway surely you had to have been brought up in the northern provinces of Italy. Perhaps I should just buy the finished dish from those who know, I thought. In reality, like many Italian dishes, it has a well-defined method that can be mastered if approached carefully and intelligently. Be aware, though, of the many sins that are committed in risotto's name: a rice dish that has not been made with specific Italian varieties of rice (which allow the soft starch to be released and dissolved into the liquid, thus creamily binding the grains with the other ingredients) will never be a risotto.

The basic method holds for all the styles – the Veneto style is looser, while in Piedmont and Lombardy risotto is more compact and substantial. The latter is often served with sausages, grilled pork, osso bucco (see page 124) and the like. Almost any vegetable combination can form the basis of a risotto – notwithstanding the more ridiculous frivolities of *la nuova cucina*. As ever, my favourite recipes are the simplest.

These are the rules:

- Choose a superfino classified rice, i.e. with large, fat grains. Arborio is the most popular. It has a thin outer layer which releases its starch easily but leaves the grains nutty and separate. Carnaroli is prized for the perfect texture it provides. Vialone nano is a semifino variety and best for the Venetian loose style – terrific for Seafood Risotto (see page 92) and risotto made with young vegetables. In all cases allow about 50–60g / 2–2¼ oz rice per person as a starter and 75g / 3oz as a main course.

- You will need a heavy, thick-bottomed pan for cooking the risotto in. Stainless steel and enamelled cast iron are the best. Aluminium is not suitable, as the risotto will catch and cook unevenly.

- The stock must be light and well strained, so its flavour will not overpower the base ingredients. Make a chicken stock by putting some wings or drumsticks in a large saucepan with a leek, a carrot, an onion, a stick of celery, some bay leaves and some peppercorns. Cover with cold water and bring to a simmer – don't let it boil, even for a minute, or it will become cloudy with emulsified fat. Simmer for 45 minutes, then strain and return to the stove over a low heat – the stock must be hot when it is added to the risotto base. Substitute about 50g / 2oz broken dried porcini mushrooms (known as *bricciollini*, and much cheaper than the sliced ones) for the chicken if making a vegetarian mushroom risotto. If making a seafood risotto, simply steam open the shellfish with a splash of white wine in a covered pan to release their juices, then dilute these with water to use as the cooking liquid.

- Start the risotto by frying the finely chopped vegetables in butter. Salt added at this stage will help the vegetables to release moisture and become transparent without browning. Follow with the rice and continue cooking for a few minutes until it is toasted or opaque and beginning to stick to the pan, but don't let anything brown.

- I often add some wine at this stage, let it reduce and then follow with the stock. Add the stock to the rice mixture in stages, adding only enough to be absorbed within a few minutes. Keep stirring the mixture gently and repeat the applications of stock perhaps up to 6 times. Cooking times will vary, you must judge it by taste, but 20 minutes is my estimate. The objective is for the rice to be tender and luscious but never too soft in the centre.

- The last stage is performed off the heat, when the risotto is judged to be nearly done, and is known as *il mantecatura*: melt a large knob of butter on the surface of the cooked risotto, with the lid on, and then beat in a good tablespoon of Parmesan. Don't use any cheese with seafood risotto – it is regarded, quite correctly, as very, very wrong.

Risotto with Broad Beans & Mint

This is my favourite risotto. Although you can make a risotto with frozen broad beans, this one relies on the starchiness of fresh beans. It is incredibly simple to make but there is one fiddly task ahead of cooking. After you have podded the broad beans they must be shucked – i. e. taken out of their little grey sacs. This not only makes them more digestible but also reveals their true colour, a stunning bright green. Here is how to make it easy. Drop the podded broad beans into a pan of boiling salted water and leave for about 30 seconds, then drain and cool them quickly under cold running water. Take a bean in one hand and aim it at a large bowl. Squeeze gently between your forefinger and thumb. The bean will pop out of the membrane and fall into the bowl in two neat halves. Remember that the skill is in a gentle squeeze. Don't be brutal or you will squash the bean and miss the bowl. It takes some time but don't cheat.

You could use fresh, but not frozen, peas instead of broad beans and you could also substitute basil, marjoram or oregano for mint.

Ingredients (serves 5–6 as a starter)

- about 3kg / 6½ lb fresh broad beans (400g / 14oz podded and shucked weight – see above)

- 2 tablespoons extra virgin olive oil (optional)

- about 2 litres / 3½ pints vegetable or chicken stock

- 150g / 5oz unsalted butter

- 2 onions, finely chopped

- 2 garlic cloves, finely chopped

- 300g / 11oz arborio rice

- a glass of white wine

- a bunch of mint, chopped

- about 75g / 3oz Parmesan cheese, freshly grated

- salt and freshly ground black pepper

Method

The first thing I do for this recipe involves a food processor and is entirely optional. I put roughly half the broad beans in a food processor with the olive oil and pulse them roughly for about 20 seconds to make a loose paste. If the paste is too stiff, add a drop of water and pulse again very quickly. This adds a creamy base to the risotto and makes the colour a little more intense.

Put the stock in a pan and bring it to simmering point. Gently heat 100g / 4oz of the butter in a separate pan, add the onions and garlic with a little salt and fry gently until tender. Do not let them brown. Turn the heat up high and pour in the rice. Stir it with a wooden spoon for about half a minute, coating it with the butter; do not let it stick to the pan. Add the wine and let it bubble fiercely for about a minute, stirring gently all the time. Quickly stir in the broad bean paste, if using, then reduce the heat and start to add the hot stock in stages, as described on page 87. When the rice is done, remove from the heat, add the rest of the butter and cover the pan until it has melted. Stir it in with the broad beans and mint, then add the Parmesan and some seasoning. Serve immediately.

Risotto with Sage & Lemon

Like the classic Milanese risotto (see page 124), **this is incredibly simple to make,** so it is worth being picky about the ingredients. Buy unsprayed, unwaxed lemons because you will be grating the rind from them. Good stock and well-aged Parmiggiano Reggiano (Parmesan) cheese are essential. The herb I love for this risotto is sage but any of the woody herbs will do, rosemary or thyme in particular.

Ingredients (serves 5–6 as a starter)

- **about 2 litres / 3½ pints vegetable or chicken stock**

- **2 tablespoons olive oil**

- **100g / 4oz unsalted butter**

- **2 onions, finely chopped**

- **2 garlic cloves, finely chopped**

- **300g / 11oz arborio rice**

- **juice and grated rind of 2 lemons**

- **a bunch of sage, finely chopped**

- **1 teaspoon dried chilli flakes (optional)**

- **about 75g / 3oz Parmesan cheese, freshly grated**

- **salt and freshly ground black pepper**

Method

Put the stock in a pan and bring it to simmering point. Heat the olive oil and 75g / 3oz of the butter in a pan, add the onions and garlic with a little salt and fry gently until soft and translucent. Do not let them brown. Add the rice and turn the heat up high. Stir thoroughly for half a minute or so, until the rice is coated with the butter. Add the lemon juice and sage, plus the dried chilli if using. Turn the heat down and start adding the stock in stages, as described on page 87. When the rice is done, remove from the heat, add the remaining butter and cover the pan until it has melted. Stir the butter in with the lemon rind and Parmesan, then season to taste and serve immediately.

Smoked Haddock Risotto with Saffron, Fennel & Peas

A sort of arty kedgeree for six.

Ingredients (serves 6)

- 750g / 1lb 10oz skinned, undyed smoked haddock
- 1 leek
- 1 carrot
- 2 fennel bulbs
- 1 small onion
- a good bunch of parsley
- a good bunch of coriander
- 175g / 6oz butter
- 450g / 1lb risotto rice (arborio is fine)
- 1g (a decent pinch) of saffron threads
- 175g / 6oz peas (frozen petits pois will do)

- 100ml / 3½ fl oz white wine
- a squeeze of lemon juice
- salt and freshly ground black pepper

For the court-bouillon:

- 1 small onion, chopped
- 1 carrot, chopped
- 1 bay leaf
- a few parsley stalks
- 3 litres / 5 pints water
- a splash of white wine

Method

To make the court-bouillon, put all the ingredients in a large pan and bring to a gentle simmer. Add the smoked haddock and poach until just cooked, then remove the fish, flake it and set aside. Strain the poaching liquid and dilute it sufficiently to achieve a lightly flavoured stock – keep hot.

Finely chop the leek, carrot, fennel, onion, parsley and coriander – in a food processor if you have one. Soften this mixture in 100g / 4oz of the butter with a pinch of salt in a heavy pan. Add the risotto rice and cook for a couple of minutes at a moderate rate until most of the rice has turned opaque. Add the saffron threads, peas and white wine. After a minute, add enough hot stock just to cover the rice mixture and stir gently until most of it has been absorbed. Continue adding the stock in stages, as described on page 87, until the rice is done. The grains should have fluffed up and the mixture become creamy. Stir in the smoked haddock, remove from the heat, then add the remaining butter and cover the pan. When the butter has melted, stir it in with a squeeze of lemon, check the seasoning and serve.

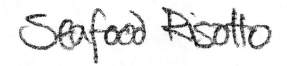
Seafood Risotto

This is a truly classic risotto from the Veneto, and fortunately all the seafood
is easily available outside Italy. Use any combination of mussels, clams, scallops, prawns, small squid or cuttlefish.

Ingredients (serves 6)

- about 500g / 1lb 2oz mussels
- about 500g / 1lb 2oz clams
- a glass of white wine
- 1 onion, finely chopped
- 1 carrot, finely chopped
- 1 fennel bulb, finely chopped
- 1 celery stick, finely chopped
- 2 garlic cloves, finely chopped
- 75ml / 2½ fl oz olive oil

- 175g / 6oz unsalted butter
- 200g / 7oz cleaned small squid, cut into strips
- 200g / 7oz raw prawns, shelled
- 450g / 1lb risotto rice, preferably vialone nano
- about 4 tablespoons chopped flat-leaf parsley
- 200g / 7oz cleaned fresh scallops, cut in half if they are king scallops
- juice of 1 lemon
- salt and freshly ground black pepper

Method

Scrub the mussels and clams, discarding any open ones that don't close when tapped, then purge them
of grit by soaking them in several changes of cold water. Put the mussels in a large saucepan with the white
wine, cover and leave over a high heat for a few minutes, until just opened. Remove them from the pan with a
slotted spoon and set aside, then add the clams to the pan and cook them in the same way. Remove them
from the pan and dilute the cooking liquid with 2 litres / 3½ pints of water. Strain this stock and keep it hot
in a pan over a low heat.

In a heavy pan, fry the vegetables and garlic in the olive oil and 100g / 4oz of the butter with black pepper
and a little salt for a couple of minutes. Add the squid and prawns and continue cooking for a few more
minutes. Add the rice and fry until it becomes opaque. Stir in the chopped parsley, then add the scallops,
mussels and clams. Add the stock in stages as described on page 87. Aim for a fairly loose, almost runny risotto. Remove from the heat, add the remaining butter and cover the pan. When it has melted, stir it
in with the lemon juice and serve.

fish

Grilled Tuna with Salmoriglio & New Potatoes

Salmoriglio is a southern Italian herb sauce that goes well with grilled fish and meat. It is strongly flavoured and should be treated with respect. Use the best olive oil you can afford. I have made it with oregano here but you can also make a very flavourful thyme salmoriglio as long as you use young, green thyme that will crush to a paste easily.

When buying the tuna, make sure you get fresh, not frozen, loin and ask the fishmonger to slice it for you rather than buying it ready sliced. Check that the fish doesn't look old and tired or grey but has a shiny complexion. It can be quite dark or pale, depending on which part of the loin and what type of tuna it is.

Ingredients

- **675g / 1½ lb new potatoes such as Jersey Royals, or waxy potatoes such as Pink Fir Apple or La Ratte, scrubbed clean**

- **a sprig of mint (optional)**

- **red wine vinegar, olive oil and chopped herbs for dressing the potatoes (optional)**

- **4 x 150g / 5oz fresh tuna steaks, about 1.5cm / ⅔ inch thick**

- **salt and freshly ground black pepper**

For the salmoriglio:

- **½ cup of clean, well-dried oregano leaves**

- **1 heaped teaspoon Maldon sea salt**

- **2 tablespoons lemon juice**

- **6–8 tablespoons good olive oil**

Method

First make the salmoriglio: put the oregano leaves and salt in a pestle and mortar and crush to a smooth paste. Mix in the lemon juice and then gradually add enough olive oil to make an emulsion.

Put the potatoes in a pan of cold water with some salt and the mint, if using, and bring to the boil. Simmer until tender, then drain well. If you like, you could toss the cooked potatoes with a few shakes of some very fine red wine vinegar and then with a little olive oil and whatever chopped herbs you fancy. I would probably use flat-leaf parsley and maybe a little mint, but there is no reason why you shouldn't use coriander, rocket or whatever else you have available.

To grill the tuna you need either a barbecue, in good weather, or a ridged grill pan or heavy-based frying pan. Whatever you use, it should be extremely hot before you add the fish. Season the tuna, going easy on the salt as the sauce will be quite salty, and then sear for about 45 seconds on each side, so it is medium rare. If it is cooked all the way through it will become dry and take on a rather different taste. If you don't like undercooked tuna, eat another fish.

Put the tuna on serving plates and spoon over the sauce, then serve with the potatoes.

Good Things to Go with Fish

Sweet, aromatic herbs such as flat-leaf parsley, coriander, tarragon, dill, chervil, oregano and basil can be used either in marinades for fish or in chopped raw salsas – see salmoriglio on page 94, for example. Herbs, chopped tomatoes, black olives and capers, mixed with lemon juice and olive oil, then warmed gently to make a dressing, make a good foil for simple grilled or baked fish. Lemon is essential for all fish. Gremolata, a barely-oiled chopped garnish of flat-leaf parsley, garlic, lemon rind and lemon juice (see page 124), is particularly good with simply cooked seafood.

The Provençal tapenade (see page 110) and *aioli* (a type of garlic mayonnaise) are very successful with cod and hake. Try very thinly sliced fennel embellished with parsley leaves, lemon and olive oil for oily fish such as tuna, swordfish and mackerel. Or thinly sliced, partially peeled and seeded cucumber, salted to purge it of excess moisture, then washed and dried and dressed with sherry vinegar and coriander leaves.

Other possibilities include roast or grilled fennel and tomatoes; spinach or young Swiss chard sautéed with lemon or black olives and garlic; roast pepper salads using anchovies, basil and capers with grilled fish; quickly fried chanterelles or field mushrooms with garlic for firm white fish such as turbot, brill or halibut; mashed potatoes with baked cod or hake. And some people say they don't like fish?

About Grilled Fish

Round, firm fish, such as sea bass, grey or red mullet, bream and sardines, are fantastic for grilling and, as with all fish, are tastier if cooked on the bone. This means a little more work for the eater but it is well worth it. As far as quantities go, 200g / 7oz cleaned and gutted per person is a fair rule of thumb.

Heat a griddle pan or overhead grill. If you are using a whole fish, make 2 or 3 slashes to the bone on each side. If using a fillet, score or slash the skin to stop it curling up, but don't cut through the flesh. Lightly oil and season with sea salt and a good grinding of pepper. Fillets should be grilled for 2–4 minutes per side, depending on thickness, until the flesh is firm to the touch and just beginning to flake. Whole fish will take longer, and if they weigh over 200g they should be cooked on a medium heat. They are done when the flesh is firm and just beginning to come away from the bone.

Baked Sea Bream or Sea Bass with Tomatoes

Serves 4

This is the easiest and most forgiving way to cook fish at home. Since the heat is less direct than with other methods, it may take a little longer than, say, grilling, but the trade-off is that timing is less critical and all you need is a shallow ovenproof dish or steel frying pan by way of equipment. Run the oven up to maximum heat, then reduce it to 200°C/Gas Mark 6 when putting the fish in.

You'll need a single fish weighing around 800g / 1lb 12oz (or 2 smaller ones) scaled, gutted and trimmed of its fins. Slash the fish twice on each side so that it will cook evenly, season it well inside and out and put it in an ovenproof dish. Slice 8 large, properly ripe tomatoes and lay them around the fish. Scatter sliced, not chopped, garlic, basil leaves and a couple of chopped anchovies over the tomatoes. Lubricate with olive oil and a little white wine. Bake at 200°C/Gas Mark 6 for around 25 minutes, or until the fish is firm to the touch and the flesh just starts to flake when prodded with a knife. Leave the fish to rest for a few minutes, then serve with something as uncomplicated as plain rice or bread, or nothing at all.

Smoked Haddock with Horseradish Mash & Poached Egg

One of the best light lunches ever. Buy undyed smoked haddock, which has a creamy colour (not yellow). The English smoked style is lighter in flavour than the Scottish, which is brined and then smoked over peat. The former uses larger fish; the latter is normally Finnan haddock, which are small split haddock.

Ingredients (serves 6)

- 6 x 200g / 7oz pieces of smoked haddock
- 6 free-range eggs

For the court-bouillon:

- 1.5 litres / 2½ pints water
- 1 tablespoon white wine vinegar
- bay, thyme and a few parsley stalks
- 6 black peppercorns
- a pinch of salt

For the horseradish mash:

- 1kg / 2¼ lb potatoes (such as Desiree, King Edward, Maris Piper or Spunta), peeled and halved
- up to 300ml / ½ pint milk (depending on the potato variety)
- 150g / 5oz butter
- 2 tablespoons finely grated fresh horseradish
- salt and freshly ground black pepper

Method

Boil the potatoes until tender in just enough salted water to cover. Drain well, return to the pot and dry over a low heat until all the remaining moisture evaporates. Heat the milk, then add it to the pan and crush the potatoes with a potato masher. Beat in the butter, horseradish and a good grind of pepper. Adjust the seasoning and keep warm.

Meanwhile, make the court-bouillon. Put all the ingredients in a pan big enough to hold all the fish and bring to the boil. Turn down to a simmer and remove the herbs and peppercorns. Drop in the fish and cook gently until it is firm and no longer translucent. Give it a prod with a knife to check – it must be lightly cooked.

If you are feeling confident, poach the eggs alongside the fish. If not, do them in a separate pan.

Divide the mash and fish between 6 serving plates and put an egg on top of each portion. This tastes even better served with buttered sautéed spinach.

Variation

We often replace the horseradish mash with saffron mash – a very fine invention that appears all
over the place but has to be attributed to (the guru) Simon Hopkinson, formerly of Bibendum restaurant.
Infuse a gram of saffron in the milk (you may use a mixture of milk and cream) while it is heating through,
and omit the horseradish. The in-joke here is that real smoked haddock and mash has white haddock and
yellow mash instead of the other way round.

Bacalhau com Batatas – Baked Salt Cod with Peppers & Potatoes

This was one of the first dishes I saw being cooked at the Eagle – the smell of the salt cod, peppers, onions and potatoes took me back home to Brazil. It is sometimes called by the Lisboan slang name, bacalhauada. The flavours complement each other really well.

Ingredients (serves 6)

- **800g / 1¾ lb dried salt cod, soaked (see page 101)**
- **6 tablespoons olive oil, plus extra for drizzling**
- **2 large Spanish onions, sliced**
- **4 garlic cloves, finely chopped**
- **2 green peppers, sliced**
- **12 large Cyprus potatoes, peeled and quartered**
- **2 bay leaves**

- **juice of 1 lemon**
- **2 handfuls of chopped parsley**
- **4 tablespoons black olives**
- **3 vine-ripened tomatoes, sliced**
- **3 hard-boiled eggs, sliced**
- **freshly ground black pepper**

Method

Put the soaked salt cod in a large saucepan of simmering water and cook gently for 15–20 minutes, until the flesh is beginning to flake. Drain and leave to cool a little – pick out any bones while it is still warm. Toss the fish with a couple of tablespoons of the oil to keep it moist.

Fry the onions in the remaining oil until soft and brown, then add the garlic and green peppers and cook for 2–3 minutes. Meanwhile, in a separate pan, cover the potatoes with salted cold water, bring to the boil and simmer for 5 minutes. Drain them and add them to the onion and peppers. Add the bay leaves, lemon juice, half the parsley, the salt cod and some black pepper and mix carefully. Transfer the mixture to a baking dish and cook in an oven preheated to 200°C/Gas Mark 6 for 30 minutes. Remove from the oven and sprinkle over the olives and tomatoes. Cook for a further 5 minutes, then put the sliced hard-boiled eggs on top, sprinkle with the remaining parsley and drizzle with olive oil. Serve hot, with a bowl of green salad.

Baccalà alla Palmeritana – Salt Cod with Prunes & Pickling Onions

The sweet and sour flavours of this Sicilian salt cod stew are a reminder of the Arabic influences in Sicily. My grandmother always cooks this dish for Christmas Eve.

Ingredients (serves 4)

- 4 tablespoons olive oil
- 1 onion, finely chopped
- 750g / 1lb 10oz salt cod, soaked (see below)
- 250g / 9oz tomatoes (tinned or fresh), chopped

- 100g / 4oz prunes
- 200g / 7oz pickling onions (you can use *cipollini* – silverskin onions – or the white bulbs from spring onions), peeled but left whole
- salt and freshly ground black pepper

Method

Heat the oil in a heavy pan, add the onion and cook until lightly browned. Add the soaked and drained salt cod, then cover and leave for 10 minutes over a medium heat. Add the tomatoes and prunes and simmer gently for 20 minutes, then add the pickling onions. Cook for 30 minutes more on a very gentle heat, until the pickling onions are tender. Carefully stir in some seasoning, then serve. *Buon appetito!*

About Salt Cod

A good fishmonger should stock salt cod, or be able to get it for you. You can also find it in delicatessens and even some supermarkets. Buy salt cod that is as thick as possible, without any yellowing, which happens when it has been badly stored. Wash as much salt from the fish as you can and then soak it, skin side up, in plenty of cold water in the fridge for a day. Change the water two or three times during this period. Even better, and quicker, would be to have a constant flow of water running over the fish, although I admit this is hardly feasible in the average kitchen. The fish should not taste overly salty at the end of the soaking period; the only way to check it is to taste a bit.

Some recipes ask that the flesh is removed from the bones at this stage, others require you to poach the fish first. In the latter case, bring a large pan of water to a barely moving simmer, add the cod and cook for 15–20 minutes, until it begins to flake. Drain the fish and remove any bones and skin.

Rape en Adobo – Fried Marinated Monkfish

This is an old gypsy recipe from the coast near Cadiz. Adobo is a kind of marinade that will preserve the fish for a few days, simultaneously giving it a wonderful flavour. A very easy recipe, it would also be suitable for hake, shark, cod or mackerel. It can be eaten as a light tapa dish or as a main course with rice, fried potatoes, tomato salad or sautéed spinach with garlic and lemon.

Ingredients (serves 4 as a main course)

- 600g / 1lb 5oz monkfish tail, skinned, boned and cut into large chunks
- 2 tablespoons plain flour
- 200ml / 7fl oz olive oil
- a squeeze of lemon
- lemon wedges, to serve

For the adobo:

- 2 tablespoons olive oil
- 1 large onion, chopped
- 1 carrot, finely chopped
- 4 garlic cloves, chopped
- a little bay, thyme and parsley
- 2 slices of lemon
- 1 tablespoon paprika
- 1 tablespoon vinegar
- salt

Method

To make the adobo, heat the oil in a frying pan and fry the onion, carrot and garlic in it for 3 minutes. Add the bay, thyme, parsley, lemon slices, paprika, vinegar and some salt, then turn down the heat and cook gently for 8 minutes. Leave to cool.

Toss the monkfish with the adobo and leave for 2–3 hours in a cool place – the longer you leave it, the stronger the flavour will be.

Remove the fish from the adobo and toss it with the flour. Fry in the olive oil over a medium heat for about 4 minutes. Squeeze on a little lemon juice and serve immediately, with lemon wedges.

Caldeirada de Mariscos – Big Portuguese Fish Stew

Almost every restaurant on the Cascais / Estoril coast has some kind of fish
caldeirada. The combination of fish used depends on what's available, so modify the suggestions below if you have to.

Ingredients (serves 6)

- **18 raw king prawns**
- **about 40 large mussels**
- **2 onions, finely chopped**
- **3 garlic cloves, finely chopped**
- **4 tablespoons olive oil**
- **2 bay leaves**
- **a pinch of saffron**
- **2 green and 2 red peppers, cut into eighths**
- **3 large baking potatoes, peeled and chopped**
- **400g tin of peeled plum tomatoes, drained and chopped**
- **1 tablespoon tomato purée**
- **a pinch of hot paprika**
- **100ml / 3½ fl oz white wine**

- **500g / 1lb 2oz monkfish cheeks or tail, cut into about 18 pieces**
- **500g / 1lb 2oz sea bass or sea bream, cleaned and cut into 3cm / 1¼ inch pieces**
- **500g / 1lb 2oz mackerel or sardines, cleaned and cut into 3cm / 1¼ inch pieces**
- **salt and freshly ground black pepper**
- **lemon halves, to serve**

For the stock:

- **1 celery stick, roughly chopped**
- **1 carrot, roughly chopped**
- **1 garlic clove, roughly chopped**
- **1 bay leaf**
- **3 peppercorns**
- **1 litre / 1¾ pints water**

Method

Pull off the heads and shells of the prawns and set aside. Remove the black vein from the back of each prawn with the tip of a knife. Put the heads and shells in a pan with all the ingredients for the stock and bring to the boil. After 3 minutes, lower the heat to a simmer and cook for a further 45 minutes, skimming off the scum with a ladle. Pour the stock through a sieve and set aside.

Scrub the mussels, removing any barnacles and their beards and throwing away any open ones that won't close when tapped on a work surface. In a large saucepan, gently fry the onions and garlic in the olive oil until softened. Add the bay leaves and saffron and fry until the onions are light brown. Add the peppers and potatoes and fry for 3 minutes, then stir in the tomatoes and cook for a further 3 minutes. Add 750ml/11/4 pints of the hot stock, plus the tomato purée, paprika and wine. Boil for 3 minutes and then reduce to a medium heat. If you want a thicker consistency, break up some of the potato pieces with the back of a spoon. Season with salt and pepper to taste.

Increase the heat and add the monkfish and prawns, then 2 minutes later add the bass or bream and mussels. After a further 2 minutes add the mackerel or sardines and turn off the heat. The mackerel or sardines will cook in the residual heat. Serve in large bowls, with halved lemons.

Octopus Stew with Spices from Goa

In Goa I once ate squid cooked with a violently hot red paste, accompanied by
Portuguese bread, not rice. Some swift detective work led me to the discovery of *recheado*, which had given the dish its fierce
heat. It can be used as a marinade, like piri-piri (see page 108), or cooked gently with onions and other vegetables to start a stew,
as we do in this recipe. In Goa the stew might be enriched with coconut milk but at the Eagle we bring the flavour closer to
Mediterranean shores by using wine – unorthodox but it tastes good. Usually I would baulk at putting wine and Indian spices
in the same pan, but *recheado* is an exception.

You can make this stew with squid and it will be faster to cook if you do, but at the pub we have found that octopus likes a long,
slow cooking time, perhaps more than any other fish. So we often make this stew a day ahead of eating it. You might already know
that this trick does wonders for all 'curries'. An excellent variation is to add chunks of potato near the end of the cooking time.
We sometimes use a pulse such as white beans or chickpeas instead.

Ingredients (serves 6)

- 2 or 3 medium-sized octopus
  (around 500g / 1lb 2oz each)

- 3 tablespoons olive oil

- 2 onions, roughly chopped

- 2 or 3 red or green peppers

- a glass of white wine

- 1 teaspoon sugar

- a bunch of fresh coriander,
  roughly chopped

- salt and freshly ground black pepper

For the *recheado*:

- 1 teaspoon cumin seeds

- 2 tablespoons dried red chillies

- 1 cinnamon stick, broken up

- 1 teaspoon cloves

- 1 teaspoon cardamom pods

- 3 bay leaves

- 2 tablespoons smoked paprika

- 1 tablespoon olive oil

- 1 onion, finely chopped

- 4 or 5 garlic cloves, finely chopped

- 1 teaspoon salt

- 100ml / 3½ fl oz white wine vinegar

Method

First make the *recheado*: heat a heavy-bottomed frying pan, throw in all the spices and give them a dry roasting on the hob for about a minute, until you smell them unlocking their flavours. It is obvious when this happens. Transfer the spices to a food processor or blender and grind them thoroughly. Heat the oil in the same pan and fry the onion and garlic until tender. Add them to the ground spices with the salt and vinegar and blend again until you have a smooth paste. If it seems too stiff, add a little more oil.

Here is how to attack a whole octopus: lay it flat on the chopping board with the tentacles to the right. Remove them with a sharp knife and keep to one side. Where the tentacles meet the body is the head. You should be able to see the eyes. Octopus have no bones but there is a hard, shell-like beak. Cut the beak and eyes away and discard them. The body will contain all sorts of gunk, and is best cleaned by turning it inside out, like a rubber glove. Then you can wash everything away. What you are left with (the tentacles and body) can be cut up like a pepper or sliced into rings.

Heat the oil in a large pan and fry the onions and peppers in it until tender. Add the octopus and a generous tablespoon of the *recheado* paste (the rest can be stored in the fridge in a tightly sealed jar, where it should keep for ages). Turn the heat up high and stir thoroughly. Add the wine and let it bubble fiercely. Cover the pan, lower the heat and cook gently for 1½–2 hours or until the octopus is very tender. Check the stew often to make sure that it doesn't dry out. If it does, add a little water. Stir in the sugar and some salt and pepper, plus more *recheado* if you want more heat. But be careful if leaving it to rest overnight, it may become hotter by itself – chillies have a way of doing this.

Serve the stew on mounds of rice, with the coriander sprinkled on top, or with lots of bread.

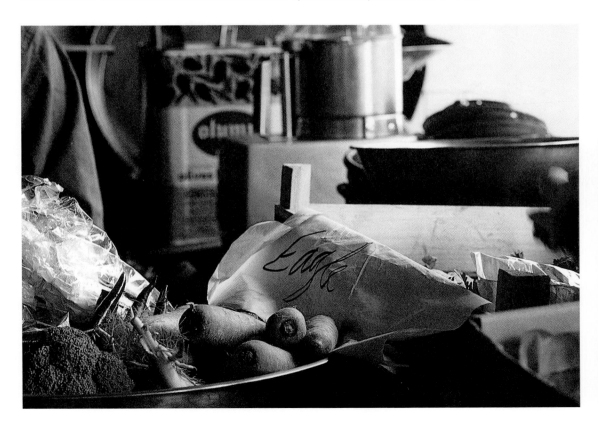

Grilled Squid Piri-Piri

David Eyre

Piri-piri is a fierce Portuguese marinade and basting sauce, made originally from the small hot chillies of the same name, grown in Portugal's former African colonies. Grilled chicken is the more usual vehicle for piri-piri, but squid is the thing; though I would also recommend fresh tiger prawns and, if the occasion should arise, roast suckling pig. The squid should really be barbecued rather than grilled conventionally.

Ingredients (serves 6)

- 2 red peppers
- 2kg / 4½ lb fresh, not frozen, squid – this will provide just over 1kg / 2¼ lb cleaned squid (see below)
- 6 fresh red chillies (or more), seeded
- 2 garlic cloves, chopped

- 3 bay leaves
- 2 teaspoons ground coriander
- 200ml / 7fl oz olive oil
- 2 teaspoons sea salt
- 3 tablespoons wine vinegar

Method

Grill the red peppers all over until the skin has blackened, then leave until cool enough to handle. Peel and seed them, then set aside.

Clean the squid. They are easier to clean than they look. Pull the head and tentacles away from the body, bringing the innards with them. Remove the plastic-like quill from inside the body, then wash the body – cut it open along its length to facilitate cleaning if necessary. Cut the tentacles off the head in one piece, just in front of the eyes, and trim the longer tentacles. Discard the head. Remove the 'beak' from the centre of the tentacles and discard it.

To make the marinade, purée the red peppers, chillies, garlic, bay and coriander in a blender or food processor. Stir in enough of the oil to make a loose paste. Marinate the squid in half of this paste for at least 4 hours. Mix the remaining paste with the salt, remaining oil and the vinegar to make the basting sauce, then taste to check that it is hot enough.

Grill the squid on a steady fire, basting it every minute or two (use a new paintbrush with natural bristles). Serve with a tomato salad and rice.

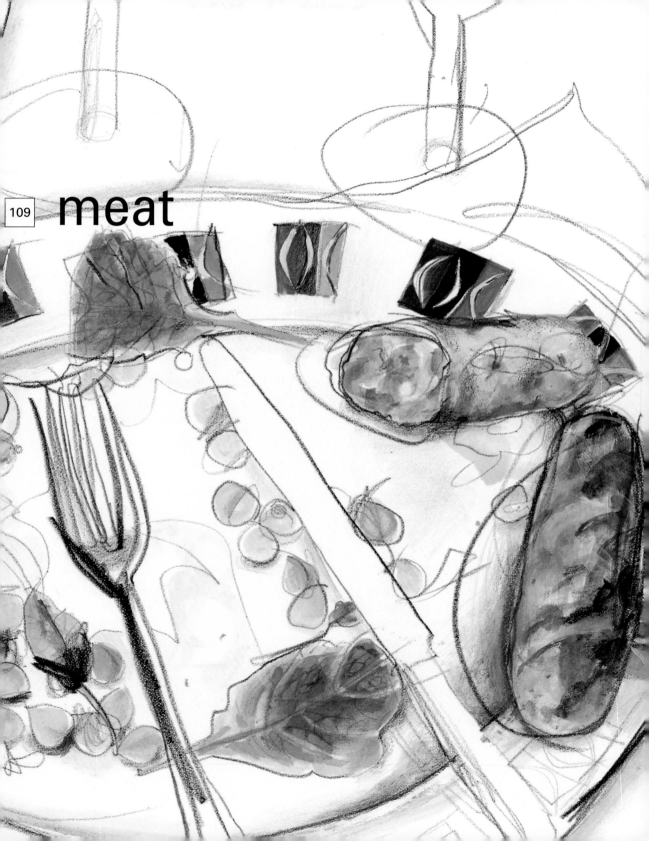

meat

Saddle of Lamb Stuffed with tapenade

Ask your butcher to bone the saddle of lamb and leave it untied. It's best to
stuff it a few hours before you roast it to let the flavours seep in. The quantities given below for the tapenade make a large jar, which will keep well if you cover it with olive oil and store it in the fridge. Use for grilled fish or meat.

Ingredients (serves 6)

- **1 saddle of lamb (without the chump)**
- **4 tablespoons olive oil**
- **salt and freshly ground black pepper**

For the tapenade:

- **about 500g / 1lb 2oz black olives, pitted**
- **3 garlic cloves, chopped**
- **juice of 1 large lemon**
- **150ml / ¼ pint olive oil**
- **a handful of capers, soaked in cold water for 30 minutes and then squeezed**
- **½ small tin of anchovies, drained**
- **1 heaped teaspoon Dijon mustard**
- **a shot of brandy**

Method

Put all the ingredients for the tapenade in a food processor and pulse until the mixture is nearly smooth but still retains some texture.

Put the saddle skin-side down and open it out. Spread about 4 tablespoons of the tapenade on to and into all the surfaces of the meat. Fold it up and turn it over. You will need to tie it up. First tie a piece of string around the whole thing horizontally and then a few pieces in a row perpendicular to the first string. The tapenade will do most of the seasoning but lightly salt and pepper the outside of the meat. Set aside for a few hours so it can absorb the flavours of the tapenade.

Heat the olive oil in a roasting tin on the hob and brown the saddle all over. Transfer to an oven preheated to 200°C/Gas Mark 6 and roast for about 45 minutes. To check if the meat is done, insert a skewer right into the centre and leave it for 10 seconds, then lay it on your lips; it should be blood temperature. Leave the meat to rest in a warm place for 20–30 minutes, then carve into thick slices and serve with roast potatoes and French beans or salad.

Lamb Shanks with Chickpeas

A dish for patient people. The key to tasty lamb shanks and soft chickpeas is time, lots of it. The meat should be cooked until it is almost falling off the bone; the chickpeas should be creamy, with very little bite. This dish is quite brothy – the stock pretty much makes itself, due to the long cooking process.

Ingredients (serves 6)

- **5 tablespoons olive oil**
- **6 lamb shanks**
- **2 large onions, roughly chopped**
- **3 garlic cloves, roughly chopped**
- **3 leeks, roughly chopped**
- **3 celery sticks, roughly chopped**
- **about ½ bottle of white wine**

- **1 teaspoon dried mint**
- **a generous pinch of saffron**
- **2 tablespoons tomato purée**
- **about 250g / 9oz chickpeas, soaked in cold water overnight, or 2 x 400g / 14oz tins of chickpeas (look for a brand that adds nothing but salt and water)**
- **a bunch of parsley or coriander, chopped**
- **salt and freshly ground black pepper**

Method

Heat the olive oil in a large frying pan over a fierce heat. Brown the lamb shanks in it and then put them to one side. Pour the fat and juices from the pan into a large casserole and use them to fry the onions, garlic, leeks and celery, adding a little more oil if you need to. When the vegetables have softened but not browned, add the wine, mint and saffron. As soon as it is bubbling, stir in the tomato purée. Add the lamb shanks and turn to coat them with the other ingredients. Add enough water for the shanks to be just about covered, but not swimming. Cover and cook over a low heat for about 2 hours.

Meanwhile, deal with the chickpeas, if you are using dried ones. Drain them of their soaking water, put them in a large pan of unsalted water and bring to the boil. Boil them rapidly for 10 minutes, then drain again. Now cover them with fresh water again and simmer until tender. The best way to get chickpeas right is to keep tasting the odd one. If the water evaporates before the chickpeas are tender, just add more boiling water from the kettle.

When the lamb has been cooking for about 2 hours, add the chickpeas and enough of their cooking liquid to cover. If they look as if they will swamp the stew, don't add them all. Continue cooking until the lamb is tender and the chickpeas are a little overcooked; make sure the stew does not dry out – add a little more liquid if necessary.

Serve in bowls with plenty of the liquid, garnished with the parsley or coriander and accompanied by some good bread for mopping up the juices.

Lamb, Olive & Artichoke Stew

Phil Pickering

This Sardinian dish starts off with a _soffritto_ – a mixture of finely chopped vegetables stewed gently in plenty of olive oil until tender. It's a classic Mediterranean technique that gives the stew a rich flavour base.

Ingredients (serves 6)

- **1 leg of lamb, boned and cut into 3cm / 1¼ inch pieces, or cut into fist-sized chunks with the bone in**
- **150ml / 5fl oz olive oil**
- **1 tablespoon tomato purée**
- **400g / 14oz tin of plum tomatoes, drained and chopped**
- **a good bunch of flat-leaf parsley, leaves and stalks chopped separately**
- **2 bay leaves**
- **a glass of sherry or white wine**

- **about 300ml / ½ pint vegetable stock or water**
- **20 kalamata olives, pitted**
- **400g / 14oz fresh globe artichokes, prepared (see below) – or, if you must, 2 tins of globe artichokes in brine, drained and rinsed**
- **rind and juice of 2 lemons**
- **salt and freshly ground black pepper**

For the _soffritto_:

- **3 onions, finely chopped**
- **2 garlic cloves, finely chopped**
- **2 carrots, finely chopped**
- **2 celery sticks, finely chopped**

Method

In a large, heavy pan, fry the lamb in 3 tablespoons of the oil until browned all over. Drain, remove from the pan and set aside while you prepare the base for the stew. Pour off the fat from the pan, add the rest of the oil and sweat the _soffritto_ vegetables in it with a pinch of salt and pepper for about 10 minutes, until the onions are glassy. Stir occasionally to keep them from sticking.

Add the tomato purée, plum tomatoes, parsley stalks, bay, the lamb, the sherry or wine and half the stock or water. Cover and simmer, stirring occasionally, for 50 minutes, or about 1½ hours if using lamb on the bone. The meat should be tender.

Skim away any fat from the surface by using the base of the ladle in a circular motion to spread the fat to the side and then remove it. If necessary, add the rest of the stock or water to cover the meat. Now add the olives, artichokes and the rest of the parsley and heat gently for 10 minutes. Squeeze in the lemon juice, then taste for more salt and pepper to suit. Serve garnished with the lemon rind and accompanied by rice, potatoes, mash or polenta.

Preparing Globe Artichokes

There are two things you must have to hand when preparing artichokes: a really sharp paring knife and a supply of halved lemons. The dark green, inedible parts of an artichoke are notoriously tough, and any cut surfaces will oxidise or blacken within a minute unless rubbed with lemon.

The simplest way to cook and eat an artichoke is to boil it in salted water containing a couple of lemon halves until the tip of a knife finds the heart or base to be tender (I don't like to cook them in anything other than stainless steel pans). First trim the tips of the petals by about a third and rub with lemon, then remove the first layer or so of the outer petals. Cut off the stem and carefully trim the remaining dark green bits from the base of the artichoke. Rub with lemon and put it in the saucepan. After cooking, open out the top of the artichoke and remove all of the hairy choke with a teaspoon (I use a worn, and thus sharp, one). To eat the artichoke, remove the leaves, each with a nugget of edible heart attached, and nibble this off until all that is left is the prize – the heart. Use a classic vinaigrette as a dip or sauce.

If you want to braise the artichokes or use them in a dish such as the Lamb, Olive and Artichoke Stew on page 112, then a little more work is needed. Snap off all the dark outer leaves until you are left with pale green ones; rub these with lemon. Cut off the top of the artichoke half way down, remove the purple inner parts and the choke (all of it!) and rub with lemon. Trim the stem, leaving about 5cm / 2 inches attached – less if the artichokes are large or not very fresh – then peel the woody outer layer of the stem. Again, lemon! Trim the remaining green parts as above. The artichoke can now be cut into slices or quarters, if large, not forgetting to rub them with more lemon. For the lamb stew I generally quarter them. Keep in water acidulated with the spent lemon halves until needed.

Feijoada – Portuguese Pork & Bean Stew

114

Feijoada roughly means 'beany', and combines various fresh pork cuts
and charcuterie with creamy beans. In Brazil it is made with black beans but this is the Portuguese (white bean)
version from the Tras-os-Montes region.

Ingredients (serves 8–10)

- **5 tablespoons olive oil**

- **1kg / 2¼ lb pork belly, trimmed of skin and some fat and cut into large chunks**

- **500g / 1lb 2oz pancetta, chopped into chunks**

- **500g / 1lb 2oz ham hocks, chopped into large chunks**

- **3 onions, chopped**

- **3 carrots, sliced**

- **3 garlic cloves, finely chopped**

- **2 green peppers, chopped**

- **2 bay leaves**

- **400g / 14oz tin of tomatoes**

- **500g / 1lb 2oz cured chorizo, roughly chopped**

- **½ teaspoon freshly ground black pepper**

- **1 teaspoon hot paprika**

- **500g / 1lb 2oz dried cannellini beans, butter beans or similar, soaked overnight in cold water**

- **a bunch of coriander, chopped**

Method

Heat 2 tablespoons of the oil in a large casserole and brown the pork, pancetta and ham hocks in it a few pieces at a time. Transfer the meat to a dish. Add the remaining oil to the pan and gently fry the onions, carrots, garlic, green peppers and bay for 10 minutes. Add the tomatoes, chorizo, browned meat and spices, then pour in sufficient water to barely cover the meat. Bring to the boil, cover and bake for 2½ hours in an oven preheated to 160°C/Gas Mark 3.

Meanwhile, drain the beans, cover with fresh water, then bring to the boil and drain again. Cover with fresh water again and bring to the boil, then simmer for about 1–1½ hours, until tender. Drain and add to the stew. Mix and taste – you may not need any salt if the chorizo and pancetta are salty. Sprinkle with the chopped coriander and serve in bowls, with crusty bread on the side.

Belly Pork Stew with Peas & Saffron

This stew is from Galicia in northwest Spain, where a lot of vegetables are grown because of the wetter climate. Although we often make pork stews at the Eagle, this one doesn't appear on the menu very often because of the peas, which we tend to cook only in the summer. A word about peas: I am not shy of using frozen peas or broad beans in most dishes. Not only does it save time podding but the growers pack them so fresh that they often beat hands down the weary real McCoy arriving in London. If you have a garden and grow your own, that is, of course, another matter. The peas in this recipe are cooked for a long time so it may be prudent to use frozen peas anyway, saving your fresh ones for a chance to steal the show another day.

Our favourite cuts of pork for stewing at the Eagle are shoulder and belly, off the bone. We tend to use belly when there are other bulky ingredients such as beans or potatoes, since it is the fattiest cut. You may wish to trim the thick layer of fat (which makes crackling when you roast the meat) from either cut – it's entirely up to you.

Ingredients (serves 6)

- 4 tablespoons olive oil
- 1.5kg / 3¼ lb belly or shoulder of pork, boned and cut into large chunks
- 2 onions, finely chopped
- 3 garlic cloves, finely chopped
- a glass of dry white wine
- 2 tablespoons sherry vinegar

- a pinch of saffron
- 1 teaspoon tomato purée
- 1kg / 2¼ lb peas
- 3 large waxy potatoes, peeled and roughly chopped
- a bunch of flat-leaf parsley, roughly chopped (about a handful)
- salt and freshly ground black pepper

Method

Heat half the olive oil in a large frying pan and brown the chunks of pork. This is a job best done in 2 or 3 batches. Be careful not to brown too many pieces at a time or they will stew rather than fry. When the pork is browned, put it to one side in a bowl to catch any escaping juices.

Gently heat the remaining oil in a large casserole and fry the onions and garlic until translucent and tender. Do not let them brown. Add the pork and its juices and stir briefly. Turn up the heat and add the wine and vinegar. When the wine is bubbling, add the saffron and tomato purée and stir thoroughly. Now turn the heat down low and let the stew reach a gentle simmer. Refill the wine glass with water and cover the meat with this. The pork should be just submerged enough to stew but not swim; add a little more water if necessary. Season with a pinch of black pepper and a good teaspoon of salt.

Cook gently until the pork is tender, which may take 1½–2 hours. About 30 minutes before serving, add the peas and potatoes and cook until the potatoes are tender but not falling apart. Check the seasoning again and serve in large bowls, garnished with the chopped parsley.

Arista — Roast Pork, Tuscan Style

David Eyre

116

This Tuscan pork loin roast with garlic and fennel seed has never failed me.

The dry marinade subtly perfumes the meat and somehow prevents the pork drying out. The loin is normally prepared with the skin removed, which certainly helps in the marinating process. In Italy all the skin seems to be saved for use in their very fine sausages. Thus crackling is unknown, which is a shame as surely that's the whole point of roast pork.

Ask your butcher to leave the bone on the loin but loosened from the meat to make carving easier. Ask, too, that the roast be cut from the rib end of the loin and, if you want the crackling, for the skin to be scored and removed — it can be roasted alongside.

Ingredients (serves 6–8)

- **5 garlic cloves, chopped**
- **2 tablespoons fennel seeds**
- **3 tablespoons chopped parsley**
- **2 teaspoons salt**

- **fruity olive oil**
- **1 loin of pork weighing 2–3kg / 4½–6½ lb, prepared as described above**
- **freshly ground black pepper**

Method

In a food processor or pestle and mortar, grind together the garlic, fennel seeds, parsley, salt and some freshly ground pepper, then mix in enough olive oil to make a paste. Rub this thoroughly all over the meat and tie the meat up with string. If you can leave it in the fridge overnight, all the better.

Roast uncovered in an oven preheated to 180°C/Gas Mark 4 for about 1½ hours, then turn the oven up high and continue roasting for half an hour or so. A meat thermometer in the centre of the joint should read 80°C. To make crackling, rub plenty of salt (but no oil) into the skin and roast separately — remove from the oven if it is done before the meat is ready.

Leave the meat to rest for 20 minutes or so, then carve it into thick slices and serve with any form of Oven Potatoes (see page 148) and perhaps Roast Red Onions (see page 145).

Fabada Asturiana – Asturian Pork & Butter Bean Stew

It can be cold in northern Spain and they are famous in Asturias and Cantabria for their dried beans, which lend themselves to winter dishes. This is my favourite version of pork with beans. It uses large dried butter beans, known as *judiones* or simply *faves*, and seven different types of pork. I might occasionally include a pinch of saffron threads, added when all is gently boiling, but it would not be an authentic thing to do. It's a good idea to make this dish the day before eating it.

Ingredients (serves 8–10)

- 500g / 1lb 2oz dried butter beans, soaked overnight in cold water

- about 500g / 1lb 2oz raw ham or gammon hock

- 1 raw pork hock or a trotter

- 500g / 1lb 2oz streaky bacon in one piece, smoked or not

- 200g / 7oz Spanish *tocino* (salted pork belly fat), Italian lardo salato, the fat trimmings from serrano or Parma ham, or really fat bacon

- 700g / 1lb 9oz fresh belly pork, in slices, or veal shin in pieces (as would be cut for osso bucco)

- 4 bay leaves

- a few sprigs of thyme

- 1 or 2 dried chillies

- 300g / 11oz morcilla (Spanish blood sausage)

- 400g / 14oz good-quality cooking chorizo

- 10 large garlic cloves, peeled

- 2 onions, sliced

- salt and freshly ground black pepper

Method

Put the drained beans and the hocks in a large pot, cover with cold water and boil for 15 minutes. Drain, then return to the pan and cover with hot water. Add the bacon, *tocino*, belly pork and herbs and cook for 1 hour at a steady simmer. Add the remaining ingredients and cook for another hour or until the beans are tender. Make sure that the stew is always just covered with water.

Remove the hocks and pick off the meat, then return it to the pot. Cut the bacon and chorizo into chunky pieces – the morcilla will have broken up. Check the seasoning but it is unlikely that salt will be needed. I sometimes stir in a handful of chopped flat-leafed parsley. Another good thing to eat with bread.

Porco à Alentejana – Pork & Clams, Alentejo Style

David Eyre

119

Although it is from the south of the country, this dish is a great favourite with all Portuguese and, while the idea might sound a little wacky, I guarantee it will become a favourite of yours as well. It is typically cooked in a *cataplana* – a unique cooking vessel in the form of two copper bowls that are hinged rather like a giant clam shell, which can be used on the stove, in the oven or even in a fire. I invariably make it in a heavy saucepan with a tightly fitting lid.

The Portuguese would use tiny clams but in my temperate island version I like to use well-washed cockles. You must fry the pork in lard or the flavour will not be right.

Ingredients (serves 6)

- 500g / 1lb 2oz lean pork (leg or loin), cut into 2cm / ¾ inch dice
- 500g / 1lb 2oz belly pork, cut into 2cm / ¾ inch dice
- 3–4 garlic cloves, finely chopped
- 1 heaped teaspoon paprika, preferably smoked
- ½ bottle of white wine
- 2 bay leaves
- 2 cloves
- 1kg / 2¼ lb live cockles or small clams
- 125g / 4½ oz good-quality lard
- 75ml / 2½ fl oz olive oil
- 1 onion, finely chopped
- 3 tablespoons chopped parsley
- 1 generous tablespoon tomato purée
- salt and freshly ground black pepper

Method

Mix the meat with the garlic, paprika, wine, bay and cloves and leave to marinate for 3–6 hours. Scrub the cockles or clams well, throwing away any open ones that won't close when tapped. Leave them in a colander within a large pan or sink full of cold water to purge them of sand and grit. This may take several hours; shaking them about occasionally will speed things up.

Remove the pieces of meat from the marinade and strain it. Melt the lard in a large frying pan, add the meat, season with salt and pepper and fry steadily until nicely browned. You may have to do this in two batches. Pour the marinade into the pan and continue cooking the meat until it is tender – about half an hour.

Heat the olive oil in a separate pan and cook the onion in it with the parsley until softened. Stir in the tomato purée and simmer for 5 minutes, then add the cockles or clams. As soon as they have started to open, add the meat and cook, covered, for another 3–5 minutes. Check the seasoning and serve.

About Roasting Meat

The basic techniques for roasting meat successfully are logical enough. If the cut is lean, I would tend to seal the outside all over by either dry frying it or starting the roasting in a hot oven and then lowering the temperature for the final period of cooking. Conversely, a fattier cut of meat or bird might benefit from initial roasting in a moderate oven to start the fat running and then at a higher oven temperature for the last 30 minutes or so to crisp it up.

Lean joints of beef and veal are often barded with pork fat or rolled and tied with a thin layer of fat to prevent them becoming too dry. However, avoid lean birds that are advertised as 'self basting', as they have probably been injected with animal fats in order to lubricate otherwise dry and tasteless meat. I prefer most joints to have the bone still attached whenever possible, as I think they taste better, although they will take longer to cook – the bone takes longer to heat up sufficiently to cook the surrounding meat – so the roasting has to be done at a lower temperature.

I have always believed that precise cooking times cannot be adhered to on account of all the variables: the differences between ovens, the position of the roast in the oven, the cut, the size of any bones, the density of the meat, and so on. Besides, the gradations on thermostat knobs are never more than approximate. So faithfully following recipes that recommend you to cook for 20 minutes per pound at such and such a temperature will often lead to failure. I generally check the roast by cutting into it and seeing if the juices are beginning to run clear, which would indicate that it is at the medium-rare stage. Even better, invest in a meat thermometer, which tells you the temperature at the centre of the roast. More primitive – but, with practice, just as successful – is the chefs' trick of pushing a steel skewer into the meat, counting to ten before removing it and then touching the tip to your lip. If it is barely warm, then the meat is medium rare. Blood temperature is rare.

Never serve a roast straight from the oven. Instead, cook it to a degree before you want it, then let it rest for 20 minutes in a warm place, covered in foil, shiny side in (or leave it in the turned-off oven), to cook through. The meat will relax and become more tender. In the case of beef or lamb, it will be uniformly pink inside if it was removed from the oven when rare. The juices that run into the pan while the meat is resting could be used to dress the roast or become the basis of a gravy.

A word also on domestic ovens. They rarely have the necessary capacity or power to maintain a constant high temperature, so don't expect a 5.5kg / 12lb goose to cook evenly if it only just fits into the oven. Fan-assisted ovens overcome this problem, as they help keep all parts of the oven at the same temperature. If your oven is not so equipped, preheat it for at least 30 minutes to a higher temperature than needed, then turn the thermostat down to the required temperature as the roast is put in and keep your checks on it to a minimum.

Filetto Freddo - Cold Rare Beef Fillet

If you like rare beef, this is one of the most delicious and simple ways to eat it.

The meat is grilled to a crust and roasted very briefly, then allowed to rest for at least 30 minutes. There is something very special about having a piece of fillet on your board and preparing it in such a simple way that the quality of the meat speaks for itself – it is just the best cut of beef available. At the Eagle we are lucky enough to use the whole fillet – a rare sight for most domestic cooks, but well worth it if you're cooking for a crowd.

In terms of both quality and expense, I would advise you to buy fillet from your local butcher – supermarket prices make this dish exorbitant.

Ingredients (serves 4)

- **1kg / 2¼ lb beef fillet**
- **a little olive oil**
- **sea salt and freshly ground black pepper**

Method

Trim any fat off the fillet. Lightly oil it and roll it in plenty of coarsely ground black pepper. Heat a grill or griddle pan to very hot and season the fillet well with salt. Grill on all sides until a crust forms (2–3 minutes per side). Place on a hot baking tray and roast on the top shelf of an oven preheated to 200°C/Gas Mark 6 for 3–6 minutes, depending on whether you have the thin (tail) end or the thick end of the fillet. Remove the beef from the oven and leave to rest for at least 30 minutes before cutting it into thin slices and sprinkling over more salt.

Serve with hot new potatoes and salsa verde (see below).

Salsa Verde

This raw parsley sauce is traditionally served in Italy with boiled meats, but it makes a pleasant sharp foil for any cold cuts or grills. You have to chop all the ingredients separately with a good chef's knife, otherwise the result will be a kind of pesto. The proportions are not that important: you'll need a measuring jug filled to the 500ml / 18fl oz mark with chopped flat-leaf parsley (curly English parsley won't do), with (or without) other sweet herbs such as tarragon, mint, basil, chervil and chives; 5 anchovy fillets; 2 tablespoons capers; 2 tablespoons small gherkins; a teaspoon of (preferably fresh) horseradish or mustard; and a tablespoon of red wine vinegar. Chop everything finely, mix together and stir in about 150ml / ¼ pint olive oil; the sauce should be runny and spoonable rather than a thick paste. Taste and adjust the seasoning if necessary.

Casseroled Beef with Cinnamon, Thyme & Shallots

A rich beef stew in the classic manner. This method can be used with almost any appropriate ingredients. I can't remember where I came across cinnamon as something good for beef stews but its sweetness is very welcome. As for shallots – well, beef and onions is a famous combination.

Possible additions or substitutions include olives, juniper berries and small white onions; brandy or more red wine could be used instead of the vinegar.

Ingredients (serves 6–8)

- 100g / 4oz streaky bacon, chopped
- 100g / 4oz salt pork fat (sold as *lardo salato* in Italian grocer's), washed and chopped
- 1.5kg / 3¼ lb shin of beef, cut into 3cm / 1¼ inch cubes
- ½ glass of red wine vinegar
- olive oil
- 10 shallots, peeled but left whole with the root intact (you may find it easier to peel them if they are soaked in cold water first)
- 5 fat garlic cloves, peeled but left whole

- 1 tablespoon tomato purée
- a handful of flat-leaf parsley, chopped, plus extra to garnish
- 2 fresh bay leaves
- a large sprig of thyme
- 2 strips of orange peel
- 2 cinnamon sticks
- 2 glasses of strong red wine
- water or meat stock
- salt and freshly ground black pepper

Method

Slowly melt the streaky bacon and pork fat in a wide, heavy casserole. Take the bacon out and put it in a warm bowl. Brown the beef in the pan – in batches if necessary – then add it to the bacon in the bowl. Pour the red wine vinegar into the hot pan and stir to deglaze, letting it bubble until slightly reduced. Pour it over the meat. Heat some olive oil in the pan, add the shallots and garlic cloves with some salt and a generous amount of black pepper and fry for a few minutes over a moderate heat. Stir in the tomato purée and chopped parsley and cook for a minute longer, then return the meat to the pan with any resulting juices.

Make a bouquet of the bay, thyme and orange peel and bury it in the pot with the cinnamon sticks. Heat the red wine, then pour it over the meat and add enough water or stock to bring the level of the liquid to no more than an inch below the surface of the meat. Cover the meat with an inner lid made of foil and then a close-fitting pan lid. Turn the heat to very low or place in a slow oven (150°C/Gas Mark 2). It will take around 3 hours to cook, but I would cook it for 2 hours one day, refrigerate it and then finish it the next. Garnish with lots of roughly chopped parsley.

Osso Bucco, Risotto Milanese & Gremolata

Osso bucco (which means 'bone with a hole') is one of those luxurious down-home dishes that any cook loves to make. It is sometimes cooked *in bianco* – without tomatoes – but I prefer this version, with the tomatoes liaising the vegetables and vermouth. Ask for the osso bucco to be cut for you and pay extra to have the centre cuts of each shin.

The Milanese style is to serve the meat with a plain saffron risotto and the gremolata – a mixture of finely chopped lemon rind, garlic and parsley – as a seasoning.

Ingredients (serves 4)

- 50g / 2oz butter
- 3 tablespoons olive oil
- 4–8 pieces (depending on their diameter) of veal shin (osso bucco), cut 4cm / 1½ inches thick
- 50g / 2oz plain flour, seasoned with salt and pepper
- 2 carrots, finely chopped
- 1 onion, finely chopped
- 2 celery sticks, finely chopped
- 4 garlic cloves, finely chopped
- 175ml / 6fl oz dry vermouth
- 400g / 14oz tin of Italian plum tomatoes, chopped
- salt and freshly ground black pepper

For the gremolata:

- 2 teaspoons finely grated lemon rind
- 1 garlic clove, very finely chopped
- 2 tablespoons finely chopped parsley
- 1 tablespoon olive oil
- a pinch of salt

For the risotto:

- 2 litres / 3½ pints chicken stock
- a pinch of saffron
- 150g / 5oz butter
- 2 tablespoons olive oil
- 1 red onion, finely chopped
- 1 celery stick, finely chopped
- 250g / 9oz arborio rice
- 4 tablespoons dry vermouth or white wine
- 4 tablespoons freshly grated Parmesan cheese

Method

Heat the butter and oil in a large, heavy-based casserole with a tight-fitting lid. Dust the osso bucco in the seasoned flour and then brown it carefully in the hot fat. Remove the meat and add a little more fat to the pan if needed. Add the carrots, onion, celery and garlic and turn the heat down, then cook, stirring occasionally, for 10 minutes. (If the vegetables start to stick to the pan, add a little of the vermouth, which should loosen them.) When the vegetables have softened, turn the heat up and add the tomatoes. Boil vigorously for 2–3 minutes to drive off some of the liquid and intensify the flavour. Then add the rest of the vermouth and carry on the fierce cooking for another few minutes to drive off the alcohol. Check the seasoning. Place the osso bucco back in the pan, cover with a circle of wet greaseproof paper and put the lid on tightly. Turn the heat down to its lowest setting and cook for 2 hours or until the meat is completely tender. Alternatively, this last part of the cooking can be done in an oven preheated to 150°C/Gas Mark 2.

Mix together all the ingredients for the gremolata and set aside.

To make the risotto, put the stock in a pan and bring to boiling point. Put the saffron in a cup, pour over some of the stock and set aside. Melt 75g / 3oz of the butter with the oil in a heavy-based pan, add the onion and celery and cook gently with a little salt for about 15 minutes, until tender. Add the rice, turn the heat up and stir to coat the rice with the fat. After a couple of minutes, add the vermouth or wine and let the alcohol evaporate for a moment or two. Then stir in a couple of cups of the hot stock and the saffron stock. Add the remaining stock in stages, as described on page 87, until the rice is done. Remove from the heat, put the remaining butter on top and cover with a lid. When the butter has melted, stir it in with the Parmesan.

Serve the risotto immediately, topped with the osso bucco. Either sprinkle the gremolata on top or pass it round for everyone to help themselves.

Pollo al Ajillo – Braised Garlic Chicken

I love this way of cooking chicken because it's simple and tasty. Cook this dish slowly and you will notice an amazing distinction of flavours. First the aromatic bay, then the garlic, whose power is lessened by the alcohol, and finally the sherry, typical of southern Spain. Pollo al ajillo goes well with roast potatoes or with Coriander Rice (see page 155).

Ingredients (serves 4)

- 100ml / 3½ fl oz olive oil
- 1 large corn-fed chicken, jointed
- 2 heads of garlic, separated into cloves but not peeled
- 3 bay leaves
- 500ml / 18fl oz dry sherry
- 250ml / 8fl oz water
- salt and freshly ground black pepper

Method

Heat the olive oil in a large, deep pan and brown the chicken pieces all over on a medium heat. Take out the chicken, then add the garlic and bay to the pan and fry gently until golden. Add the sherry, return the chicken to the pan and add the water. Bring to a simmer, then reduce the heat and cook slowly for 35 minutes or until the chicken is done, stirring it every few minutes to spread the garlic flavour. Season to taste.

If you're going to eat this with roast potatoes, put the chicken on top of the potatoes and then thicken the sauce by turning up the heat and boiling off some of the liquid. Pour it over the chicken and serve.

Roast Chicken with Tarragon, Garlic & Olives

There is nothing like tarragon, olives and garlic for elevating a humble roast chicken in a SW France manner. Choose a medium-sized, organic or decent free-range roasting chicken, which may well be costly – I really think that we've become used to thinking of chicken as everyday food, when really it should be more special than that. Don't bother with the small, meritless poussins, or spring chickens, as they invariably lack flavour. 'Black leg' chickens (a.k.a. *poulet noir* if imported from France) are a favourite at the Eagle for roasting. Some supermarkets and good butcher's shops now stock them.

Ingredients (serves 4)

- a 1.5kg / 3¼ lb roasting chicken

- rind and juice of 1 lemon

- 4 garlic cloves, roughly chopped

- 1 streaky bacon rasher, finely chopped

- 1 heaped tablespoon chopped tarragon

- about 20 black olives,
  pitted and roughly chopped

- 2 tablespoons olive oil

- coarse sea salt and freshly
  ground black pepper

Method

Wash the bird well and dry it thoroughly. Rub the chicken all over with coarse salt, pepper and the lemon rind, working it under the skin and into the body cavity. Mix the garlic with the chopped bacon, tarragon and olives and put all into the cavity. Squeeze the lemon juice over the bird and rub it with the olive oil. Place in a roasting tin, breast side up, and wrap it loosely, but airtight, with foil. Roast in an oven preheated to 180°C/Gas Mark 4 for about 35 minutes (this method keeps the meat moist), then remove the foil, baste the chicken and cook at 220°C/Gas Mark 7 for 20 minutes or more to crisp it up. The juices from a cut made in the thick part of the thigh should run clear when the bird is ready. Leave to rest for 10 minutes, then pour off the juices and carve the chicken. Eat with potatoes of some kind or simple rice.

Codornices con Granadas – Pot-roast quail with Pomegranates

Although quails and pomegranates are used together in Persian cooking, this is a Spanish dish, whose origins lie in Catalunya. The sweet meat of the quails is offset by the bittersweet flavour of the pomegranates, and this simple combination of ingredients yields a surprisingly deep-flavoured dish.

Ingredients (serves 4)

- 100ml / 3½ fl oz olive oil
- 8 quails
- 1 white onion, finely chopped
- 2 garlic cloves, finely chopped
- 4 vine-ripened tomatoes, finely chopped

- 4 tablespoons white wine
- 2 pomegranates, seeded as best you can and slightly crushed
- about 150ml / ¼ pint light chicken stock (hot)
- a few sprigs of parsley
- salt and freshly ground black pepper

Method

In a casserole that is just big enough to hold the quails in a single layer, heat the olive oil over medium heat. Lightly season the quails, place them in the oil and cook, turning, until browned all over. Remove and keep warm. Drain off a good amount of the oil, then add the onion and garlic and cook slowly until translucent. Stir in the tomatoes and cook for 5 minutes, stirring every minute. Add the white wine, increase the heat and boil until reduced by a third. Add the juice from the pomegranates and a tablespoon of their seeds. Return the quails, upside down, to the casserole and stir them into the other ingredients. Add enough hot stock to barely cover the birds, then cover the casserole and place in an oven preheated to 160°C/Gas Mark 3 for about 35 minutes or until the flesh begins to soften.

This dish seems to benefit from a rest, to relax and compose itself. So remove it from the oven and let it stand for 15 minutes before serving. At this point you can strain the sauce if you like, but I prefer the chunky texture and being able to see all the ingredients. Adjust the seasoning, then place the quails on a serving dish and spoon the sauce over the top. Use the parsley and a few pomegranate seeds for garnish.

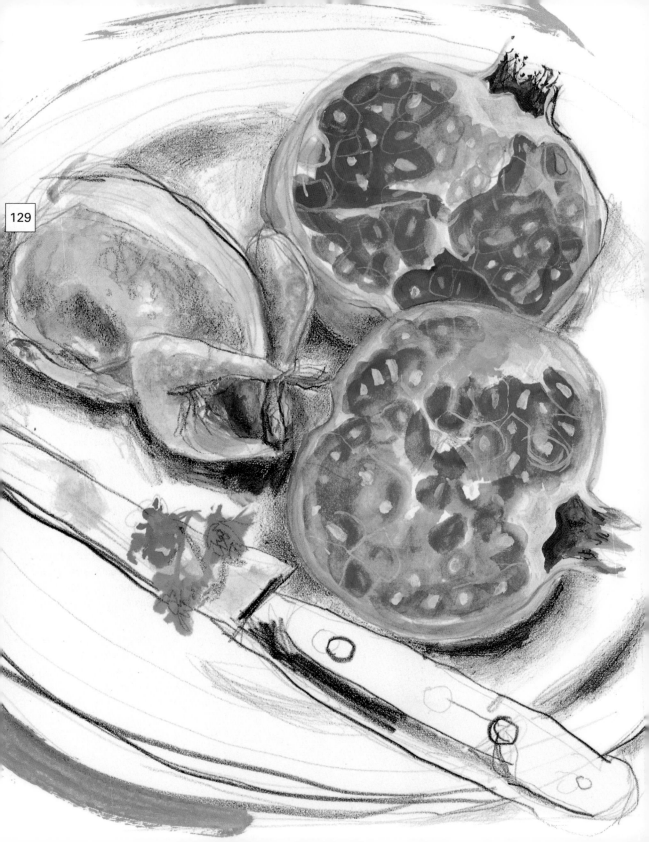

Grilled Chicken Breasts with Oregano, Lemon & Black Pepper

Chicken breasts simply grilled and served with some form of leaf and herb salad are always going to be a favourite. Whether grilled on a ridged pan for a mid-week supper or on the barbecue at the weekend, this is all about giving a dull chicken breast some big flavours. Chicken breasts need to be cooked steadily on a medium heat; the aim is that the breast meat should not be dry by the time the meat around the wing bone is just cooked.

Ingredients (serves 4)

- **4 large (225–250g / 8–9oz) free-range chicken breasts**

- **2 tablespoons finely chopped fresh oregano (or marjoram) – you could use dried for a different result, but use less than half the quantity**

- **3 tablespoons olive oil**

- **1 small dried chilli, crushed**

- **more freshly ground black pepper than you would expect – about 1 level tablespoon**

- **2 lemons**

- **sea salt**

Method

Wash and dry the chicken breasts. Mix with the oregano, oil, chilli, black pepper and the grated zest of one of the lemons and leave to marinate whilst the grill heats up or the charcoal dies down to an even medium heat. When ready to cook, salt the chicken and squeeze one of the lemons all over it. Cook the breasts, turning them 90 degrees once on each side, then remove from the heat. Squeeze the juice of the other lemon over them, sprinkle with a little more olive oil and leave to rest for a moment. If you happen to have some truffle oil, now is the time to make good use of it. Serve with a mixed leaf salad containing chives, parsley and spring onions.

131

Pheasant Casserole with Chestnuts, Ceps & Bacon

David Eyre

132

A wonderful casserole for the depths of winter. The chestnuts and dried mushrooms make a dark, earthy stew that I'd serve with mashed potatoes or soft polenta. Dried chestnuts, which must be soaked for an hour before they reach the pot, are a good thing to have in your storecupboard. Fresh ones will need to be roasted and peeled – a laborious and often painful way to spend time in the kitchen. Vacuum-packed chestnuts are the stuff of chefs' dreams; they are already cooked and peeled and are definitely a good thing. If you use either roasted or vacuum-packed chestnuts, they should be added to the pot towards the last half hour of cooking.

Ingredients (serves 4)

- 75g / 3oz dried ceps (sold as porcini in Italian grocer's)
- 2 large pheasant, cut into 4 pieces each
- 1 tablespoon olive oil
- 1 tablespoon butter
- 200g / 7oz smoked fat bacon, chopped
- 2 celery sticks, chopped
- 4 garlic cloves, chopped

- 1 onion, chopped
- 1 carrot, chopped
- a glass of red wine
- a bouquet of sage, bay, parsley and thyme
- 20 vacuum-packed, dried or fresh chestnuts, prepared as described above
- a good bunch of parsley, chopped
- salt and freshly ground black pepper

Method

Soak the dried ceps in some warm water. Meanwhile, season the pheasant pieces and brown them well in the olive oil in a heavy casserole. Remove the pheasant, turn the heat down and melt the butter in the pan. Add the bacon, celery, garlic, onion and carrot, then cover and cook gently for about 10 minutes, until softened. Now add the red wine, bouquet of herbs, drained soaked mushrooms, and the chestnuts, if using soaked dried ones. Return the fowl to the casserole, trying to arrange the pieces in a single layer, and add enough of the mushroom-soaking water to almost cover the pheasant. Cover the pan again and cook slowly for around 1½ hours, adding vacuum-packed or cooked fresh chestnuts after about an hour. It doesn't matter if the chestnuts collapse but they will thicken the sauce if they do. Adjust the seasoning and stir in the chopped parsley before serving.

Grilled Leg of Venison

This is something a bit different to do with venison – a meat that not long ago was considered a luxury but is now a fairly affordable option. It has started to gain popularity, probably due to its lack of fat. This does make it susceptible to dryness if it is overcooked. Aim for rare and juicy with this one. Perfect for a posh barbecue.

Ingredients (serves 10)

- 2–2.5kg / 4½–5½ lb leg of venison (boned and trimmed weight)
- 4 garlic cloves, crushed
- 100ml / 3½ fl oz olive oil
- a handful of rosemary and thyme, chopped
- freshly ground black pepper

Method

First you need to butterfly the leg of venison. Slice through the thinnest part of the boned leg – the underside – then open it up and flatten out. Trim off any sinew and slash through the larger muscles to give a more uniform thickness for even cooking.

Put the flattened leg in a glass or ceramic dish. Mix together the garlic, oil, herbs and some black pepper to make a marinade and pour it over the meat, massaging it in well. Cover and refrigerate for about 8 hours or overnight, turning occasionally.

Bring the meat back to room temperature. Season with sea salt and another grinding of pepper. Heat a barbecue or large chargrill pan to the highest point. Slap on the meat and leave till brown and crisp, then turn, doing the same for the other side. Reduce the heat and cook slowly for 30 minutes. It is important that the heat is reduced or the meat will burn on the outside and be raw in the middle. Leave to rest on a warm plate, loosely covered, for about 20 minutes before carving.

Venison & Pancetta Casserole

This is a rich, gamey winter stew. Get the butcher to bone the venison for you. Buy your pancetta or bacon at the butcher's too, then cut the rind off and use it to give the stew juices extra flavour. Serve with Celeriac Mash (see page 142).

Ingredients (serves 8)

- 2 tablespoons vegetable oil

- 200g / 7oz pancetta or streaky bacon, without rind, chopped into small pieces

- 1 shoulder of venison (about 1.5kg / 3¼ lb), boned, cut into chunks and sprinkled with salt

- ½ bottle of red wine

- 2 onions, chopped

- 2 carrots, cut into small dice

- 2 leeks, cut into small dice

- 3 celery sticks, cut into small dice

- 2 garlic cloves, finely chopped, and 4 whole cloves, peeled

- a few parsley stalks, finely chopped

- 3 tablespoons olive oil

- 1 tablespoon tomato purée

- 1 bunch of thyme, tied together

- salt and freshly ground black pepper

Method

Heat the vegetable oil in a large frying pan, add the pancetta and fry until browned. Take the pancetta out of the pan, then brown the venison in the same fat, a few pieces at a time. Put all the browned meat in a casserole dish. Pour a slosh of the wine into the frying pan and scrape up any meaty bits that may have stuck to the bottom. Pour this over the meat. Gently fry the vegetables, chopped garlic, whole garlic cloves and parsley stalks in the olive oil for 15 minutes, then add the tomato purée, thyme, the rest of the red wine and the bacon rind. Pour this mixture over the meat. Add sufficient water to half submerge the meat. Dip your finger into the liquid to taste and then adjust the seasoning as necessary. Cook, covered, for 2 hours at 160°C/Gas Mark 3, until tender.

Cozido de Cabrito – Braised Goat with Rosemary, Tomatoes & Wine

Kid or young goat is a much underappreciated meat in the UK.

The texture of its pale flesh is not unlike milk-fed veal or spring lamb, while the flavour is slightly stronger. The prime cuts, such as saddle and leg, are good for roasting or grilling. Treat them as you would lamb. The neck and shoulder, or even a whole small animal, are delicious slowly roasted with wine and aromatics. This casserole makes good use of the cheaper cuts.

Ingredients (serves 6–8)

- 100ml / 3½ fl oz olive oil
- 3kg / 6½ lb goat shoulder or neck, on the bone
- 2 large onions, chopped
- 4 carrots, chopped
- 4 celery sticks, chopped
- 8–10 garlic cloves, sliced
- 500g / 1lb 2oz tomatoes, chopped
- 250g / 9oz black olives, pitted
- 2 bay leaves
- a sprig of thyme
- 4–5 stalks of rosemary
- 450ml / ¾ pint white wine
- salt and freshly ground black pepper

Method

Heat the oil in a large, heavy-based casserole, add the goat and brown all over. Remove the meat from the pan. Add the onions, carrots and celery and fry until lightly golden. Add the garlic, tomatoes, olives and herbs, then return the meat to the pan and pour the wine over it to come two-thirds of the way up the meat – if necessary, top up with water. Bring to a simmer, add a good pinch of salt and a grinding of black pepper, then cover and transfer to an oven preheated to 160°C/Gas Mark 3. Cook for around 2 hours, then remove the lid and cook for another 30 minutes or so, until the meat is falling away from the bone. The liquid should be slightly reduced, the meat crusty and brown on top and melting underneath.

Serve with potatoes – boiled, steamed or mashed.

137

Hare Casserole

This makes a good, rich winter evening meal. Don't omit the chocolate, which is essential to thicken and enrich the casserole. The beauty of this dish is that it really looks after itself. It is best reheated the next day, as it develops a fuller flavour overnight. Any leftovers can be stripped from the bone and served with pappardelle to make one of the finest pasta dishes ever.

To joint the hares, follow the bone structure: remove the front and back legs and chop the saddle into 3 or 4 pieces, keeping the liver and kidneys intact. Try to keep as much of the blood as you can. Alternatively you can ask your butcher to joint the hares and save the blood for you.

Ingredients (serves 8–10)

- 2 good-sized hares (around 1.5kg / 3¼ lb) each, jointed (see above)
- 2 white onions, cut into chunks
- 3 carrots, cut into chunks
- 2 celery sticks, cut into chunks
- 2 leeks, cut into chunks
- 8–10 garlic cloves, chopped
- 2 bay leaves
- a sprig of thyme

- 6 juniper berries, bruised
- 1 bottle of red wine
- 200g / 7oz smoked streaky bacon in a piece, cut into big lardons
- olive oil for frying
- 1 tablespoon plain flour
- 1 tablespoon tomato purée
- 50g / 2oz dark chocolate (about 70% cocoa solids), finely chopped
- salt and freshly ground black pepper

Method

Put the hare, chopped vegetables, garlic, herbs and juniper in a large dish, pour over the red wine to cover (top up with water if necessary), then leave to marinate overnight.

The next day, strain the meat through a colander, keeping the wine. Pat the meat dry. Sauté the bacon gently in a heavy casserole until it releases its fat. Add the vegetables and garlic from the marinade and sauté until golden, then remove from the pan.

Add some olive oil to the pan and brown the hare in it in batches. Remove from the pan and set aside. Deglaze the pan with some of the reserved marinade, then, over a low heat, add the flour, tomato purée and blood and stir until combined and thickened. Tuck in the hare and vegetables, add the herbs from the marinade and pour in the remaining wine. The hare and vegetables should be barely covered with the wine; if necessary, top up with a little water. Add the chopped chocolate, a good pinch of salt and a grinding of black pepper. Cover tightly, then transfer to an oven preheated to 160°C/Gas Mark 3 and cook for about 2½ hours, until the meat is coming away from the bones. The exact cooking time will depend on the age of the hare – older animals take longer. Eat with mash.

139

Potatatas Rellenos - Braised Wild Boar with Potatoes

Rellenos is the Spanish word for stuffing. In this case it refers to the stew hiding underneath the potatoes that have been cooked on top of it. I cheat like mad when making this. I cook the stew separately, then I layer the potatoes on top and finish them together. The potatoes still have plenty of time to soak up the juices.

You can use other game such as venison or hare for this dish.

Ingredients (serves 6)

- **4 tablespoons olive oil, plus extra for drizzling**

- **1kg / 2¼ lb shoulder of wild boar, roughly diced**

- **200g / 7oz smoked pancetta, roughly diced**

- **2 leafy celery sticks, roughly chopped**

- **2 carrots, roughly chopped**

- **2 leeks, roughly chopped**

- **1 large onion, roughly chopped**

- **3 garlic cloves, finely chopped**

- **1 teaspoon smoked paprika**

- **about ½ bottle of red wine**

- **2 tablespoons tomato purée**

- **2 bay leaves**

- **1 teaspoon sugar**

- **3 large waxy potatoes, peeled and cut into rounds no more than 5mm / ¼ inch thick**

- **salt and freshly ground black pepper**

Method

Heat the oil in a large casserole and brown the meat in it. Remove the meat from the pan, add the pancetta, vegetables, garlic and paprika and fry until the vegetables begin to soften. Turn the heat up and add the wine. When it boils, stir in the tomato purée, bay leaves and sugar. Return the meat to the casserole; you may need to add a little water to cover it. Cook the stew for 1½–2 hours or until the meat is very tender. Taste and adjust the seasoning if necessary.

Remove the casserole from the heat and layer the potato slices on top of the stew, as if you were making a gratin dauphinois. Season the potatoes with a little salt and pepper and drizzle some oil over them. Bake in an oven preheated to 180°C/Gas Mark 4 until the potatoes are soft and golden, with the stew bubbling away underneath.

side dishes

Celeriac Mash

You don't have to use sage here but it does complement the celeriac beautifully.

Ingredients (serves 6)

- 2 heads of celeriac
- 4 large potatoes, peeled
- 3 garlic cloves, peeled

- 300ml / ½ pint milk
- 150g / 5oz butter
- a handful of sage leaves, chopped
- salt and freshly ground black pepper

Method

Peel the celeriac and cut it into chunks, dropping these into acidulated water (water with a squeeze of lemon) as you go. Cut the potatoes into chunks about twice the size of the celeriac – they cook much faster. Boil the potatoes and celeriac, along with the garlic cloves, in plenty of salted water until tender. Drain really well, return to the pot and dry off any excess moisture over a very low heat. Heat the milk, then pour it into the pot and crush the vegetables with a potato masher. Beat in the butter, fold in the sage and season with pepper. Check for salt.

Celeriac Gratin

David Eyre

Celeriac is such an inexpensive and underused winter vegetable.

This is a really easy dish that is particularly good with lamb or even as a starter by itself.

Ingredients (serves 6 as a starter, more as a side dish)

- **250ml / 8fl oz double cream**
- **10 sage leaves**
- **2 bay leaves**
- **3 garlic cloves, thinly sliced**

- **3 tablespoons freshly grated Parmesan cheese**
- **3 medium-sized celeriac, peeled and cut into slices 5mm / ¼ inch thick**
- **sea salt and freshly ground black pepper**

Method

Put the cream in a pan with the herbs, garlic and Parmesan and simmer until it has reduced a little. Arrange the sliced celeriac in an ovenproof dish as densely as possible to a depth of 3–4cm / 1¼–1½ inches, seasoning each layer. Pour over the cream. Cover with foil and cook in a medium-hot oven (200°C/Gas Mark 6) for around 30 minutes or until the celeriac just yields to the tip of a knife. Brown the top under a hot grill if you wish.

Jansson's Temptation

Trish Hilferty

This traditional Swedish dish goes very well with roast lamb.

Ingredients (serves 10)

- **8 large waxy potatoes, peeled**
- **50g / 2oz butter**
- **2 onions, sliced**
- **2 garlic cloves, thinly sliced**

- **300ml / ½ pint milk**
- **300ml / ½ pint double cream**
- **75g / 3oz anchovies in oil, drained**
- **salt and freshly ground black pepper**

Method

Slice the potatoes fairly thinly, about 5mm / ¼ inch. Grease a baking dish with 20g / ¾ oz of the butter. Melt the remaining butter in a large pan and sweat the onions in it until soft. Stir in the garlic and potatoes, then pour in the milk and cream. Tip in the anchovies and mix well, making sure they are evenly distributed. Adjust the seasoning.

Tip the whole lot into the baking dish and bake in an oven preheated to 200°C/Gas Mark 6 for 1 hour or until the potatoes are tender. If the top is browning too quickly, cover the dish with foil.

Roast Red Onions

Red onions are best for roasting, as they cook to the most wonderful magenta colour and have a lovely sweetness, but any small firm onions or shallots, or a combination, would work.

Peel the onions and trim the hairy part of the root but leave the main part intact to hold the onion together. Cut the onions into quarters through the root. Put them into a roasting tin with some whole peeled garlic cloves, bay leaves, strong herbs (such as thyme, rosemary, sage), a small spoonful of sugar, enough olive oil to coat everything, salt, pepper and a couple of spoonfuls of red wine vinegar. Cover the tin with foil and roast for an hour or so in a medium oven (about 180°C/Gas Mark 4, although the exact temperature is not that important), until the onions are tender and look done. Remove the foil and cook for a further 5 minutes. If there seems to be too much liquid, take out the onions and boil the liquid on a high flame until reduced and syrupy, then return the onions to the tin.

Roast onions are equally good cold and can be excellent with charcuterie or as part of a salad – also very good on a slice of bread when home after a busy night out.

Roast Tomatoes

Probably the cornerstone dish of my repertoire, these slow-roasted – almost oven-dried – tomatoes are so versatile. Not only are they superior to grilled tomatoes as a something to partner grills, they are also good in pasta dishes, sauces and salads.

Halve some properly ripe tomatoes across the middle, scoop out the seeds with your fingertip and lay the tomatoes cut side up in a single layer in an ovenproof dish. Oil them slightly and season with salt, pepper, a tiny amount of sugar and some dried oregano. Depending on their intended use, you can spike them further with cumin, garlic, anchovies, chopped olives or whatever. Roast them, uncovered, at a low temperature (120–140°C/Gas Mark ½–1) for 3 hours or longer, until they look shrunken and ugly. Leave to cool. They can be kept in the fridge for a couple of weeks if you cover them in oil.

These tomatoes make a good pasta sauce when combined with whole or chopped pesto ingredients – garlic, toasted pine nuts and basil leaves. They're also good on bruschetta with anchovies or grilled sardines (see pages 53 and 54); with grilled polenta, rocket and slivered Parmesan as a starter; roughly chopped with a green chilli and some fresh coriander as a salsa for, say, grilled fish; with roasted aubergines and houmous for a lunchtime salad. With anything, really.

Espinacas con Piñones y Pasas – Spinach with Pinenuts & Raisins

This versatile dish is normally served as a starter but we use it as an
accompaniment to meats and especially grilled fish. The combination of nuts and fruit in a savoury dish has a typical Catalan signature and it looks great on the plate: glossy green spinach studded with pale-gold pine nuts and plump, succulent raisins. The anchovy, garlic and lemon work well as strong seasonings. In Spain, the spinach is boiled first. At the Eagle we have improved on this by wilting the spinach in a wok at high speed.

Ingredients (serves 4)

- 1kg / 2¼ lb fresh spinach
- 2 tablespoons olive oil, preferably from Catalunya and made from Arbequina olives
- 25g / 1oz pine nuts
- 1 garlic clove, very finely chopped
- 25g / 1oz raisins, soaked in hot water for an hour or so
- 2 anchovy fillets, chopped
- juice of 1 lemon
- salt and freshly ground black pepper

Method

Wash the spinach and remove the stalks, then shake it dry. In a wok or large pan, heat the oil over a high flame. Add the pine nuts and garlic and shake the wok. When the pine nuts start to colour, add the drained raisins and anchovies and cook for 30 seconds. Then add the spinach – at first it will fill the wok – stirring and tossing as it starts to wilt. Add some salt and pepper and the lemon juice and stir once more. Then serve on a warmed white plate, with a little more olive oil if you wish.

Patatas al forno – Oven Potatoes

David Eyre

148

Not really a gratin, since it doesn't include cheese, but potatoes baked in a shallow dish in this way were used to partner grills and roasts almost every day when I was at the Eagle. Endless fun can be had with the flavours added to the potatoes (see suggestions below). Use any waxy potato variety; floury baking potatoes will collapse into a mush. The Cyprus Nicola potato is the ideal but Maris Piper is a good second choice.

Ingredients (serves 6)

- sufficient potatoes, peeled and sliced 5mm / ¼ inch thick, to fill an ovenproof dish to a depth of 4cm / 1½ inches

- 1 large onion for every 500g / 1lb 2oz potatoes, sliced

- olive oil

- salt and freshly ground black pepper

Additional ingredients as you think fit:

- pitted black olives and garlic

- parsley and garlic

- sliced green or red peppers and garlic

- chopped rosemary and / or sage

- smoked streaky bacon

- saffron

Method

In a large bowl, mix the potatoes and onions with enough olive oil to coat them lightly. Layer them in the ovenproof dish, with whichever additions you are using. Cover with foil and bake in a moderate oven (about 180°C/Gas Mark 4, although the exact temperature is not important) for up to an hour, until nearly cooked. Remove the foil and brown the top for 15 minutes.

Potatoes with Braised Cabbage

This is a great accompaniment to winter roasts but it could also be eaten on its own, since the pancetta provides a good meat fix. Duck fat, bacon and cabbage is a famously good trinity, so why wait for bubble and squeak tomorrow when you can have this today?

Ingredients (serves 6)

- 3 tablespoons duck fat

- 8 large waxy potatoes, peeled and cut into thick rounds

- 300g / 11oz smoked pancetta, roughly diced

- a handful of sage leaves, very roughly chopped

- 1 teaspoon juniper berries, crushed

- 3 onions, chopped

- 2 garlic cloves, chopped

- 1 Savoy cabbage, darker green leaves only (cavolo nero in season would be even better), roughly chopped

- salt and freshly ground black pepper

Method

Heat 2 tablespoons of the duck fat in a roasting tray and let it get really hot. Add the potato slices and stir until they all have a good coating of fat. Place in an oven preheated to 200°C/Gas Mark 6.

Heat the remaining fat in a wide pan or casserole. Add the pancetta, sage, juniper berries, onions and garlic and fry on a high heat for a couple of minutes. Stir in the cabbage and add about 250ml / 8fl oz of water. Season with salt and pepper, then cover and cook gently, stirring occasionally. The potatoes will take about half an hour, by which time the cabbage mixture should be good and ready. You now add one dish to the other. For sheer visual effect, adding the cabbage to the potatoes is my favourite. Mix it all thoroughly. Do not worry if some of the potatoes break up a little. You can shove it all back in the oven to crisp the top layer up ever so slightly, but the dish will keep warm enough to serve for ages.

3 Potato Salads

You need to choose your potatoes carefully for salads. The first two salads here use waxy new potatoes such as the ubiquitous Charlottes, my beloved Rattes, a.k.a. Belle de Fontenay, Pink Fir Apples, Jersey Royals or small Nicola potatoes from Cyprus. The third can be made with any large potato apart from those suitable for baking (King Edward and the like), which will collapse when boiling. By all means peel them after boiling, when still warm, but I can never really see that the effort is justified.

1. With Mayonnaise, Capers and Onion

Ingredients (serves 4)

- 500g / 1lb 2oz new potatoes, scrubbed
- 2 egg yolks
- 1 teaspoon mustard
- 400ml / 14fl oz sunflower oil

- 1 teaspoon white wine vinegar
- 1 tablespoon salted capers, washed and soaked in several changes of cold water for 1 hour
- 1 red onion, very finely chopped
- 1 tablespoon chopped parsley
- salt and freshly ground black pepper

Method

Put the potatoes on to boil in salted water. Meanwhile, make the mayonnaise. Beat the egg yolks and mustard together in a food processor or mixer, then add the oil in the slowest possible stream with the machine running. Add the vinegar at the end and season to taste. Then thin with a tablespoon of water.

Drain the potatoes and cut them into pieces. Combine with all the other ingredients and the mayonnaise while still warm.

2. **With Green Olives,** Shallots and Sweet Herbs

Ingredients (serves 4)

- **500g / 1lb 2oz new potatoes, scrubbed**
- **3 shallots, very finely chopped**
- **100g / 4oz green olives, roughly chopped**
- **1 garlic clove, crushed and finely chopped**
- **2 tablespoons chopped mixed herbs, such as mint, chervil, tarragon, parsley, marjoram, basil**
- **4 tablespoons olive oil**
- **1 tablespoon balsamic vinegar**
- **salt and freshly ground black pepper**

Method

Boil the potatoes until tender, then drain. Mix together the rest of the ingredients. Cut the potatoes into pieces and combine with the other ingredients while still warm. Season to taste.

---

3. **With Black Olives,** Spring Onions and Olive Oil

Ingredients (serves 4)

- **500g / 1lb 2oz large potatoes (see above), scrubbed (peeled if you wish)**
- **100g / 4oz black olives, roughly chopped**
- **6 tablespoons olive oil**
- **a small bunch of spring onions, chopped**
- **freshly ground black pepper**

Method

Boil the potatoes until tender, then drain. Cut them into slices and bruise in a colander. Gently mix together with the other ingredients.

Cannellini Beans with Garlic & Sage

Beans often make an appearance in Mediterranean meals, accompanying
grilled meats such as pork or lamb. In this recipe, the handsome cannellini bean is enhanced by the traditional flavours
of sage and garlic. It is essential to use dried, but not ancient, beans and fresh herbs.

Ingredients (serves 8)

- **500g / 1lb 2oz dried cannellini beans**
- **a bunch of sage, leaves chopped and stalks kept**

- **2 large garlic cloves, very finely chopped**
- **1 red chilli, finely chopped**
- **75ml / 2½ fl oz extra virgin olive oil**
- **salt and freshly ground black pepper**

Method

Place the beans in a large saucepan, cover with twice as much water and leave to soak overnight.

The next day, drain the beans, cover with fresh water and bring to the boil. As soon as froth appears
on the surface, remove the pan from the heat and drain. Cover the beans with fresh water again (about
2.5cm / 1 inch above the level of the beans), add the sage stalks and bring to the boil. Cook for 1–1½ hours
or until the beans are soft. Do not drain them. Place one cup of the mixture in a food processor or liquidiser,
purée and return to the pot. This will give a creamy consistency to the dish. Finally add the garlic, chilli,
sage leaves, salt, pepper and olive oil. Leave to stand for 20 minutes before serving.

Coriander Rice

Some things go with nothing better than a fluffy serving of white rice.

In particular, some of our wetter dishes are grateful for it – such as Octopus Stew (see page 106), lamb shanks or Pollo al Ajillo (see page 126) – as are fish (mackerel is the best) with a really simple salsa or salad leaves.

Here we deviate from the sticky rice of Spain and Italy. Basmati is best. The name means 'fragrant', and it should have a slightly nutty, perfumed smell. Only rice grown in the Himalayan foothills of India and Pakistan should be labelled basmati. The soil and water in this region give it its special aroma and flavour. So choose a reputable brand, such as Tilda, because there is a huge difference between this and other kinds of long-grain rice.

This dish is our own, very deconstructed and not remotely authentic pilaff. If you have problems cooking rice, use this basic absorption method for plain basmati as well – it never fails.

Ingredients (serves 6)

- **4 tablespoons olive oil**
- **1 clove**
- **½ teaspoon cumin seeds**
- **enough basmati rice to fill a measuring jug to the 750ml / 1 ¼ pint level**

- **1.5 litres / 2½ pints water**
- **juice of ½ lemon**
- **a bunch of coriander, very roughly chopped**
- **salt and freshly ground black pepper**

Method

Nowadays you do not need to wash basmati rice. For this dish, however, we give it a very brief toasting. Heat 2 tablespoons of the oil in a pan (choose one with a very tight-fitting lid). Add the clove and cumin seeds, then add the rice and stir thoroughly until it is coated with the oil and looks a little opaque. Add all the water and turn the heat up full. Bring the water just to boiling point, then turn the heat down as low as it will go. The water should be just below a simmer. Cover with the lid; it must fit snugly. The rice will carry on cooking in the steam once it has absorbed all the water. Don't stir! After 10 minutes, taste a grain and see if it is as soft as you want it. As soon as it is, remove the pan from the heat, add the remaining oil and gently nudge the rice apart with a carving fork, a narrow knife or a skewer. Don't use a spoon, which would be like a bull in a china shop and smash the grains (unlike other rice, basmati elongates rather than thickens, so it is delicate). Fold in the lemon juice and coriander, add salt and pepper to taste and serve.

156

Note: Vegetarian dishes exclude eggs but include dairy products.

INDEX

157

accompaniments *see* side dishes

anchovies *see* seafood

Andalucian Garlic Soup with a Soft-boiled Egg
(Sopa al Ajillo) **16**

Arista (Roast Pork, Tuscan Style) **116**

Arroz con Conejo (Spanish Rice
with Rabbit) **82**

artichokes **113**
• Lamb, Olive and Artichoke Stew **112**
• Penne with Artichoke Hearts and Greens **70**

Asturian Pork and Butter Bean Stew
(Fabada Asturiana) **118**

aubergines
• Caponata (Sicilian Aubergine Relish) **47**
• Cold Roast Aubergine Soup
with Yoghurt **26**
• Imam Bayeldi (Baked Aubergines
Stuffed with Tomatoes) **49**

Bacalhau com Batatas (Baked Salt
Cod with Peppers and Potatoes) **100**

Baccalà alla Palermitana (Salt Cod
with Prunes and Pickling Onions) **101**

bacon *see* meat

Baked Aubergines Stuffed with Tomatoes
(Imam Bayeldi) **49**

Baked Buckwheat Pasta with Sage,
Fontina and Cabbage (Pizzoccheri) **79**

Baked Chicory Wrapped in Prosciutto **46**

Baked Salt Cod with Peppers and Potatoes
(Bacalhau com Batatas) **100**

Baked Sea Bream or Sea Bass
with Tomatoes **96**

beans **23**
• Black Bean Soup **32**
• Cannellini Beans with Garlic and Sage **154**
• Egg Fettuccine with Radicchio,
Borlotti Beans and Pancetta **74**
• Fabada Asturiana (Asturian Pork and Butter
Bean Stew) **118**
• Feijoada (Portuguese Pork
and Bean Stew) **114**
• Pasta e Fagioli (Pasta and Bean Soup) **28**
• Risotto with Broad Beans and Mint **88-9**
• Sopa de Pedra **22-3**

beef *see* meat

Belben, Mike **8, 11**

Belly Pork Stew with Peas and Saffron **115**

Bife Ana (The Eagle Steak Sandwich) **62**

Big Portuguese Fish Stew
(Caldeirada de Mariscos) **104-5**

Black Bean Soup **32**

Black Mushroom Soup **19**

Braised Garlic Chicken
(Pollo al Ajillo) **126, 155**

Braised Goat with Rosemary, Tomatoes
and Wine (Cozido de Cabrito) **136**

Braised Wild Boar with Potatoes
(Patatas Rellenos) **140**

Broccoli and Treviso with
Anchovy Dressing **40**

bruschetta **53**
• Bruschetta with Mozzarella, Treviso
and Balsamic Vinegar **55**
• Bruschetta with Roast Tomatoes
and Grilled Sardines **54**
• Bruschetta with Warm Ricotta Salad **53**

Bucatini with Cauliflower, Anchovies,
Pine Nuts and Raisins **67**

Burrill, Jemima **10, 35, 67**

Caldeirada de Mariscos (Big Portuguese
Fish Stew) **104-5**

Caldo Verde (Greens and Potato Soup
with Chorizo) **25**

Canja (Portuguese Chicken Broth with Rice,
Mint and Lemon) **18**

Cannellini Beans with Garlic and Sage **154**

Caponata (Sicilian Aubergine Relish) **47**

capone *see* meat (chicken)

Carabaccia (Florentine Pea Soup) **30**

Cardoso, Jorge **11, 44, 104-5**

Casseroled Beef with Cinnamon,
Thyme and Shallots **123**

Celeriac Gratin **143**

Celeriac Mash **142**

Chaves, Pedro **9-10, 154**

cheese
• accompaniments **47**
• Bruschetta with Mozzarella, Treviso
and Balsamic Vinegar **55**
• Bruschetta with Warm Ricotta Salad **53**
• Egg Fettuccine with Ricotta,
Peas and Smoked Pancetta **75**

chicken *see* meat

Chickpea Stew (Potaje de Garbanzos) **24**

chicory
• Baked Chicory Wrapped in Prosciutto **46**

chicory continued
• Broccoli and Treviso with
Anchovy Dressing **40**
• Bruschetta with Mozzarella,
Treviso and Balsamic Vinegar **55**

chorizo *see* meat (pork)

cod *see* seafood

Cold Rare Beef Fillet (Filetto Freddo) **122**

Cold Roast Aubergine Soup with Yoghurt **26**

Cordonices con Granadas (Pot-roast
Quail with Pomegranates) **128**

Coriander Rice **155**

Cozido de Cabrito (Braised Goat with
Rosemary, Tomatoes and Wine) **136**

Cut Seared Beef Salad (Tagliata) **43**

Eagle pub **6-11**

Eagle Steak Sandwich, The (Bife Ana) **62**

Egg Fettuccine with Porcini, Sausage
and Peas (Fettuccine alla Ciociaria) **73**

Egg Fettuccine with Radicchio,
Borlotti Beans and Pancetta **74**

Egg Fettuccine with Ricotta,
Peas and Smoked Pancetta **75**

eggs
• Huevos a la Flamenca (Gypsy Eggs) **63**
• Peas with Chouriço and Poached Egg **14**
• Smoked Haddock with Horseradish
Mash and Poached Egg **98-9**
• Sopa al Ajillo (Andalucian Garlic
Soup with a Soft-boiled Egg) **16**

Escalivada (Spanish Roast
Vegetable Salad) **56**

Espinacas con Pinones y Pasas
(Spinach with Pine Nuts and Raisins) **146**

Eyre, David **6-9, 11, 113**
• light dishes **36, 38-9, 43, 45,
53-4, 58-9, 62-4**
• meat **14, 18, 22-3, 38-9, 62, 64, 114, 116,
118-20, 123, 127, 130, 132**
• pasta and rice **66, 71, 74-5, 78, 86-7, 91-2**
• seafood **54, 58-9, 78, 91-2, 95-6, 101, 108**
• side dishes **143, 145, 148, 152-3**
• soups **14, 18-19, 22-3, 25, 30**

Eyre, Rob **8, 11**

Fabada Asturiana (Asturian
Pork and Butter Bean Stew) **118**

Feijoada (Portuguese
Pork and Bean Stew) **114**

fettuccine *see* pasta

Filetto Freddo (Cold Rare Beef Fillet) **122**

fish *see* seafood

Florentine Pea Soup (Carabaccia) **30**

Foxwell, Brad **68**

Fried Choricitos with Pimientos, Aguadiente and Garlic (Chorizo a la Llama) **64**

Fried Fillets of Fresh Anchovies **59**

Fried Marinated Monkfish (Rape en Adobo) **102**

game *see* meat

garlic
- Pollo al Ajillo (Braised Garlic Chicken) **126, 155**
- Sopa al Ajillo (Andalucian Garlic Soup with a Soft-boiled Egg) **16**

Gazpacho Andaluz **15**

goat *see* meat

Greek Salad **36**

Greens and Potato Soup with Chorizo (Caldo Verde) **25**

Grilled Chicken Breasts with Oregano, Lemon and Black Pepper **130**

Grilled Chicken Salad with Truffle Oil **34**

Grilled Leg of Venison **134**

Grilled Squid Piri-piri **108**

Grilled Tuna with Salmoriglio and New Potatoes **94-5**

Gypsy Eggs (Huevos a la Flamenca) **63**

haddock *see* seafood

ham *see* meat

Hilferty, Trish **10, 16, 40, 49, 60-61, 72, 98-9, 134, 136, 138-9, 142, 144**

Hodges, Jake **11, 94-5, 124-5**

Huevos a la Flamenca (Gypsy Eggs) **63**

Humphries, John **11, 146**

Imam Bayeldi (Baked Aubergines Stuffed with Tomatoes) **49**

Jansson's Temptation **144**

lamb *see* meat

Lasagne with Rabbit **80-81**

lentils, cooking **23**

Lewis, Kate **11, 47, 52, 56, 122**

light dishes **33-64**
- Baked Chicory Wrapped in Prosciutto **46**
- Bife Ana (The Eagle Steak Sandwich) **62**
- Broccoli and Treviso with Anchovy Dressing **40**

light dishes continued
- Bruschetta with Mozzarella, Treviso and Balsamic Vinegar **55**
- Bruschetta with Roast Tomatoes and Grilled Sardines **54**
- Bruschetta with Warm Ricotta Salad **53**
- Caponata (Sicilian Aubergine Relish) **47**
- Chorizo a la Llama (Fried Choricitos with Pimientos, Aguadiente and Garlic) **64**
- Escalivada (Spanish Roast Vegetable Salad) **56**
- Fried Fillets of Fresh Anchovies **59**
- Greek Salad **36**
- Grilled Chicken Salad with Truffle Oil **34**
- Huevos a la Flamenca (Gypsy Eggs) **63**
- Imam Bayeldi (Baked Aubergines Stuffed with Tomatoes) **49**
- Peas with Chouriço and Poached Egg **14**
- Ratatouille **52**
- Roast Pumpkin and Red Onion Salad **44**
- Salade Niçoise **45**
- Seafood Salad with Cooked Lemon and Coriander **35**
- Tagliata (Cut Seared Beef Salad) **43**
- Tortilla de Bacalao (Salt Cod Tortilla) **50**
- Vitello o Capone Tonnato (Veal or Chicken with a Tuna Dressing) **60-61**

Manners, George **11, 13, 32, 128**

Marconi, Fulvia **11, 73, 101**

meat **109-40**
- accompaniments **32, 47, 52, 56, 94-5, 110, 143-6, 148-9, 154-5**
- cooking **38-9, 86-7, 120**

meat, bacon
- Egg Fettuccine with Radicchio, Borlotti Beans and Pancetta **74**
- Egg Fettuccine with Ricotta, Peas and Smoked Pancetta **75**
- Fabada Asturiana (Asturian Pork and Butter Bean Stew) **118**
- Feijoada (Portuguese Pork and Bean Stew) **114**
- Minestrone **29**
- Pasta e Fagioli (Pasta and Bean Soup) **28**
- Patatas al Forno (Oven Potatoes) **148**
- Potaje de Garbanzos (Chickpea Stew) **24**
- Potatoes with Braised Cabbage **149**
- Sopa de Pedra **22-3**
- Venison and Pancetta Casserole **135**

meat, beef
- Casseroled Beef with Cinnamon, Thyme and Shallots **123**
- Filetto Freddo (Cold Rare Beef Fillet) **122**
- Tagliata (Cut Seared Beef Salad) **43**

meat, chicken **39**
- Canja (Portuguese Chicken Broth with Rice, Mint and Lemon) **18**
- Grilled Chicken Breasts with Oregano, Lemon and Black Pepper **130**
- Grilled Chicken Salad with Truffle Oil **34**
- Paella Valenciana **84-5**
- Pollo al Ajillo (Braised Garlic Chicken) **126, 155**
- Roast Chicken with Tarragon, Garlic and Olives **127**
- Vitello o Capone Tonnato (Veal or Chicken with a Tuna Dressing) **60-61**

meat, game **39**
- Arroz con Conejo (Spanish Rice with Rabbit) **82**
- Cordonices con Granadas (Pot-roast Quail with Pomegranates) **128**
- Grilled Leg of Venison **134**
- Hare Casserole **138-9**
- Lasagne with Rabbit **80-81**
- Patatas Rellenos (Braised Wild Boar with Potatoes) **140**
- Pheasant Casserole with Chestnuts, Ceps and Bacon **132**
- Venison and Pancetta Casserole **135**

meat, goat **39**
- Cozido de Cabrito (Braised Goat with Rosemary, Tomatoes and Wine) **136**

meat, ham
- Baked Chicory Wrapped in Prosciutto **46**
- Fabada Asturiana (Asturian Pork and Butter Bean Stew) **118**
- Feijoada (Portuguese Pork and Bean Stew) **114**
- Huevos a la Flamenca (Gypsy Eggs) **63**
- Paella Valenciana **84-5**
- Sopa de Pedra **22-3**

meat, lamb
- Lamb, Olive and Artichoke Stew **112**
- Lamb Shanks with Chickpeas **111**
- Saddle of Lamb Stuffed with Tapenade **110**

meat, pork ('s' denotes sausages)
- Arista (Roast Pork, Tuscan Style) **116**
- Belly Pork Stew with Peas and Saffron **115**
- Caldo Verde (Greens and Potato Soup with Chorizo) (s) **25**

meat, pork continued ('s' denotes sausages)
- Chorizo a la Llama (Fried Choricitos with Pimientos, Aguadiente and Garlic) (s) **64**
- Fabada Asturiana (Asturian Pork and Butter Bean Stew) (and s) **118**
- Feijoada (Portuguese Pork and Bean Stew) (and s) **114**
- Fettuccine alla Ciociaria (Egg Fettuccine with Porcini, Sausage and Peas) (s) **73**
- Huevos a la Flamenca (Gypsy Eggs) (s) **63**
- Paella Valenciana **84-5**
- Peas with Chouriço and Poached Egg (s) **14**
- Penne with Sausages, Tomato and Sage (s) **68**
- Porco à Alentejana (Pork and Clams, Alentejo-style) **119**
- Potaje de Garbanzos (Chickpea Stew) (s) **24**
- Sopa de Pedra (s) **22-3**

meat, steak **39**
- Bife Ana (The Eagle Steak Sandwich) **62**

meat, veal
- Osso Bucco, Risotto Milanese and Gremolata **124-5**
- Vitello o Capone Tonnato (Veal or Chicken with a Tuna Dressing) **60-61**

minestra **28-9**
Minestrone **29**
mushrooms
- Black Mushroom Soup **19**
- Fettuccine alla Ciociaria (Egg Fettuccine with Porcini, Sausage and Peas) **73**

Norrington-Davies, Tom **11, 20-21, 26, 46, 55, 70, 76, 79-81, 88-90, 106-7, 111, 115, 140, 149, 155**

octopus see seafood
olives
- Lamb, Olive and Artichoke Stew **112**
- Roast Chicken with Tarragon, Garlic and Olives **127**

onions
- Red Onion and Red Wine Soup with Parmesan Bruschetta **13**
- Roast Pumpkin and Red Onion Salad **44**
- Roast Red Onions **145**

Orecchiette with Butter, Sage, Garlic and Parmesan **71**
Osso Bucco, Risotto Milanese and Gremolata **124-5**
Oven Potatoes (Patatas al Forno) **148**

Paella Valenciana **84-5**

Palermo Salt Cod with Prunes and Pickling Onions (Baccala alla Palermitana) **101**
pancetta see meat (bacon)
pasta **66-81**
- Bucatini with Cauliflower, Anchovies, Pine Nuts and Raisins **67**
- cooking **66**
- Egg Fettuccine with Radicchio, Borlotti Beans and Pancetta **74**
- Egg Fettuccine with Ricotta, Peas and Smoked Pancetta **75**
- Fettuccine alla Ciociaria (Egg Fettuccine with Porcini, Sausage and Peas) **73**
- Lasagne with Rabbit **80-81**
- Minestrone **29**
- Orecchiette with Butter, Sage, Garlic and Parmesan **71**
- Pasta e Fagioli (Pasta and Bean Soup) **28**
- Penne with Artichoke Hearts and Greens **70**
- Penne with Sausages, Tomato and Sage **68**
- Pizzoccheri (Baked Buckwheat Pasta with Sage, Fontina and Cabbage) **79**
- Spaghetti with Roasted Fennel, Lemon and Chilli **76**
- Spaghettini with Walnut Sauce **72**
- Wholewheat Spaghetti with Sardines **78**

Patatas al Forno (Oven Potatoes) **148**
Patatas Rellenos (Braised Wild Boar with Potatoes) **140**
peas
- Carabaccia (Florentine Pea Soup) **30**
- Peas with Chouriço and Poached Egg **14**

penne see pasta
Pickering, Phil **10, 112**
Pizzoccheri (Baked Buckwheat Pasta with Sage, Fontina and Cabbage) **79**
Pollo al Ajillo (Braised Garlic Chicken) **126, 155**
pork see meat
Portuguese Chicken Broth with Rice, Mint and Lemon (Canja) **18**
Portuguese Pork and Bean Stew (Feijoada) **114**
Pot-roast Quail with Pomegranates (Cordonices con Granadas) **128**
Potaje de Garbanzos (Chickpea Stew) **24**
- potato salads **152-3**
Potatoes with Braised Cabbage **149**
Pritchett, Amanda **10, 110**
pumpkin, Roast Pumpkin and Red Onion Salad **44**

Quinlan, Ruth **11, 28-9, 135**

rabbit see meat (game)
Rape en Adobo (Fried Marinated Monkfish) **102**
Ratatouille **52**
Red Onion and Red Wine Soup with Parmesan Bruschetta **13**
rice **82-92**
- Arroz con Conejo (Spanish Rice with Rabbit) **82**
- Coriander Rice **155**
- Paella Valenciana **84-5**
- risotto see risotto
risotto **86-7**
- Osso Bucco, Risotto Milanese and Gremolata **124-5**
- Risotto with Broad Beans and Mint **88-9**
- Risotto with Sage and Lemon **90**
- Seafood Risotto **86-7, 92**
- Smoked Haddock Risotto with Saffron, Fennel and Peas **91**

Roast Chicken with Tarragon, Garlic and Olives **127**
Roast Pork, Tuscan Style (Arista) **116**
Roast Pumpkin and Red Onion Salad **44**
Roast Red Onions **145**
Roast Tomatoes **145**
Root Vegetable Soup with Greens **20-21**

Saddle of Lamb Stuffed with Tapenade **110**
salads **145**
- see also side dishes
- Broccoli and Treviso with Anchovy Dressing **40**
- Bruschetta with Warm Ricotta Salad **53**
- Escalivada (Spanish Roast Vegetable Salad) **56**
- Greek Salad **36**
- Grilled Chicken Salad with Truffle Oil **34**
- potato salads **152-3**
- Roast Pumpkin and Red Onion Salad **44**
- Salade Niçoise **45**
- Seafood Salad with Cooked Lemon and Coriander **35**
- Tagliata (Cut Seared Beef Salad) **43**

Salsa Verde **122**
salt cod see seafood
sandwiches, Bife Ana (The Eagle Steak Sandwich) **62**
Santos, Paulo **11, 68, 100**
sardines see seafood
sauces **80-81, 94-5, 122, 145**
sausages see meat (pork)

seafood **93-108**
- accompaniments **40, 44, 52, 56, 94-5, 110, 145-6, 155**
- anchovies **58**
- Bacalhau com Batatas (Baked Salt Cod with Peppers and Potatoes) **100**
- Baccalà alla Palermitana (Salt Cod with Prunes and Pickling Onions) **101**
- Baked Sea Bream or Sea Bass with Tomatoes **96**
- Bruschetta with Roast Tomatoes and Grilled Sardines **54**
- Bucatini with Cauliflower, Anchovies, Pine Nuts and Raisins **67**
- Caldeirada de Mariscos (Big Portuguese Fish Stew) **104-5**
- cooking **95**
- dressings **40, 60-61**
- Espinaca con Pinones y Pasas (Spinach with Pine Nuts and Raisins) **146**
- Fried Fillets of Fresh Anchovies **59**
- Grilled Squid Piri-piri **108**
- Grilled Tuna with Salmoriglio and New Potatoes **94-5**
- Jansson's Temptation **144**
- Octopus Stew with Spices from Goa **106-7, 155**
- Paella Valenciana **84-5**
- Porco à Alentejana (Alentejo-style Pork and Clams) **119**
- Rape en Adobo (Fried Marinated Monkfish) **102**
- Salade Niçoise **45**
- salt cod **101**
- Seafood Risotto **86-7, 92**
- Seafood Salad with Cooked Lemon and Coriander **35**
- Smoked Haddock with Horseradish Mash and Poached Egg **98-9**
- Smoked Haddock Risotto with Saffron, Fennel and Peas **91**
- Tortilla de Bacalao (Salt Cod Tortilla) **50**
- Wholewheat Spaghetti with Sardines **78**
shellfish *see* seafood
Sicilian Aubergine Relish (Caponata) **47**
side dishes **141-55** *see also* salads
- Cannellini Beans with Garlic and Sage **154**
- Celeriac Gratin **143**
- Celeriac Mash **142**
- Coriander Rice **155**
- Espinacas con Pinones y Pasas (Spinach with Pine Nuts and Raisins) **146**
- Jansson's Temptation **144**

side dishes continued
- Patatas al Forno (Oven Potatoes) **148**
- potato salads **152-3**
- Potatoes with Braised Cabbage **149**
- Roast Red Onions **145**
- Roast Tomatoes **145**
Smoked Haddock with Horseradish Mash and Poached Egg **98-9**
Smoked Haddock Risotto with Saffron, Fennel and Peas **91**
snails, Paella Valenciana **84-5**
Sopa al Ajillo (Andalucian Garlic Soup with a Soft-boiled Egg) **16**
Sopa de Pedra **22-3**
soups **12-32**
- Black Bean Soup **32**
- Black Mushroom Soup **19**
- Caldo Verde (Greens and Potato Soup with Chorizo) **25**
- Canja (Portuguese Chicken Broth with Rice, Mint and Lemon) **18**
- Carabaccia (Florentine Pea Soup) **30**
- Cold Roast Aubergine Soup with Yoghurt **26**
- Gazpacho Andaluz **15**
- *minestra* **28-9**
- Minestrone **29**
- Pasta e Fagioli (Pasta and Bean Soup) **28**
- Peas with Chouriço and Poached Egg **14**
- Potaje de Garbanzos (Chickpea Stew) **24**
- Red Onion and Red Wine Soup with Parmesan Bruschetta **13**
- Root Vegetable Soup with Greens **20-21**
- Sopa al Ajillo (Andalucian Garlic Soup with a Soft-boiled Egg) **16**
- Sopa de Pedra **22-3**
spaghetti *see* pasta
Spanish Rice with Rabbit (Arroz con Conejo) **82**
Spanish Roast Vegetable Salad (Escalivada) **56**
Spinach with Pine Nuts and Raisins (Espinacas con Pinones y Pasas) **146**
steak *see* meat

Tagliata (Cut Seared Beef Salad) **43**
tomatoes, Roast Tomatoes **145**
Tortilla de Bacalao (Salt Cod Tortilla) **50**
tuna *see* seafood

Vargas, Carlos **10, 15, 24, 50, 82, 84-5, 102, 126**
veal *see* meat

vegetarian dishes
- Black Bean Soup **32**
- Black Mushroom Soup **19**
- Bruschetta with Mozzarella, Treviso and Balsamic Vinegar **55**
- Bruschetta with Warm Ricotta Salad **53**
- Cannellini Beans with Garlic and Sage **154**
- Caponata (Sicilian Aubergine Relish) **47**
- Carabaccia (Florentine Pea Soup) **30**
- Celeriac Gratin **143**
- Celeriac Mash **142**
- Cold Roast Aubergine Soup with Yoghurt **26**
- Coriander Rice **155**
- Escalivada (Spanish Roast Vegetable Salad) **56**
- Gazpacho Andaluz **15**
- Greek Salad **36**
- Imam Bayeldi (Baked Aubergines Stuffed with Tomatoes) **49**
- Orecchiette with Butter, Sage, Garlic and Parmesan **71**
- Patatas al Forno (Oven Potatoes) **148**
- Penne with Artichoke Hearts and Greens **70**
- Pizzoccheri (Baked Buckwheat Pasta with Sage, Fontina and Cabbage) **79**
- potato salads **152-3**
- Ratatouille **52**
- Red Onion and Red Wine Soup with Parmesan Bruschetta **13**
- risotto **86-7**
- Risotto with Broad Beans and Mint **88-9**
- Risotto with Sage and Lemon **90**
- Roast Pumpkin and Red Onion Salad **44**
- Roast Red Onions **145**
- Roast Tomatoes **145**
- Root Vegetable Soup with Greens **20-21**
- Spaghetti with Roasted Fennel, Lemon and Chilli **76**
- Spaghettini con Salsa di Noci (Spaghettini with Walnut Sauce) **72**
venison *see* meat (game)
vitello *see* meat (veal)

Wholewheat Spaghetti with Sardines **78**
Wickham, Pola **10, 34**
wine
- Braised Goat with Rosemary, Tomatoes and Wine (Cozido de Cabrito) **136**
- Red Onion and Red Wine Soup with Parmesan Bruschetta **13**

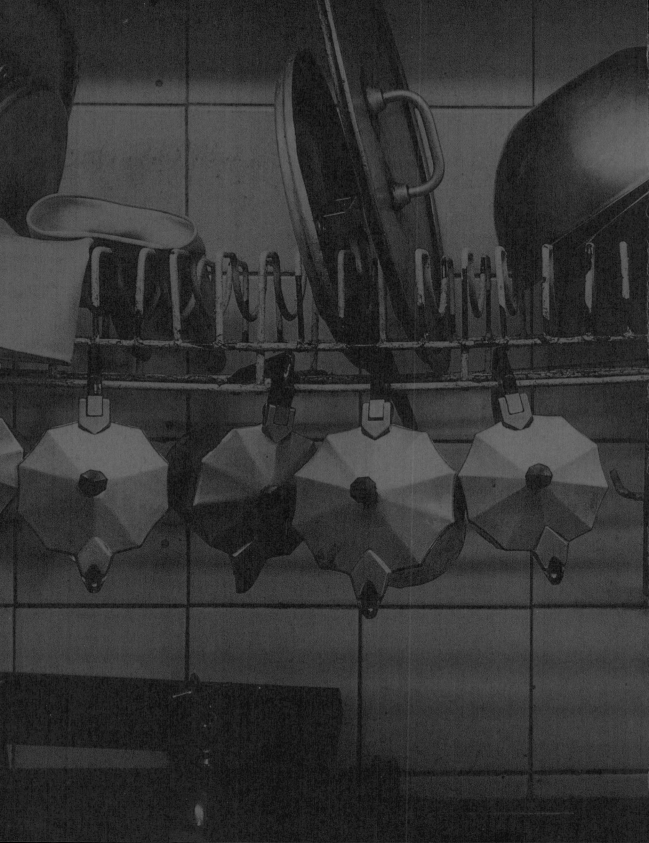

WIGAN ATHLETIC
THE FOOTBALL LEAGUE YEARS

--- DEAN HAYES ---

SUTTON PUBLISHING LIMITED

Sutton Publishing Limited
Phoenix Mill · Thrupp · Stroud
Gloucestershire · GL5 2BU

First published 2000

Copyright © Dean Hayes, 2000

Front cover: Lifting the Autowindscreen
shield, p. 57. *Back cover:* Delivering the
Freight Rover Trophy, p. 49. *Title page:* 'Up
for the Cup' – 3rd Division Champs. p. 143.
Below: The new JJB Stadium, p. 80.

British Library Cataloguing in Publication Data
A catalogue record for this book is available from the
British Library.

ISBN 0-7509-2534-5

Typeset in 10.5/13.5 Photina.
Typesetting and origination by
Sutton Publishing Limited.
Printed and bound in England by
J.H. Haynes & Co. Ltd, Sparkford

CONTENTS

Introduction   5

1.   The Managers   7

2.   The Players   15

3.   Freight Rover Trophy   49

4.   Autowindscreen Shield   57

5.   The Grounds   67

6.   Team Groups   81

7.   Through the Seasons   93

Appendices   151

Acknowledgements   160

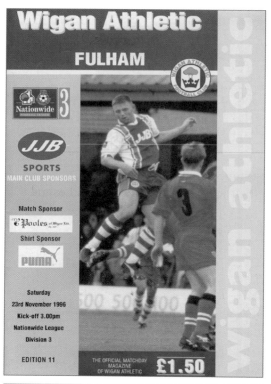

Wigan Athletic

FULHAM

Nationwide 3

JJB
SPORTS
MAIN CLUB SPONSORS

Match Sponsor
Pooles of Wigan Ltd.

Shirt Sponsor
PUMA

Saturday
23rd November 1996
Kick-off 3.00pm
Nationwide League
Division 3

EDITION 11

THE OFFICIAL MATCHDAY
MAGAZINE
OF WIGAN ATHLETIC

£1.50

wigan athletic

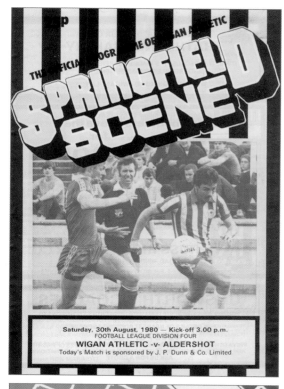

SPRINGFIELD SCENE

THE OFFICIAL PROGRAMME OF WIGAN ATHLETIC

Saturday, 30th August, 1980 — Kick-off 3.00 p.m.
FOOTBALL LEAGUE DIVISION FOUR
WIGAN ATHLETIC -v- ALDERSHOT
Today's Match is sponsored by J. P. Dunn & Co. Limited

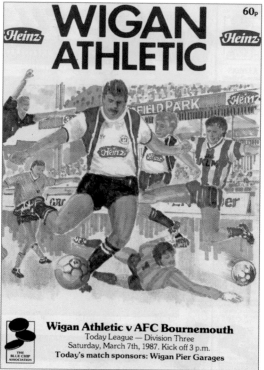

Heinz   60p   *Heinz*

WIGAN ATHLETIC

Wigan Athletic v AFC Bournemouth
Today League — Division Three
Saturday, March 7th, 1987. Kick off 3 p.m.
Today's match sponsors: Wigan Pier Garages

THE BLUE CHIP ASSOCIATION

Today's match
sponsors are
SADDLER
MOTOR
GROUP

WIGAN ATHLETIC
v
YORK CITY
Sat. Dec. 28th, 1985. Kick off 3 p.m.
CANON LEAGUE DIVISION THREE

60p

Wigan
ATHLETIC

Heinz

INTRODUCTION

Though Wigan Athletic have been in existence since 1932, this book deals specifically with the club's exploits since their admission to the Football League in 1978.

The Latics' first league game was at Hereford United on 19 August 1978. Over three thousand Wigan fans made the historic journey and the roar that greeted the team as captain Ian Gillibrand led them out at Edgar Street could be heard back in Wigan! The game ended goalless and Latics fans travelled home happy with a point. Latics ended their first season in the Football League in sixth position and, though they made challenging runs in each of their first three seasons, they were unable to sustain their form enough to earn promotion. They eventually achieved the honour in 1981–2.

In 1979–80, their second season as a Football League club, Wigan reached the fourth round of the FA Cup. In this run they beat Blackpool 2–0 after a 1–1 draw, Northwich Victoria 1–0 after a 2–2 draw and an opening game which saw Latics leading 3-0 until the game was abandoned due to fog, and Chelsea 1–0 at Stamford Bridge before going down 3–0 at Everton.

In 1981–2, Latics finished third in Division Four with 91 points, behind Bradford City and Sheffield United. That season, Eamon O'Keefe arrived from Everton for a club record £65,000 and Second Division Chelsea were sent packing from the League Cup before League Champions Aston Villa ended the run, snatching victory three minutes from time.

In 1984–5, Wigan won their first trophy as a league club when they beat Brentford 3–1 to lift the Freight Rover Trophy at Wembley. The following season the Latics finished fourth in Division Three, missing promotion by just one point – whilst in 1986–7 they again finished fourth to qualify for the play-offs which had been introduced to settle the promotion and relegation issues between divisions. They were paired against Swindon Town in the semi-finals but, after leading 2–0, suicidal defending allowed the Robins to score three goals in the last 18 minutes. In the return leg, luckless Latics hit the woodwork but not the net and went out after a goalless draw.

That season also saw the club have its most successful run in the FA Cup. Having proved themselves in the fourth round against First Division opposition in Norwich City, the Latics then beat Hull City 3–0 before facing the mighty Leeds United at Springfield Park. Latics lost 2–0 but proved that they were more than capable of handling football at a higher level.

In April 1988, Wigan were involved in the Mercantile Centenary Festival at Wembley, qualification being based on the number of league points won in the first fifteen games after 1 November 1987. Playing twenty minutes each way, Wigan and Sunderland fought out a goalless draw before Latics won 2–1 on penalties. In the quarter-finals, Wigan drew 1–1 with Sheffield Wednesday but this time lost 3–2 in the penalty shoot-out.

The 1992–3 season was without doubt the most turbulent in the club's short Football League history and ended in total disappointment as the Latics were relegated for the first time since their election to the League. If relegation was a disappointment then Latics finishing 19th in the Third Division in 1993–4, thus recording their lowest-ever position in the Football League, must have run it pretty close.

In 1996–7 the Latics won the Third Division Championship with Graeme Jones the leading scorer with 31 goals, a total which included four hat-tricks.

The 1998–9 season was a campaign of highs and lows. The Latics reached Wembley where they beat Millwall 1–0 in the final of the Autowindscreen Shield but then suffered the bitter disappointment of losing in the play-offs to Manchester City after a near super-human effort to get into the top six. In the summer of 1999 the Latics left Springfield Park to play their football at their new all-seater JJB Stadium.

Unbeaten in their opening 24 league games, the Latics had a great season in 1999–2000, finishing fourth and so qualifying for the play-offs. After beating Millwall, ten-men Wigan were seven minutes away from promotion to Division One but two late goals saw Gillingham promoted. Though they failed at the final hurdle, I am sure Latics will be back, better and stronger under new manager Bruce Rioch.

Dean Hayes
Bamber Bridge
July 2000

1

The Managers

When Wigan Athletic were elected to the Fourth Division to replace Southport in 1978, it was almost fifty years since another club from the same town, Wigan Borough had been forced by huge debts to resign from the League. The current club was founded in 1932 a year after Boroughs' demise and elected to the Fourth Division after an outstanding record in the Northern Premier League.

As a non-League club, the Latics had been able to attract some impressive names to their then-home ground of Springfield Park. These included former and future league managers – Jimmy Milne (Preston North End), his son Gordon (Coventry City and Leicester City), Ted Goodier (Derby County), Allenby Chilton (Grimsby Town) and Allan Brown (Luton Town, Nottingham Forest and Blackpool).

At the time of the club's entry into the Football League, Ian McNeill was in charge. A vastly experienced player in England and Scotland with Leicester City and Aberdeen, he remained at the helm until 1981 when he was replaced by Larry Lloyd. Lloyd had played at the highest level for Liverpool, Nottingham Forest and England among others and led the club to promotion for the first time in its history. There was a brief splash of glamour at Springfield Park for a few months in 1983 following Lloyd's departure. The unlikely figure of Bobby Charlton took over as caretaker manager, but he stepped aside when Harry McNally was appointed as the club's third manager. His pre-Wigan experience had all been in non-League football, playing for Skelmersdale and managing both Altrincham and Southport. After two seasons of struggle he was replaced by the articulate Irishman, Bryan Hamilton. The former Northern Ireland international led the club to success in the Freight Rover Trophy Final at Wembley but after taking the Latics to fourth place in Division Three, he left to take charge of Leicester City. His club coach and successor was Ray Mathias, a tough northerner who had made 637 appearances as a player for Tranmere Rovers. In his first season in charge the club reached the sixth round of the FA Cup and were involved in the end of season play-offs. In March 1989, Hamilton began his second spell as manager and despite low crowds and little success on the pitch, he managed to keep the club in the Third Division for four seasons. His second spell ended with the team floundering in the spring of 1993 and it was left to Dave Philpotts to preside over the club's first relegation months later.

The Latics next manager was Kenny Swain but after just one season in charge, he made way for former Latics favourite, Graham Barrow, who had been manager at Chester. Following his appointment, there was a dramatic improvement in the club's fortunes and the Latics almost made the play-offs. Barrow was surprisingly dismissed in October 1995 and replaced by much-travelled striker, John Deehan. He almost took the Latics to promotion via the play-offs in his first season at Springfield Park but unfortunately the club lost their last match of the season against Northampton Town. In 1996–7, Deehan led the Latics to the Third Division Championship, pipping Fulham for the title. He left the club after accepting a three-year deal at Sheffield United as assistant to Steve Bruce. His replacement was former Latics boss Ray Mathias, who in 1998–9 led the club to Wembley where they beat Millwall 1-0 to win the Autowindscreen Shield, and to the play-offs. Two days after losing 2-1 on aggregate to Manchester City, controversially, Mathias was sacked.

In June 1999, John Benson rather reluctantly took over the reins, having an agreement with the chairman that he would manage the club for twelve months and then review the situation. After leading the division for much of the season, Latics had to be content with fourth position and a place in the play-offs. After they had beaten Millwall over two legs, Benson shocked the soccer world by announcing that he would step down after the play-off final against Gillingham. Sadly Latics lost 3–2 after extra-time but Benson, who is staying on at the club in an advisory position, will work closely with new manager Bruce Rioch.

Scottish international wing-half Bruce Rioch played for Luton Town, Aston Villa, Derby County, Everton, Birmingham City, Sheffield United and Torquay United, where he gained his first experience of management. However, his first success came following his appointment by Middlesborough in February 1986. He guided the club from a dire financial position and lifted them from the Third to the First Division within two seasons. Rioch left Ayresome Park in March 1990 and in less than a month was in charge at Millwall.

In 1990–1 he took the London club to the Second Division play-offs but in March 1992 after their form slumped he took over the reins at Bolton Wanderers. In his first season the Trotters finished runners-up in Division Two and in 1993–94 he led Bolton to the sixth round of the FA Cup. The following season he took Bolton to the League Cup Final and promotion to the Premiership via the play-offs. In June 1995 he was appointed manager of Arsenal but after 15 months was sacked and joined Queen's Park Rangers. After a spell as manager of Norwich City he arrived at the JJB Stadium in the summer of 2000 to become Latics' eleventh Football League manager.

Ian McNeill, seen here in his Leicester City days, soon made an impact at Filbert Street after being signed by his former manager at Aberdeen where he began his first-class career. He scored 18 goals in Leicester's Second Division Championship winning season of 1956–7 but found goals and a regular place somewhat harder in the top flight. After later playing for Brighton and Southend United, he entered management with Ross County, leading them to their first-ever Highland League Championship in 1967.

McNeill first took charge of Wigan Athletic in May 1968 and in his first season at Springfield Park, led the Latics to runners-up to Macclesfield in the Northern Premier League. The following season McNeill, surprisingly, was sacked just six weeks after the club's epic FA Cup encounter with Port Vale.

Following a brief spell at Northwich and another with Ross County, McNeill rejoined the Latics in April 1976 and was in charge when the club entered the Football League in 1978. He took the Latics to the creditable position of sixth in their first two seasons in the League but in February 1981, was sacked for a second time. He later had a spell as manager of Shrewsbury Town with periods as assistant-manager at Chelsea and Millwall

Larry Lloyd's early footballing was with Bristol Rovers before Liverpool stepped in with a £50,000 offer in April 1969 that tempted him north. Lloyd was an immediate hit, the perfect replacement for Kop favourite Ron Yeats. He won a League Championship medal in 1973 and a UEFA Cup winners' medal the same year. Then as Bob Paisley took over, he was surprisingly sold to Coventry City for £225,000. Two years later he joined Nottingham Forest and within a season of his arrival, Forest were champions. Lloyd went on to claim two European Cup medals and two League Cup medals with his new club.

He left Forest in March 1981 to become player-manager of Wigan Athletic, making his debut in a 1–0 home defeat by Rochdale. The following season he appeared in 36 league games, leading the Latics to third position in Division Four and promotion for the first time in their history. The former England international who scored four goals in 57 League and Cup games for the Latics was sacked in April 1983 following the club's disappointing showing. He later managed Notts County before leaving soccer to run a pub in Nottingham.

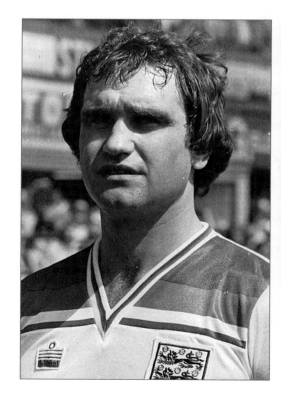

Harry McNally never appeared in the Football League, spending most of his playing career with Skelmersdale United where he was also coach in his latter days. After spells managing Altrincham and Southport, he joined Wigan Athletic as assistant manager and chief scout before being appointed manager in June 1983 following the departure of Larry Lloyd. There followed two seasons of struggle, with the club finishing 15th and 16th respectively in the Third Division. McNally resigned after being asked to let his assistant Roy Tunks and coach Alex Bruce take charge for a while.

In June 1985 McNally took charge at Chester City and in his first season as manager led the Cestrians to runners-up spot in the Fourth Division and to eighth in Division Three in 1988-9. In 1990 Chester lost their Sealand Road ground, sold off to pay massive debts – yet, despite attendances dropping off alarmingly, he managed to keep Chester in the Third Division. However, they had a constant struggle to avoid relegation to the League's basement and after a poor start to the 1992–3 season he was sacked.

Bryan Hamilton began his Football League career with Ipswich Town after moving to Portman Road from Linfield. He went on to score 56 goals in 199 games for the Suffolk club before signing for Everton for £40,000 in 1975. Remembered on Merseyside for scoring the 'goal that never was' in the FA Cup semi-final against Liverpool, Hamilton later played for Millwall and Swindon Town before joining Tranmere Rovers as player-manager. Following his sacking in 1985, Hamilton joined Wigan Athletic and led the club to success in the Freight Rover Trophy Final at Wembley. At the end of the following season in which Latics finished fourth in Division Three, Hamilton left Springfield Park to take charge of Leicester City. He got off to a fine start at Filbert Street but at the end of his first season in charge, the Foxes were relegated and when they were found to struggle the following campaign, he was sacked.

In March 1988 he returned to Springfield Park as chief executive but later reassumed control of team matters. Despite little success on the pitch and low attendances, Hamilton managed to keep the Latics in the Third Division for the next four seasons before losing his job in March 1993. After a spell as Northern Ireland team manager he is now in charge of Norwich City.

Ray Mathias holds the Tranmere Rovers record for the most League and Cup appearances, having played in 637 games over 18 seasons in the Birkenhead club's side. Though he started his career in midfield he was converted to full-back and over the years missed very few games, being ever-present in five seasons. Playing his last match in September 1984, he turned his hand to coaching before being appointed assistant manager to Bryan Hamilton at Prenton Park.

When Hamilton was dismissed in February 1985, Mathias took over as caretaker manager but was not given the chance to do the job on a permanent basis, with Frank Worthington being appointed.

Mathias followed Hamilton to Springfield Park, taking over as Latics manager in June 1986. He led the club to one of their most successful seasons with an FA Cup run to the sixth round and fourth place in the League and a play-off place. After a poor season with the Latics in 1988–9 he returned to Tranmere as the Training Centre Manager. He returned to manage Wigan for a second time in 1998 but despite leading the Latics to success in the Autowindscreen Shield and to the Second Division play-offs, he lost his job in the summer of 1999.

Dave Philpotts' playing career consisted of spells with Coventry City and Southport before he joined Tranmere Rovers in September 1974. After making his debut that month in a goalless home draw against West Ham United in a League Cup second round tie, the central defender became a regular member of the Rovers' first team and was ever-present in 1975–6 when the club won promotion to the Third Division.

He left Prenton Park to spend three-and-a-half years playing in American football before returning for a second spell with Tranmere. He had taken his career record with the club to 12 goals in 237 League and Cup games when a back injury forced his retirement in 1984.

He was appointed Wigan Athletic's coach in the summer of 1986 but later moved to assistant manager before taking over the reins in 1993. He was replaced by Kenny Swain.

Starting his Football League career with Chelsea, Kenny Swain scored 19 goals in 126 outings for the Stamford Bridge club, operating mainly as a striker or in midfield, before joining Aston Villa in December 1978. At Villa Park, the Birkenhead-born player was converted into right-back and won medals for League Championship, European Cup and European Super Cup successes in seasons 1980–1 and 1981–2. He played in 178 first team games for Villa before moving to Nottingham Forest in 1983. He later helped Portsmouth win promotion to the First Division and had a spell on loan at West Bromwich Albion before becoming player-coach at Crewe Alexandra. Swain, who had appeared in 625 league games for his six clubs, was appointed Latics' manager in 1993 – but after they finished 19th in the Third Division in 1993–4, his only season in charge, he was dismissed

After playing his early football for Altrincham, Graham Barrow joined the Latics in 1981 and went on to score 44 goals in 212 games before leaving to play for Chester City. He later became the Cestrian's player-coach before becoming assistant manager to Harry McNally in 1988. Following McNally's sacking at the start of the 1992–3 season, Barrow took over the reins at Chester but failed to prevent the club from being relegated. In 1993–4, Barrow led the Cestrians to immediate promotion as they finished runners-up to Shrewsbury Town.

In September 1994 Barrow returned to Springfield Park to become manager of Wigan Athletic. His appointment sparked a dramatic upturn in the Latics' fortunes. There was even talk of the club reaching the play-offs in 1994–5 but they had to settle for 14th place in the Third Division after results fell away towards the end of the season. Following Wigan's 6–2 home defeat at the hands of Mansfield Town in October 1995, Barrow, surprisingly, was sacked.

In May 1996 he became maanger of Rochdale but lost his job in the summer of 1999. He has recently been appointed manager of Chester City for a second time.

A striker who did his fair share of creating goals as well as scoring them, John Deehan formed splendid partnerships with both Andy Gray and Brian Little during his time with Aston Villa, where he began his league career. He helped Villa win the League Cup in 1977 and won seven England Under-21 caps but in the early part of the 1979-80 season left to join West Bromwich Albion. The move didn't work out, and in December 1981 he was transferred to Norwich City for £175,000

At Carrow Road, Deehan scored 70 goals in 197 games, winning a League Cup winners' medal in 1985 and a Second Division Championship medal the following year. When he left Norwich he stayed in East Anglia, signing for Ipswich Town whom he helped into the Division Two play-offs. He later had spells with Manchester City and Barnsley and, after coaching Norwich City, became the Canaries' manager. However, during 1994–5 when the club were relegated they adopted a policy to sell their best players and Deehan resigned.

He took over as manager of Wigan Athletic in October 1995 and led the Latics to promotion to the Second Division in 1996–7. At the end of the following season he left Wigan to take up a three-year deal at Sheffield United with Steve Bruce, whom he has since followed to Huddersfield Town

A wing-half, John Benson's league career began in the First Division with Manchester City in 1962 before moving to Torquay United two years later. He played in 240 league games for the Plainmoor club, helping them to promotion from the Fourth Division in 1965–6. He joined Bournemouth in 1970 and in 1973 moved to Norwich City as player-coach. He returned to Dean Court in 1975 as player-manager, a position he held until 1979. After another spell at Norwich as youth coach, Benson became John Bond's assistant at Manchester City, taking over the reins when Bond resigned in February 1983. However, following City's relegation at the end of the season, Benson lost his job and teamed up with Bond again, this time at Burnley. Again he replaced the outspoken Bond following his departure but after the Clarets were relegated, he resigned.

After a spell as Barnsley's chief scout, he joined Wigan Athletic as assistant-manager to John Deehan, a position he continued to hold under Ray Mathias. He was appointed Latics' boss in June 1999 and took the club to fourth place in Division Two and a place in the play-offs. Sadly, Latics lost in the Wembley Final to Gillingham – but Benson, as agreed with chairman Dave Whelan, has stepped down, though he is staying at the club in an advisory capacity.

2

The Players

Tommy Gore spent four years at Anfield, helping Liverpool reach the FA Youth Cup Final in 1972, where they were beaten by Aston Villa. He followed Liverpool and Scottish international Ron Yeats to Prenton Park; but, after being unable to win a regular place in the Tranmere side, he joined Wigan Athletic, initially on loan, midway through the 1973–4 season. The club's regular penalty-taker, he helped them win the Northern Premier League Championship in 1974–5 and was ever-present in 1977–8 when they were runners-up, as well as being voted the Latics' Player of the Year.

He made his league debut for Wigan in the club's inaugural game in the competition, a goalless draw at Hereford United. An ever-present in the club's first two seasons of league football, he is one of only three players to have appeared in over 100 consecutive league games following his debut. The scorer of a number of spectacular goals, he took his tally to 56 in 367 games in all competitions since his arrival at Springfield Park before leaving to end his first-class career with Bury.

Jeff Wright played his early football for Tow Law Town before joining Netherfield. A virtual ever-present over the next two-and-a-half seasons, Wright had played in over 120 games when Les Rigby brought him to Springfield Park in February 1974. In his first full season with the Latics, he helped the club win the Northern Premier League Championship, and over the next three seasons of non-League football missed very few games.

He made his Football League debut in the club's inaugural game, a goalless draw at Hereford United, and scored his first goal in the competition in a 3-0 home win over Rochdale in September 1978. Wright was ever-present in the Latics' side for the first two seasons of league football, going on to make 110 consecutive league appearances from his debut. He went on to appear in 163 League and Cup games after the club entered the Football League, scoring 20 goals, before leaving to continue his career with Barrow.

Peter Houghton was playing for South Liverpool when Wigan Athletic signed him towards the end of the 1977–8 season. He scored nine goals in 15 games, helping Latics finish as runners-up to Boston in that season's Northern Premier League. He was the club's leading scorer in their first season in the Football League, his total of 14 goals including a hat-trick in the 5–3 defeat of Port Vale. He topped the club's scoring charts again the following season, whilst in 1980–1 he netted his second hat-trick for the club in a 3–2 win at Tranmere Rovers, despite it being a campaign in which he was hampered by a series of niggling injuries. When Latics won promotion in 1981–2, Houghton, who formed a formidable strike partnership with Les Bradd, netted 17 goals including another hat-trick in a 6–3 win at Doncaster Rovers.

He had scored 68 goals in 219 games when in October 1983 he was allowed to join Preston North End. He later played for Chester City, whose manager was former Latics' boss Harry McNally, before ending his career with Runcorn.

Liverpool-born midfielder Frank Corrigan began his career with Blackpool; but, being unable to break into the Bloomfield Road club's league side, he joined Walsall. After just one appearance for the Saddlers, he left League football to play for Burton Albion. He later had spells with Bangor City and Northwich Victoria before joining Wigan Athletic in March 1978. He appeared in 13 Northern Premier League games for the Latics before making his league debut for the Latics in their inaugural game in the competition at Hereford United.

His first goal for the club came in Wigan's first win in the Football League, their sixth game of the season, as Rochdale were beaten 3–0. He missed just one game in 1978–9 and was a regular in the Wigan side for three seasons, scoring 15 goals in 131 League and Cup games before moving on to play non-League football for Stafford Rangers.

After joining Derby County as an apprentice, Mick Quinn began his league career with Wigan Athletic, making a goalscoring debut in a 3–1 win over Halifax Town in April 1980. He became a regular goalscorer and in 1980–1 headed the club's scoring charts with 14 goals, including a hat-trick in the 3—0 defeat of Doncaster Rovers. However, after a disappointing campaign in 1981–2 when he took his tally of goals to 21 in 77 games, he was released and joined Stockport County.

An immediate success at Edgeley Park, scoring 24 goals in his first season with the Hatters, he was soon on the move again, this time to Oldham Athletic. Leading scorer at Boundary Park, he was soon snapped up by Portsmouth. Quinn helped the Fratton Park club win promotion to the top flight but, when his contract expired, he chose to join Newcastle United, the fee of £680,000 being decided by the transfer tribunal.

He scored four goals on his debut for the Magpies against eventual champions Leeds United and had scored 71 goals in 140 games for the north-east club when he was transferred to Coventry City, where he ended his first-class career.

(*Left*) Although born in India, Colin Methven is a Scot with an unrivalled passion for football. He began his career with East Fife before moving to Wigan Athletic in October 1979 for a fee of £30,000. After making his Latics debut as a substitute for Derek Brownbill in a 4–0 defeat at Huddersfield Town, Methven missed very few games in his seven seasons with the club. He was strong, skilful and had tremendous leadership qualities. His contribution at the heart of the Wigan defence was outstanding, and he became a firm favourite with the Latics' faithful, who elected him Player of the Year in 1979–80 and 1984–5. Methven, who helped the Latics win the Freight Rover Trophy in this latter season, received his greatest honour in 1981–2 when his fellow professionals voted him into the Fourth Division Select XI. Methven, who scored 28 goals in 340 games for Wigan, left Springfield Park in July 1986, joining Blackpool for £20,000.

He was a virtual ever-present for the next four years, being voted Player of the Year for two consecutive seasons, before leaving Bloomfield Road in November 1990 to see out his career with Walsall.

(*Right*) After making just three appearances for Rotherham United, Les Bradd was transferred to Notts County in October 1967, a move which transformed his career. During the following 11 seasons, Bradd made over 400 League and Cup appearances for Notts County whilst setting a club League scoring record of 125 goals.

In the summer of 1978 he joined Stockport County, where his total of 35 goals in 132 games included a seven-minute hat-trick in a 4–4 draw with Barnsley.

In July 1981, Bradd moved to Wigan Athletic and made his debut in the opening match of the 1981–2 season, scoring one of the Latics' goals in a 3–3 draw. After forming an effective strike partnership with Peter Houghton he ended the season with 20 goals, including a hat-trick in the 7–2 win at Scunthorpe United. Not surprisingly he was voted the club's Player of the Year. Sadly injuries restricted his appearances in 1982–3 and at the end of that campaign in which he had taken his tally of goals to 27 in 75 games, he retired.

He joined the backroom staff at Notts County, holding a number of positions including that of Commercial Manager, before crossing the River Trent to take up a similar position with Nottingham Forest.

A great utility player who could operate in several positions, Alex Cribley was spotted playing football for his Youth Club by Liverpool. After a number of appearances in Liverpool's Youth side, he was offered professional terms and, though he was a regular member of the Anfield club's Central League side, there appeared little chance of him breaking into the club's first team. A tough, skilful player, he decided to accept Ian McNeill's offer of first team football with Wigan Athletic and joined the Springfield Park club in November 1980.

He made his league debut at Bournemouth and went on to appear in 30 games that season. In 1981–2 he helped Wigan win promotion to the Third Division and the following season, in which he missed just a handful of games, he scored his first goal for the club in a 3–1 win over Wrexham. Cribley was a virtual ever-present in the Latics' side for the next six seasons but in October 1987 he was badly injured in a 4–1 defeat at Sunderland and had to retire. Cribley, who had scored 17 goals in 316 games, is now the club's physiotherapist.

German-born goalkeeper Roy Tunks began his Football League career with Rotherham United where he made the first of 138 league appearances for the Millmoor club shortly after his 17th birthday. During his time with the Yorkshire club, he became dissatisfied and had trials with Newcastle United, Ipswich Town and York City. In November 1974 he joined Preston North End for the knock-down price of £7,000. In seven seasons at Deepdale, Tunks kept goal in 277 league games but in November 1981, Latics' manager Larry Lloyd persuaded him to join the Springfield Park club.

Tunks played his first game for the Latics against Hereford United in a 1-1 draw and kept 12 clean sheets in 31 games to help the club win promotion to the Third Division. He was ever-present the following season and missed very few games over the next five campaigns, taking his total of appearances for the Latics to 284 before leaving to join Hartlepool United. His stay at the Victoria Ground was brief and he rejoined Preston North End for a second spell towards the end of the 1988–9 season.

Midfielder Graham Barrow joined the Latics from non-League Altrincham in the summer of 1981 and made his debut in a 3–3 draw at Bradford City on the opening day of the 1981–2 season. Barrow's 12 goals from midfield were instrumental in the Latics winning promotion to the Third Division at the end of that campaign. Over the next three seasons he missed very few games and Wigan won the Freight Rover Trophy Final at Wembley in 1985. Barrow was voted Latics' 'Man of the Match'. He played the last of his 212 games for the Latics in the same competition in May 1986 as they lost 2–1 to Bolton Wanderers in the Northern Area Final.

Barrow joined Chester City in July 1986 for a tribunal-fixed fee of £6,000. He went on to play in 248 league games for the Cestrians, being employed as player-coach. In 1992 he replaced Harry McNally as manager before two years later returning to Springfield Park to take charge of the Latics. Surprisingly dismissed in October 1985, Barrow has recently been appointed Chester's manager for a second time following their relegation to the Conference.

After playing his early football for Stalybridge Celtic, Eamon O'Keefe was given the chance to play league football with Plymouth Argyle but after failing to make the grade, returned to non-League action with Mossley following a spell in Saudi Arabia. His performances for Mossley led to Everton paying £25,000 for his services and he made his debut for the Toffees against Bolton Wanderers on Boxing Day 1979. A Republic of Ireland international, winning the first of his five caps against Wales in 1981, he had scored eight goals in 51 games for Everton when in January 1982 he joined Wigan Athletic for what was then a club record fee of £65,000.

He scored on his Latics debut in a 3–2 win over Northampton Town and towards the end of his first season with the club netted hat-tricks in the 3–0 defeat of Crewe Alexandra and a 3–1 victory over Mansfield Town. Though not a prolific scorer, he scored another treble the following season in a 4–0 win over Southend United; but in the summer of 1983, after scoring 26 goals in 61 games, he left to join Port Vale.

In March 1985 he moved to Blackpool and helped the Seasiders gain promotion to the Third Division. He later ended his career with Chester City.

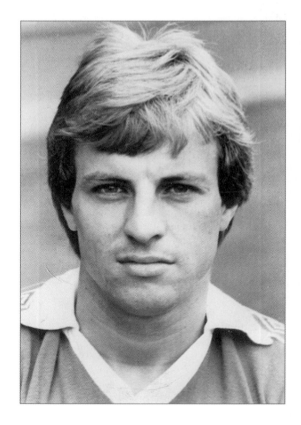

After playing his early football for Prescot Cables, John Butler joined the Latics in January 1981 and made a goalscoring debut as Wigan beat Bradford City 3–2. It was 1982–3 when Butler established himself in the Latics side and over the next six-and-a-half seasons he missed very few matches. Surprisingly, at Christmas 1988, Butler was allowed to join Stoke City, the Potters paying £75,000 for his services.

At the Victoria Ground, Butler won a Second Division Championship medal and helped the Potters win the Autoglass Trophy. He had scored nine goals in 319 games for Stoke when in August 1995 he returned to Springfield Park for a second spell.

Butler is one of the most versatile players to have worn the colours of Wigan Athletic, having the distinction of having played in every position including goalkeeper. His spell between the posts came against Bury in a Freight Rover Trophy match when Roy Tunks was injured.

One of the most popular players ever to represent the club, John Butler holds a unique record, winning promotion with the Latics in his first and last seasons with the club, having scored 18 goals in 368 games in his two spells at Springfield Park.

After working his way up through the ranks, Steve Walsh made his first team debut for the Latics in a 2–0 League Cup defeat at Manchester City in October 1982, going on to make 32 appearances in what was the club's first season in the Third Division. He soon established himself as a first team regular, and in 1984–5 helped the Latics win the Freight Rover Trophy as they beat Brentford 3–1 in the Wembley final. Walsh had scored four goals in 138 games for the Latics when, in June 1986, the strapping central defender followed Bryan Hamilton to Leicester City for a fee of £100,000.

After winning the Foxes' Player of the Year award in 1988, injuries began to hamper his progress; but no matter who managed the Filbert Street club, he remained at the heart of the defence, that is until 1993 when he was moved up-front. Here, he top-scored with 15 goals and netted an additional goal in the play-off final against Swindon Town. A year later he scored twice against Derby County to lift Leicester into the Premiership and now, having scored 61 goals in 431 games, is at the age of 35 still the Foxes' first-choice centre-half.

Kevin Langley was working as a painter and decorator when he wrote to Wigan Athletic asking for a trial. Though Ian McNeill offered him an apprenticeship, it was Larry Lloyd who gave Langley his first taste of league football, as he made his debut in a 3–1 win over Northampton Town in September 1981. It was towards the end of the following season, the club's first in the Third Division, when Langley established himself as a first team regular. Over the next three seasons he missed very few games but in the summer of 1986 he was transferred to First Division Everton for £120,000.

Unable to make much headway with the Goodison club, he joined Manchester City but could not settle at Maine Road and was even loaned out to Chester City. In March 1988 the tall, elegant midfielder joined Birmingham City but he never looked comfortable with the Blues' style of play and in September 1990 he rejoined the Latics. He went on to give the club a further four years' service, taking his total of first team appearances to 366, which includes the club's Football League appearance record of 317 in his two spells with the club.

An outstanding goal scoring record for Altrincham in the Northern Premier League led to Bury giving Steve Johnson the opportunity to play league football. He didn't disappoint and in his six seasons with the Shakers he scored 52 goals in 159 league outings. In August 1983 he was transferred to Rochdale for the first of three spells with the Spotland club, but midway through the following season he joined Wigan Athletic after Latics boss Harry McNally paid £20,000 for his services.

He scored twice on his debut in a 3–0 home win over Sheffield United and ended the season with seven goals in 21 games. In 1984–5 he was joint-top scorer with Mike Newell, both strikers netting 16 League and Cup goals. Sadly, Johnson, who scored 23 goals in 58 games for the Latics, had left for Bristol City just before the Freight Rover Trophy Final.

Unable to settle at Ashton Gate, he had loan spells with Rochdale and Chester City before joining Scunthorpe United. The much-travelled striker later joined the Cestrians on a permanent basis before ending his first-class career with Rochdale following a spell in Sweden playing for Haskvarna.

Wigan-born utility player Warren Aspinall began his career as an apprentice with his home-town club and made his debut in a 1–1 draw with Leyton Orient in March 1985. Forming a formidable strike force with Mike Newell, Aspinall was the Latics' leading scorer in 1985–6 with 26 League and Cup goals, including a hat-trick in a 5–3 home win over Wolverhampton Wanderers on the final day of the season. His goalscoring exploits – 28 goals in 65 games – attracted the attention of the top clubs and in May 1986, Everton paid £150,000 for his services.

Finding his first team opportunities at Goodison Park limited, he moved to Aston Villa for £300,000 a year later. He had scored 14 goals in 42 games for the Villans when Portsmouth paid a club record £315,000 to take him to Fratton Park.

The former England Youth international was a virtual ever-present in his four seasons with Pompey but, following loan spells with Bournemouth and Swansea, he joined the Cherries on a permanent basis. The much-travelled Aspinall later joined Carlisle United before moving to Brentford where he won a Third Division Championship medal. Now with his ninth league club, Colchester United, Aspinall has appeared in well over 500 first-class games.

After failing to make the grade with Liverpool, Tony Kelly joined Derby County before moving to non-League Prescot Cables. After a series of impressive performances, Harry McNally signed him for Wigan Athletic and he made his debut at right-back in a 1–0 home defeat by Walsall in November 1983.

After moving into midfield, Kelly established himself as a first team regular, helping the Latics win the Freight Rover Trophy in 1985 when he scored one of the goals in Wigan's 3–1 win over Brentford. He had scored 22 goals in 127 games for the Latics when Stoke City paid £80,000 for his services in the summer of 1986.

After 45 games for the Potters, he joined West Bromwich Albion before, following loan spells with Chester and Colchester, he teamed up with Ian McNeill at Shrewsbury. He became captain at Gay Meadow, making 120 appearances before moving to Bolton Wanderers. Affectionately known as 'Zico', he reached a creative peak during the club's FA Cup run of 1993–4. After losing form he was allowed to join Port Vale and, after a spell with Peterborough, returned to Wigan. Things didn't work out and he left to play for Altrincham.

A former Liverpool junior, Mike Newell was not offered terms at Anfield and made his league debut while on trial with Crewe Alexandra. After failing to impress Dario Gradi, he joined Wigan Athletic, playing his first game against Rotherham United in December 1983. After winning a regular place in the Latics side, he scored one of the goals in the club's Freight Rover Trophy Final win over Brentford and in 1985–6, netted 16 goals in 24 games including a hat-trick in a 5–1 defeat of Darlington. He had scored 35 goals in 92 games before being transferred to First Division Luton Town.

Newell was the Hatters' leading scorer in 1986–7 but shortly afterwards joined Leicester City where he was the Foxes' top-scorer for two seasons before Everton paid £1.1 million for him in the summer of 1989. Despite struggling to score goals he became Blackburn Rovers' first £million player. After scoring the winning goal in the play-off final he formed an effective partnership with Alan Shearer and went on to score 42 goals in 157 games before joining Birmingham City. Unable to settle, he had loan spells with West Ham and Bradford City before joining Aberdeen. He later played for Crewe Alexandra before joining Blackpool.

Despite his early football being restricted to school and local league level, David Lowe's teacher recommended him to Harry McNally, and after a week's training with the Latics first team, he was offered an apprenticeship. After injuries had decimated the first team squad, Lowe made his Wigan debut against Reading in October 1982 and though he appeared out of his depth, the club stuck with him. He won a Freight Rover Trophy medal in 1985, scoring one of the goals in a 3–1 win over Brentford. He had scored 53 goals in 231 games when Ipswich Town paid £80,000 for his services.

Leading scorer in his first three seasons with the Portman Road club, he won England Under-21 honours but in July 1992, having scored 45 goals in 159 games, he moved to Leicester City. Unable to settle at Filbert Street he had a brief loan spell with Port Vale before rejoining the Latics in March 1996 for £125,000.

In 1996–7 he won a Third Division Championship medal, his goal against Mansfield Town assuring the club of the title. In 1997–8 he was the club's top scorer with 18 goals and was voted Player of the Year but, at the end of the following season, he was released having scored 84 goals in 358 games.

(*Left*) Paul Beesley was playing for Marine in the Northern Premier League before signing professional forms for Wigan Athletic. He made his league debut in a 1–0 win at Reading in October 1984 but only appeared once more that term. Gradually establishing himself at the heart of the Wigan defence, Beesley had scored three goals in 185 games for the Latics before Leyton Orient paid a club record £175,000 to take him to Brisbane Road.

After just one season in which he was voted the London club's Player of the Year, he moved to Sheffield United; where, forming a highly effective defensive partnership with Brian Gayle, he showed his versatility by appearing in a number of positions. He went on to appear in 195 games for the Blades before joining Leeds United for a fee of £250,000 in the summer of 1995. After less than six months at Elland Road, he was on the move again, this time to Manchester City for £500,000. Knee and ankle injuries restricted his appearances; and, after loan spells with Port Vale and West Bromwich Albion, he joined the Valiants on a permanent basis before being released in the summer of 1999.

Right) Liverpool-born Paul Jewell was an apprentice with the Anfield club but was snapped up by Wigan Athletic manager Harry McNally who paid £15,000 for his services in December 1984. Jewell made his debut for the Latics in a 3–3 draw with Rotherham United later that month. It was 1986–7 before he established himself as a first team regular when he netted some important goals in the club's run to the sixth round of the FA Cup, including the winner against Norwich City. That was his best campaign in terms of goals scored as he netted 15 in League and Cup competitions. The following season he scored his only hat-trick for the club in a 4–0 win over Aldershot but in July 1988, after scoring 47 goals in 171 games, he was sold to Bradford City for £80,000.

A versatile performer who could play in midfield or as a striker, Jewell, who had a brief loan spell with Grimsby Town, went on to score 66 goals in 308 games for the Valley Parade club before hanging up his boots in the summer of 1996.

Appointed the Bantams' manager, he kept them in the Premier League after they had won promotion to the top flight in 1998–9 but is now in charge at Sheffield Wednesday.

Left-back Barry Knowles began his career with Barrow before signing for his home-town club Wigan Athletic in the summer of 1984. His first game in Latics' colours came in a 1–1 home draw against Newport County in October of that year. Knowles, who suffered a spate of niggling injuries during his first season at Springfield Park, liked nothing better than to get forward and support the attack, scoring his first goal for the club in a 4–2 win over Orient in only his fifth appearance. At the end of his first season he picked up a Freight Rover Trophy winners' medal as Latics beat Brentford 3–1 in the Wembley final.

Knowles, who missed just one game in 1985–6 as Latics finished fourth in Division Three, had an outstanding season – as he did the following campaign when the club repeated the achievements. His only goal that season was the winner on the final day as Latics won 3–2 at Brentford. His third league goal for the club came on the opening day of the 1987–8 season in a 4–4 draw at Notts County but, at the end of the campaign, the popular defender who had appeared in 148 games was released.

Liverpool-born Paul Cook began his career with Marine before turning professional with Wigan Athletic in the summer of 1984. He played his first game for the Latics in March 1985, wearing the number two shirt in a 2–1 home defeat by Walsall. Cook, who went on to wear five different numbered outfield shirts, was an important member of the Wigan side for the next three seasons but in June 1988, after scoring 15 goals in 100 games, he was transferred to Norwich City for £73,000.

Unable to win a regular first team place with the Canaries he moved to Molineux in November 1989, joining Wolves for a fee of £250,000. After impressing with his probing passes and powerful long-range shooting, he suffered a loss of form and was allowed to join Coventry City. The Sky Blues had paid £600,000 for his services but patchy form restricted his appearances and he moved to Tranmere Rovers.

He later joined Stockport County for a club record fee of £250,000 and, despite fracturing his skull in a fall at home, he has made an unexpected comeback, having a loan spell with Burnley.

Mark Hilditch began his Football League career with Rochdale, signing professional forms for the Spotland club in November 1978. After five seasons in which he scored 40 goals in 197 league games, Hilditch moved on to Tranmere Rovers. In September 1986, Ray Mathias brought him to Springfield Park. He made his debut in a 2–1 home defeat at the hands of Newport County and four days later scored his first goal for the club in a 5-1 rout of Walsall. In his first season with the club, the Latics reached the sixth round of the FA Cup only to lose to Swindon Town in the promotion play-offs.

Though injuries restricted his appearances over the next few seasons, the versatile Hilditch returned to lead the attack in the 1989–90 season, and after wearing nine different outfield shirts, he netted his first hat-trick for the club in a 4-0 win at Mansfield Town. He went on to score 29 goals in 118 first team games before financial restrictions forced Latics not to renew his contract. He returned to Spotland for another season before becoming assistant manager at Northern Premier League side, Mossley.

England Schoolboy international goalkeeper Nigel Adkins began his league career with Tranmere Rovers and played his first game for the Prenton Park club in a 4–2 defeat at Colchester United in November 1982. However it was 1984–5 before he won a regular place in the Tranmere side. After appearing in 98 League and Cup games for the Birkenhead club, he was transferred to Wigan Athletic.

Adkins made his Latics debut as a replacement for the injured Roy Tunks at Blackpool in September 1986 but didn't have the best of days as the Seasiders ran out winners 5–1. Even after Tunks had left the club, Adkins found stiff competition from Northern Ireland international Phil Hughes, with whom he shared the goalkeeping duties for the next few seasons before winning a spot on a regular basis in 1991–2. That season the Latics finished 15th in Division Three and Adkins, who was ever-present, kept 12 clean sheets. He went on to appear in 179 games for the Latics before losing his place to Simon Farnworth.

Belfast-born centre-forward Bobby Campbell began his Football League career with Aston Villa before moving to Huddersfield Town in April 1975. Unable to win a regular place in the Terriers' side, he joined Sheffield United before signing for Halifax Town. There was no doubt about his ability to score goals but a question mark hung over his temperament, for the Shaymen sacked him for persistant misconduct! After trying his luck in Australia with Brisbane City he returned to these shores to play for Bradford City.

Whilst at Valley Parade he made two appearances for Northern Ireland and his form led to Derby County paying £70,000 for his services in August 1983. Unable to settle at the Baseball Ground, he rejoined Bradford City and took his tally of league goals to 121, a club record.

In October 1986 he joined Wigan Athletic for £25,000, making a goalscoring debut in a 3–1 defeat at Swindon Town. He ended the campaign as the club's leading scorer with 20 goals and the following season netted a magnificent hat-trick in the 3–2 League Cup win at Bolton Wanderers. Despite heading the scoring charts for a second successive season, the popular Irishman decided to retire having scored 36 goals in 80 games for the Latics.

Manchester-born winger Dave Thompson played his early football for North Withington before Rochdale gave him the chance to play in the Football League. He made his debut for the Spotland club in September 1981 and over the next five seasons terrorised full-backs in the lower divisions. He left Rochdale in the summer of 1986 and had just over a season with Notts County before Wigan Athletic paid £35,000 for him in October 1987.

'Tommo' made his debut for the Latics in a 3–3 home draw against Brighton and Hove Albion but suffered an injury and was forced to sit out the next seven games before returning to play in the final 26 games of the season. Over the next two campaigns, Thompson missed very few games and scored some vital goals. His only hat-trick for the club came in March 1990 when he netted all the goals in a 3–1 win at Shrewsbury Town. He had scored 17 goals in 123 games for the Latics when in August 1990, Preston North End paid £27,500 to take him to Deepdale.

He later had a spell with Chester before rejoining Rochdale where he took his tally of goals to 24 in 307 games.

Wigan-born midfielder Andy Pilling joined Preston North End on a Youth Training Scheme in 1985 but in two years on the Deepdale staff, his only appearance in the club's first team came in the 4–0 defeat at Aldershot on the final day of the 1985–6 season when the Lilywhites finished one off the bottom of the Fourth Division. After another season of Central League football, he moved to Wigan Athletic and made a goalscoring debut when, coming on as a substitute for Peter Atherton, he netted in the 2–1 defeat at Brentford.

Pilling was an important member of the Wigan side for the next six seasons but in the summer of 1993, following the club's relegation to the Third Division, he was released after having scored 21 goals in 170 games for the Latics.

Orrell-born defender Peter Atherton first came through Wigan Athletic's junior ranks as an associated schoolboy before signing as a trainee in July 1986. Prior to turning professional he made his Football League debut at Blackpool in October 1987, having an outstanding game in a goalless draw. After claiming a regular place the following season, Atherton did not miss another match for the Latics, apart from one when he was substitute, until he signed for Coventry City for a fee of £300,000 in August 1991.

Twice voted Wigan's Player of the Year, his only goal for the club in 177 games came against Sheffield United at Bramall Lane in October 1989.

Within two months of arriving at Highfield Road, he had been selected for the England Under-21 side. A tenacious defender, he played in 120 games for the Sky Blues before joining Sheffield Wednesday for £800,000 in June 1994. Midway through his first season with the club he was appointed the Owls' captain and, over the next six seasons, inspired his colleagues by his never-say-die attitude. After the Owls lost their Premier League status, Atherton, who had scored eight goals in 240 games, left to play for Bradford City.

After serving his apprenticeship with Manchester United, goalkeeper Phil Hughes was snapped up by Leeds United. But the Northern Ireland Youth international, who qualified via parentage, was unable to budge veteran David Harvey and after just seven games joined Bury on a free transfer.

A member of the Northern Ireland World Cup squad in 1986, he was one of several young 'keepers earmarked as a possible successor to Pat Jennings. He made the first of three full international appearances for Northern Ireland against England at Wembley in April 1987 but a shoulder injury cost him his place at Bury and so in November 1987 he moved to Wigan Athletic for £35,000.

He kept a clean sheet on his Latics debut as Wigan won 1-0 at Chesterfield, going on to keep a further 11 clean sheets in the remaining 31 games of the season. Injuries restricted his appearances the following season but early in 1989–90 he returned to first team action, replacing Nigel Adkins. However in October 1991, after appearing in 106 games, he joined Scarborough.

He later played for Guiseley for a couple of seasons before moving to Pontefract Collieries.

A lively central midfield player, Eccles-born Joe Parkinson joined the Latics on a YTS scheme and after some impressive displays for the club's reserve side, made his debut as a substitute for Andy Hilditch in a 2–1 win over Blackpool in September 1988. In his first full game four months later, Parkinson scored the only goal of the match as Latics beat Mansfield Town 1–0 at Field Mill. He established himself as a first team regular early the following season but in the summer of 1993, having scored seven goals in 147 games and been a member of the Wigan side relegated to the Third Division, he left to play for Bournemouth.

Before his first season at Dean Court was over, Parkinson had returned to the north-west with Premier League Everton paying £250,000 for his services. He won an FA Cup winners' medal in 1995 as the Toffees beat Manchester United but a persistent knee problem forced him to give up the game after making 107 appearances for the Merseyside club.

Don Page joined Wigan Athletic from Runcorn in March 1989 and made his debut in a 2–1 reversal at Gillingham. After playing in the remaining 15 games of the season, hopes were high that this prolific scorer at non-League level would find his shooting boots in the Third Division. However, though he scored in both major cup competitions, Page failed to find the net in 25 league appearances. He made amends the following season when he was joint-top scorer with Bryan Griffiths, his total of 17 goals including a hat-trick in the 4–0 Leyland Daf Cup win over Chester City. At the end of that season, the pacy striker who held the ball up well joined Rotherham United, having scored 22 goals in 90 games for the Latics.

He continued to find the net for the Millmoor club but after two seasons fell out with the manager and following a loan spell with Rochdale, joined Doncaster Rovers. The much-travelled striker later played for Chester City before he ended his career with Scarborough, having scored 57 league goals in 259 games for his six clubs.

A former England Schoolboy and Youth international, Neill Rimmer began his Football League career with Everton, making his debut as a substitute for Paul Wilkinson in a 2–0 defeat at Luton Town on the final day of the 1984–5 season. It was his only appearance in the Goodison club's first team and in the summer, he moved to Ipswich Town. He spent two years at Portman Road before joining Wigan Athletic on a free transfer in the summer of 1988.

He scored in his first game for the Latics as they won 2–0 at Bristol Rovers on the opening day of the 1988–9 season. He was an important member of the Wigan side for the next eight seasons and during his last campaign with the club, he became the Latics longest-serving player.

A great midfield competitor, strong tackler and ball-winner, he suffered his fair share of injuries during his time at Springfield Park. But this willing worker, who was also the club captain, was freed in the summer of 1996 after scoring 15 goals in 228 games for the Latics.

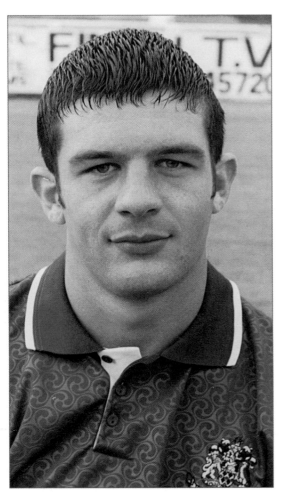

England Youth international Alan Johnson worked his way up through the ranks at Springfield Park to make his Wigan Athletic debut alongside the club's other debutant, Joe Parkinson, in a 1–0 win at Mansfield Town in January 1989. His first goal for the club came towards the end of that season in a 1–0 defeat of Bury, a result which ensured Latics' Third Division status. Johnson missed very few games over the next four seasons but after the club were relegated in 1992–3 he failed to agree a new contract with the Wigan board. He signed a week-to-week contract but in February 1995, after scoring 19 goals in 222 games, he left to join Lincoln City, the Imps being Wigan's opponents in Johnson's last game.

A transfer tribunal set the fee at £65,000 but injuries hampered his progress on his arrival at Sincil Bank. Following a loan spell with Preston North End, Johnson, who had made 72 appearances for the Imps, joined Rochdale on a free transfer.

An ever-present and Player of the Year in his first season at Spotland, he missed the whole of the 1997–8 campaign through injury and at the end of the following season, after making 70 appearances, he was released.

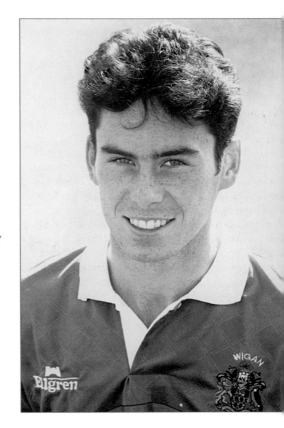

An England Youth international, Allen Tankard began his league career with Southampton but after failing to establish himself in the Saints' side he joined Wigan Athletic on a free transfer in the summer of 1988. After making his debut in a 3–2 defeat at Bristol Rovers on the opening day of the 1988–9 campaign, Tankard missed very few games in his five seasons with the club, being ever-present in 1990–1 when Latics finished tenth in the Third Division. Following the club's relegation in 1992–3, Tankard, who had scored five goals in 257 games from his position at left-back, left to join Port Vale for £87,500.

The attacking full-back who had also had spells in midfield is a great favourite with the Vale fans and, after suffering a series of hamstring injuries in the early part of his Vale Park career, has been a virtual ever-present. Despite the club's relegation in 1999–2000, Tankard remains an important member of the Vale side, having played in almost 300 games for the Potteries club.

Bryan Griffiths began his career with his home-town club, St Helens Town before joining Wigan Athletic in November 1988. He made his league debut in a 3–1 defeat at the hands of Northampton Town and went on to top the club's scoring charts in his first season at Springfield Park with eight goals in 29 games. Griffiths was the club's top scorer in 1990–1 and 1992–3. Without doubt, Griffiths' most spectacular strike for the Latics was the free-kick which left Bruce Grobbelaar standing in the 5–2 League Cup defeat at Liverpool in September 1989. A regular in the Wigan side for five seasons, Griffiths, who had the knack of scoring some important goals, found the net 52 times in 220 League and Cup games before refusing terms and leaving to join Blackpool in the summer of 1993.

He continued to find the net for the Seasiders, scoring 17 goals in 57 games as well as spending a short loan period with Scarborough.

Northern Ireland international Darren Patterson began his career with West Bromwich Albion but in April 1989 after being unable to make the grade at the Hawthorns, joined Wigan Athletic on a free transfer.

He had to wait until the fifth game of the following season before making his league debut as a substitute for Steve Senior in a 1–0 defeat at Leyton Orient and, though he appeared in 29 games in that campaign, more than half were in the role of substitute. It was a similar story the following season – but in 1991–2, this versatile player established himself as a first team regular. His form was so impressive that at the end of the season, Crystal Palace paid £225,000 for his services. Patterson, who had scored 10 goals in 121 games for the Latics, spent two seasons in Palace's reserve side before finally being given his chance in the league side.

Shortly afterwards he was sold to Luton Town for £100,000 but his debut for the Hatters was delayed owing to a tendon injury. The strong-tackling defender, who had a brief loan spell with Preston North End, appeared in 69 games for the Kenilworth Road club and had taken his total of Northern Ireland appearances to 11 when, surprisingly, he was released in 1998.

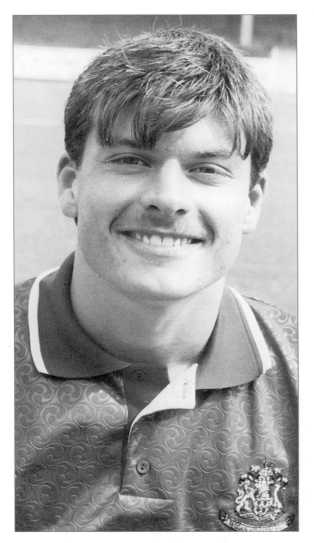

Phil Daley joined Wigan Athletic from Newtown in October 1989 and made his first team debut in a goalless home draw against Shrewsbury Town later that month. His first goal for the club came on his next appearance as Walsall were beaten 3–1 and he ended his first season at Springfield Park with eight goals in 40 games. The following season he formed a prolific strike force with Bryan Griffiths and Don Page and then in 1991–2 with Gary Worthington. This was Daley's best season in terms of goals scored, the Liverpool-born striker finding the net 14 times in 38 outings. Injuries hampered his last two seasons with the club and in the summer of 1994 after scoring 46 goals in 204 games he moved to Lincoln City for a fee of £40,000.

During his first few weeks at Sincil Bank, Daley suffered a bad knee injury which necessitated a cartilage operation. Unfortunately he never fully recovered, and after two seasons with the Imps, was released in the summer of 1996.

Unable to make the grade with Everton, Gary Powell had loan spells with Lincoln City, Scunthorpe United and Wigan Athletic before signing for the Latics on a permanent basis in the summer of 1991. He had made his league debut as a substitute for Don Page in a 1–0 home defeat at the hands of Tranmere Rovers in March 1991.

Though not a prolific scorer, he did score some vital goals during his two seasons with the club but, in the summer of 1993, after scoring 20 goals in 97 League and Cup outings, he left to play for Bury where he saw out his first-class career.

A member of a famous footballing family, the most famous being his uncle, England international Frank Worthington, Gary Worthington trained with Manchester United from the age of 13 but was released when his apprenticeship at Old Trafford ended. He joined Huddersfield Town but after only one season was again released without making a first team appearance. He moved to Darlington and had scored 15 goals in 40 games for the Quakers when they were relegated to the Conference and he joined Wrexham. After two seasons at the Racecourse Ground in which he scored 27 goals in 88 games, he moved to Wigan in exchange for Ian Griffiths.

He made his debut as a substitute for Andy Pilling in a 1–0 home win over Crewe Alexandra, ending the season with five goals in ten starts. In 1991–2, Worthington was the club's leading scorer with 18 goals but midway through the following season after scoring 24 goals in 76 games he was released, later joining Exeter City. Unable to settle at St James' Park he had a loan spell with Doncaster Rovers before being released in the summer of 1994.

Phil Jones began his Football League career at Everton but in almost three years with the Goodison club his only experience of first team football came in an appearance as substitute for Neil Adams in a 1–0 home win over Southampton. The Liverpool-born defender had a brief loan spell with Blackpool, making six appearances for the Seasiders before joining Wigan Athletic in January 1991.

He made his debut as a substitute for Ronnie Hildersley in a 2–0 home win over Fulham the following month before appearing in 19 of the remaining 20 games. His first goal for the club came in the Latics 6–1 win at Swansea city in April 1991.

Jones, who wore eight different numbered outfield shirts during his time with the Latics, was a first team regular for three seasons but, following the club's relegation in 1992–3, he was released after appearing in 98 games and joined Bury as a non-contract player.

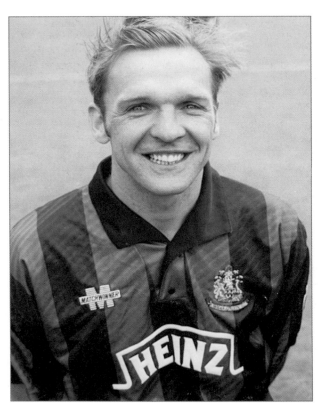

Hull-born central defender Peter Skipper began his league career with his home-town club until, following a brief loan spell with Scunthorpe United, he joined Darlington. After two seasons at the Feethams he rejoined the Tigers and in his first campaign back at Boothferry Park, helped the club win promotion to the Third Division. Two seasons later, Skipper was instrumental in Hull winning promotion to Division Two; but in October 1988, after scoring 19 goals in 288 league games in his two spells with the club, he joined Oldham Athletic.

After just one season at Boundary Park he was on the move again, this time to Walsall but, after the Saddlers dropped into the Fourth Division, he moved to Wrexham. Unable to win a regular place he joined the Latics on a non-contract basis.

He played his first game for the club as a substitute for Darren Patterson in a 1–0 home win over Stoke City. He appeared in 18 of the games that remained that season before leaving to play for Stafford Rangers. In November 1992 he rejoined the Latics on a permanent basis and over the next two seasons was a virtual ever-present, scoring five goals in 97 games before being released.

Tough-tackling central defender John Robertson joined the Latics as a trainee and after working his way up through the ranks, made his debut in a 2–1 defeat at Stoke City in August 1992. A first team regular for four seasons, Robertson, who was very good in the air, was voted by his team-mates as the club's Player of the Year in 1994–5. Following the signings of Colin Greenall and John Pender, Robertson, who had scored four goals in 142 games, was allowed to move to Lincoln City for £15,000 in December 1995.

After an impressive first few games he was kept out of the Lincoln side for most of the club's promotion-winning season of 1996–7 by Grant Brown. A wholehearted player, Robertson's never-say-die attitude was very rarely required and, in the summer of 1998, after making just 44 appearances in his two-and-a-half seasons at Sincil Bank, he was released.

A former England Schoolboy goalkeeper, Simon Farnworth began his Football League career with Bolton Wanderers, making his debut for the Trotters in a 2–0 win over Wimbledon on the opening day of the 1983–4 campaign. He was the club's first-choice 'keeper for the next three seasons and appeared for the Wanderers in the 1986 Freight Rover Trophy Final at Wembley. Following loan spells with both Stockport County and Tranmere Rovers, Farnworth, who had appeared in 138 games for Bolton, left Burnden Park to join Bury.

Highly popular with the Shakers' fans, he had appeared in 124 games for the Gigg Lane club when in the summer of 1990 he moved to Preston North End. He missed very few games in his three years at Deepdale, having turned out 97 times before his move to Wigan in July 1993.

He made his debut for the Latics in a 2–0 defeat at the hands of Scunthorpe United at the start of the 1993–4 season. A virtual ever-present during his time at Springfield Park, the experienced 'keeper went on to appear in 151 games for the Latics before being appointed the club's physiotherapist at the end of the 1995–6 campaign.

Lively winger Andy Lyons played his early football for Fleetwood Town in the Lancashire Combination where his performances led to a number of inquiries from league clubs. Crewe Alexandra paid £15,000 for his services in October 1992. Unable to establish himself as a first team regular at Gresty Road, by the time he left to join Wigan twelve months later, he had scored three goals in 12 games.

He made his league debut for the Latics in a 6–3 home win over Chester City and though he didn't get on the scoresheet in that game he ended the season as the club's leading scorer with 11 goals. He repeated the feat the following season when his total of 15 goals included a hat-trick in a 4–1 win over Darlington.

Sadly he was unable to recapture the form of the previous two seasons in 1995–6 – and after failing to hold down a regular place, the Blackpool-born player who had scored 28 goals in 100 games was allowed to join Partick Thistle.

Bristol-born midfielder Ian Kilford joined Wigan Athletic on a free transfer from Nottingham Forest in the summer of 1994, having made his debut in a goalless home draw with Rochdale whilst on loan in December 1993. An established member of the Latics side, he helped the club win the Third Division Championship in 1996–7 when his versatility and goal-scoring were vital as he was called upon to fill a number of roles. Comfortable on the ball, he also has an eye for goal and in 1997–8 was the club's second-top league scorer with 10 goals.

Over the last two seasons, Kilford, who is the club's longest-serving player, has found it difficult to hold down a regular first team spot; but, as always, a player who has now scored 33 goals in 221 games for the club, the central midfielder is a willing servant.

Mark Leonard joined Everton from Witton Albion in February 1982 but failed to make the grade with the Goodison club and made his league debut in a 1–0 defeat at Darlington whilst on loan with Tranmere Rovers. At the end of the 1982–3 season, he joined Crewe Alexandra but, after scoring 17 goals in 60 games, he moved to Stockport County. In 1985–6 he was County's top scorer with 23 goals, a feat that prompted Bradford City to pay £40,000 for his sevices. He scored 39 goals in 195 games for the Bantams before spending brief spells with Rochdale, Chester City and Preston North End prior to joining Wigan in September 1994.

He made his Latics debut in a 2–0 defeat at home to Carlisle United and in two seasons at Springfield Park showed great aerial power to score 16 goals in 78 games before rejoining Rochdale in the summer of 1996. He took his tally of league goals to 95 in 17 seasons of football with his eight clubs before injury forced his retirement.

Canadian-born Kevin Sharp was one of two youngsters signed by Leeds United following their release by French First Division club Auxerre in October 1992. He had a great first season at Elland Road as a prominent member of the FA Cup winning youth team. An England Youth international, Sharp had made 18 first team appearances for the Yorkshire club when, in November 1995, he became Wigan Athletic's first £100,000 signing.

A skilful left-sided midfielder, he made his Latics debut in a 3–1 defeat at Plymouth Argyle before scoring in his first home game against Hereford United the following week. In 1996–7 his impressive performances helped the Latics win the Third Division Championship and, though he was often made the scapegoat for some poor team performances the following season, he remained a firm favourite with the Latics fans. Playing throughout the 1998–9 season on a week-to-week contract, he picked up an Autowindscreen Shield winners' medal and has now clocked up 11 goals in 171 games.

Billinge-born central defender Colin Greenall began his Football League career with Blackpool where, in August 1980, at the age of 16 years 237 days he became the Bloomfield Road club's youngest-ever debutant. Greenall won England Youth honours and at the age of 20 was voted the Fourth Division Player of the Year by the PFA. Following a contractual dispute, Greenall, who had played in 206 games for Blackpool, joined Gillingham for £40,000.

Midway through the 1987–8 season, Oxford United paid £285,000 to take Greenall to the Manor ground but he was unable to settle and after a loan spell at Bury, joined the Shakers on a permanent basis. There followed spells with Preston North End, Chester City and Lincoln City before he joined Wigan for £45,000 in September 1995.

Appointed club captain he made his debut in a 1–0 home defeat at the hands of Plymouth Argyle, later forming an effective central defensive partnership with John Pender. In 1996–7 he was ever-present and was instrumental in the club winning the Third Division Championship, earning him the Supporters' and Players' Player of the Year awards.

Now the club's first team coach, Greenall won the Man-of-the-Match award in Wigan's Autowindscreen Shield success at Wembley in 1999.

John Pender won Irish Youth international honours
before joining Wolves in November 1981. He became
a regular in the Molineux club's defence, helping
them win promotion to Division One in 1982–3. After
two successive relegations, he joined Charlton Athletic
and helped them win promotion to the top flight in
1985–6. In October 1987 he joined Bristol City for
£50,000 and although they were a Third Division
club he helped them reach the League Cup semi-finals
in 1988–9. In the summer of 1990 he moved to
Burnley where he led the Clarets to the Fourth
Division Championship in 1991–2. After lifting the
Endsleigh Trophy at Wembley as Burnley beat
Stockport in the 1994 play-off final, Pender was no
longer an automatic choice and in August 1995,
joined Wigan for £40,000.

After making his debut in a 2-1 home win over
Scunthorpe he formed an imposing partnership at the
heart of the Latics defence with Colin Greenall. In
January 1997 in the match against Swansea he had
the misfortune to suffer a severe knee injury –
although he returned to play in a total of 29 matches
and thus pick up a Third Division Championship
medal. Pender, whose only goal came against Torquay
United in February 1996, had made 81 appearances
for the Latics before joining Rochdale.

Hard-working midfielder Gavin Johnson began his league
career with Ipswich Town, making his debut against
Burnley in February 1989. Though he played in only a
handful of games over the next couple of seasons, he was
a first team regular when the Portman Road club won the
Second Division Championship in 1991–2. He scored the
club's first goal in the new Premier League when he fired
home from fully 30 yards against Aston Villa. He went on
to make 159 appearances for the Suffolk club before
joining Luton Town. His stay at Kenilworth Road was
short and in December 1995 he joined Wigan Athletic for
a fee of £15,000. He made his debut in a 2–1 home win
over Hereford United, going on to play in the last 27
games of the campaign.

Over the next three seasons he proved that he could
play anywhere down the left flank and scored some
spectacular goals, especially from dead ball situations.
After helping the Latics to win the Third Division
Championship in 1996–7 he found his time at Springfield
Park dogged by groin problems and, in the summer of
1998, after scoring eight goals in 98 games, he was
released.

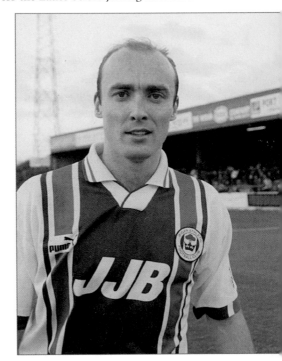

Wayne Biggins scored on his league debut for Lincoln City but was released in May 1981 and drifted into non-League football with King's Lynn and Matlock. He was working as a hod carrier on a building site when Burnley gave him the chance to resurrect his league career. A prolific scorer at Turf Moor, Norwich City paid £40,000 for his services in October 1985 and he helped the Canaries win the Second Division Championship. After leaving Carrow Road, Biggins joined Manchester City, also helping the Maine Road club reach the top flight. He moved to the Victoria Ground in the summer of 1989, later helping the Potters win the Autoglass Trophy. He then had spells with Barnsley, Celtic, Luton Town and Oxford United before joining Wigan in January 1996 after an earlier loan spell.

It was the third time in his career that he had been recruited by John Deehan. After making his debut in a goalless draw at Northampton Town, injuries restricted his appearances to just 15 starts and two goals. He later relished his new central midfield role and in 1996–7 chipped in with some vital goals as the Latics won the Third Division Championship, but was still released at the end of the season.

Northern Ireland international defender Pat McGibbon began his career with Portadown before Manchester United paid £100,000 to take him to Old Trafford. He made his debut for the Reds in the League Cup at York City but was sent off after giving away a penalty.

Following a loan spell at Swansea, McGibbon joined Wigan Athletic on loan in March 1997 and scored the goal that beat Colchester United 1–0 to ensure promotion to the Second Division. The move was made permanent in the summer of 1997, Latics paying £250,000 for his services.

Dominant in the air and strong in the tackle, he has been a virtual ever-present since joining the club and in 1998–9 was an important member of the Latics side that won the Autowindscreen Shield at Wembley. The reliable defender whose aerial ability makes him a dangerous proposition at set-pieces, has now scored seven goals in 145 games for the Latics.

Signed from the Spanish Second Division side FC Balageur, Roberto Martinez was one of a trio of Spanish players to join the Latics in the summer of 1995. He made his Football League debut on the opening day of the 1995–6 season, scoring Wigan's goal in a 2–1 defeat at Gillingham. In a season in which he was able to leave opponents spellbound with a string of match-winning performances, he was the club's leading scorer with 13 goals. Voted the Latics Player of the Year, he had earlier been chosen for the PFA Third Division team.

He helped the Latics win the Third Division Championship in 1996–7 and though he didn't take the division by storm, he was still the club's most exciting player and was again selected for the PFA side.

The cultured right-footed midfielder, the last of the 'Three Amigos' still at the club has now scored 24 goals in 180 games for the Latics, winning an Autowindscreen Shield medal in 1999.

Hard-working midfielder, Paul Rogers was playing non-League football for Sutton United when Sheffield United paid £35,000 for his services in January 1992. A first team regular at Bramall Lane for four years, he had scored 11 goals in 138 games before a change of management saw him transferred to Notts County. In his first season at Meadow Lane he helped the Magpies to the Second Division play-off final where they lost to Bradford City. However, midway through the following season he lost his place and joined Wigan Athletic on loan. He made his debut as a substitute against Cambridge United in December 1996 and, after signing on a permanent basis, was instrumental in the club winning the Third Division Championship.

A player who relishes a challenge, Rogers scored the injury-time winner at Wembley in the 1999 Autowindscreen Shield Final. He had scored six goals in 117 games for the Latics when, after rejecting a new contract with the club, he moved to Brighton and Hove Albion.

Bustling centre-forward Graeme Jones began his Football League career with Doncaster Rovers whom he joined from Bridlington Town in the summer of 1993 for a fee of £10,000. Leading scorer for the Belle Vue club in 1994–5 and 1995–6, he had scored 29 goals in 105 games when he joined the Latics for a club record fee of £150,000 in July 1996.

He scored on his Wigan debut in a 1–1 draw at Barnet in the club's second game of the 1996–7 season. He ended the campaign as the Football League's highest scorer with 33 goals, including hat-tricks in the wins over Chester City (Home 4–2), Torquay United (Home 3–2), Leyton Orient (Home 5–1), and Darlington (Home 3–2). Voted the club's Player of the Year, he was also selected for the Third Division side at the PFA awards night and won a Third Division Championship medal. Thanks to a succession of injuries he was unable to discover his goalscoring form of the previous season and, after damaging his cruciate ligaments, was forced to miss the majority of the 1998–9 campaign. Jones had scored 52 goals in 115 games when he was allowed to leave the club.

Enniskillen-born goalkeeper Roy Carroll began his Football League career with Hull City, making his debut for the Tigers in a 3–0 defeat at Swindon in January 1996. He retained his place with a series of eye-catching performances, displaying a presence and maturity beyond his years. At the end of his first season at Boothferry Park he was voted the club's Player of the Year. He got his first international call-up in October 1996 for Northern Ireland's World Cup qualifier against Armenia but, after making 50 appearances for the Tigers, was sold to Wigan Athletic for £350,000 in order to help Hull out of a financial dilemma.

Despite being the Latics' record signing, Carroll did not start the 1997–8 season as the club's first-choice 'keeper and had to wait until the fourth game of the season before making his debut at Bristol City. Since then he has been a virtual ever-present in the Wigan goal and in 1998–9 won an Autowindscreen Shield winners' medal as Latics beat Millwall 1–0. Despite stories of his moving to a top flight club, Carroll, who missed the end of the 1999–2000 season, is still with the Latics having made 134 appearances for the club.

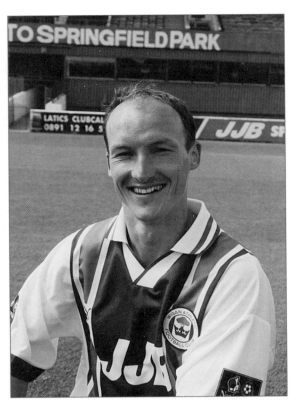

Winger David Lee began his career with Bury whom he helped to the Division Three play-offs. He scored 40 goals in 249 games for the Shakers before moving up to the top flight with Southampton, who paid £350,000 for his services in the summer of 1991. Unable to settle on the south coast he joined Bolton on loan, later signing for the club on a permanent basis for £300,000.

In his first season with the club he helped the Wanderers win promotion to the Second Division. He continued to torment the opposition defences and, in the club's FA Cup run of 1993–4, he ran Arsenal and England full-back Nigel Winterburn ragged in the fourth round replay at Highbury. However, in July 1997 following a broken ankle and a resulting loss of confidence, he joined Wigan Athletic for £250,000.

He made his debut on the opening day of the 1997–8 season, helping Latics beat Wycombe Wanderers 5–2. After taking time to settle in at Wigan, the speedy player who can run all day and take his markers on with ease, proceeded to become a great favourite with Latics fans. The scorer of a number of spectacular goals, Lee, who had a brief loan spell with Blackpool, has found the net 16 times in 107 games for Wigan.

Stuart Barlow began his Football League career with Everton but despite his ability to poach crucial goals, especially from set pieces, he was essentially a fringe team player at Goodison Park. The majority of his 71 league appearances for the Toffees were as a substitute and in November 1995, after previously having a brief loan spell with Rotherham United, he joined Oldham Athletic for £450,000.

In 1996–7 he was Oldham's leading scorer with 12 goals including hat-tricks against Bradford City (Away 3–0) and Swindon Town (Home 5–1). He was Oldham's leading scorer the following season but in March 1998 was sold to Wigan Athletic for £45,000. Barlow, who had scored 32 goals in 106 games for Oldham, scored his first goal for the Latics in a 3–2 win over First Division bound Watford.

In 1998–9, Barlow enjoyed the best goalscoring season of his career, netting 26 goals and helping the Latics reach the Second Division play-offs and win the Autowindscreen Shield at Wembley. Barlow's goal against Manchester City in the play-off semi-final first leg was the last to be scored at Springfield Park. Barlow scored 52 goals in 106 games for the Latics before leaving to play for Tranmere Rovers.

As a schoolboy, Scott Green had played for Stoke City, West Bromwich Albion and Walsall and looked set to join the Saddlers until manager Alan Buckley left the club. Derby County took him on trial but he failed to get into the Rams' first team. In March 1990, Bolton Wanderers' manager Phil Neal paid £50,000 for his services and he made his league debut against Shrewsbury Town. He made a Wembley appearance in the 1991 play-off final against Tranmere and in February 1992 celebrated a memorable substitute appearance against First Division Southampton, scoring a late equaliser in the fifth round FA Cup tie. In 1994–5 Green switched to full-back, helping the Wanderers win promotion and reach the League Cup Final. He had scored 31 goals in 286 games for Bolton when in June 1997 he moved to Wigan for £300,000.

He scored on his debut in a 5–2 win over Wycombe Wanderers on the opening day of the 1997–8 season, a campaign in which for the most part, he occupied the right-back spot. A highly versatile and valuable member of Wigan's squad, he won an Autowindscreen Shield medal in 1999 and has at the time of writing scored three goals in 138 games for the Latics.

A former England Youth international, Carl Bradshaw began his career with Sheffield Wednesday but was on loan with Barnsley when he made his league debut against Crystal Palace in August 1986. Despite scoring, the 'Tykes' lost 3–2. He played his first game for the Owls later that year. With his first team chances at Hillsborough limited, he moved to Manchester City in exchange for Imre Varadi. He played only one full match before returning to his home-town of Sheffield and signing for United.

He helped the Blades win promotion to the First Division, going on to play in 175 games before joining Norwich City for £500,000 in the summer of 1994. Sadly, injuries blighted his time at Carrow Road and, unable to hold down a regular place, once fully recovered he joined Wigan on a free transfer in October 1997.

He made his debut in a 1–1 home draw against Luton Town, going on to prove himself a revelation in the Latics' defence and winning the club's Player of the Year award. Appointed club captain, he has proved his versatility by playing in a number of positions including keeping goal. Bradshaw, who lifted the Autowindscreen Shield at Wembley, has now scored ten goals in 109 games for the Latics.

Scottish Under-21 international, Andy Liddell began his career with Barnsley where, after working his way up through the ranks, he made his league debut as a substitute against Portsmouth in the last game of the 1991–2 season. Though on the small side for a striker, he scored his fair share of goals as well as having the ability to unlock defences and provide chances for his colleagues. His goalscoring in the early games of the 1996–7 season gave the Yorkshire club just the impetus they needed as they went on to win promotion to the Premiership. However, he found his opportunities in the top flight limited and after scoring 38 goals in 223 games, left to join Wigan Athletic in October 1998 for a fee of £350,000.

He made his debut in a 1–0 home defeat by Manchester City, going on to score 10 goals in 28 games including two against Chesterfield in the final league game at Springfield Park. A member of the team that won the Autowindscreen Shield, he has now scored 19 goals in 84 games for Wigan.

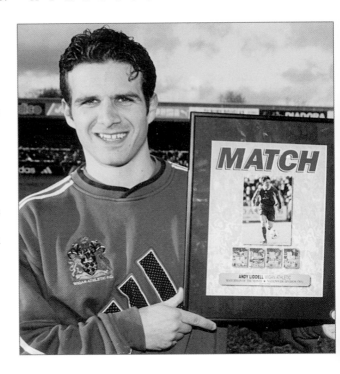

Cardiff-born striker Simon Haworth began his Football League career with his home-town club, making his debut against Rochdale on the opening day of the 1995–6 season. However, it was midway through the season before he made any real impact, scoring some superb goals. His form led to him winning international honours for Wales when he played against Scotland in a performance which attracted a number of top-flight clubs.

In June 1997, Coventry City paid £500,000 for his services, but though he scored on his Sky Blues debut against Everton, he struggled to win a regular place in the Coventry side and in October 1998 joined Wigan Athletic for £600,000, the club's record signing.

After making his debut against Northampton Town (Home 1–0) his progress was hampered by hamstring problems, though he returned to play in the club's victory in the Autowindscreen Shield Final at Wembley. Strong in the air, with an excellent first touch, he has now scored 34 goals in 78 games for the Latics, including a superb effort in the play-off final against Gillingham.

3

Freight Rover Trophy

It was during the season of 1984–5 that Harry McNally masterminded what was nearly one of the shock results of the FA Cup. Chelsea were the opponents and Wigan travelled to Stamford Bridge for their third round tie as 'no-hopers'. Goals from Mike Newell and Paul Jewell seemed to have set up a sensational victory but the Blues pulled two goals back to get a draw. After going down 5–0 in the replay, Wigan's Wembley dream seemed over – but, thanks to the Freight Rover Trophy, they achieved their ambition.

Two goals from Mike Newell helped the Latics draw 2–2 at Wrexham, and then another brace from Paul Jewell in the replay, along with a super strike from Steve Johnson, gave Wigan a 3–1 win. In the second round, Latics won 1–0 at Bury courtesy of a Tony Kelly penalty to set up a home tie with Tranmere Rovers. Kelly was on the scoresheet again but it was two outstanding individual goals from David Lowe that gave Latics a comfortable 3–1 victory. Lincoln City were beaten by a similar score in the Northern Area semi-final, with Lowe, Barrow and Bennett netting the Wigan goals.

After being held to a 1–1 draw at Mansfield Town in the Northern Area Final, Latics won 3–1 on penalties to go through to the first-ever Freight Rover Trophy Final against Brentford.

The Latics, outnumbered off the field by fans who could virtually walk to the stadium, made up for that with an almost faultless display. After Tunks had made a couple of early saves, Wigan gradually got on top and took the lead in the 25th minute when Barry Knowles looped a ball to the right for Mike Newell to control and crash home a great shot. The Latics scored again twelve minutes later when Graham Barrow back-heeled the ball for Tony Kelly to beat the Brentford 'keeper with a well-struck long shot. Soon after the restart, Cooke scored for Brentford but Latics soon hit back, and after Newell had a shot cleared off the line, David Lowe scored a spectacular third for the Latics with a overhead kick.

The final whistle confirmed what all Latics' fans had known for the majority of the second half, the Freight Rover Trophy was on its way to Springfield Park. The Latics team was: R. Tunks; A. Cribley; B. Knowles; T. Kelly; S. Walsh; C. Methven; D. Lowe; G. Barrow; G. Bennett; M. Newell; K. Langley; subs W. Aspinall/P. Jewell.

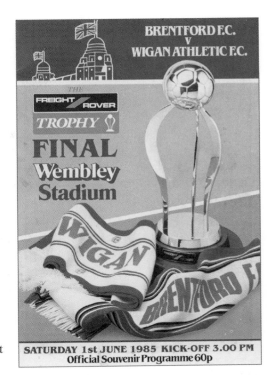

Official souvenir programme cover for the Freight Rover Trophy final against Brentford.

Latics' manager Bryan Hamilton and Brentford boss Frank McLintock lead their teams out at Wembley.

Midfielder Graham Barrow acknowledges the cheers of the Wigan fans. Referee Terry Bune of Newbury is in the background.

Graham Barrow in action, racing through the Brentford defence to set up another chance for the Latics' forwards.

One of the Latics' goalscorers, Mike Newell heads for goal, leaving Bees' defender Jamie Murray in his wake.

Graham Barrow outjumps Brentford defender Keith Millen whilst Colin Methven, up supporting the attack, waits to pounce.

The Wembley scoreboard showing the final score from the Freight Rover Trophy Final.

Gary Bennett and Kevin Langley show off the Freight Rover Trophy to the Latics fans.

The victorious Wigan Athletic side after goals from Newell, Kelly and Lowe had helped them beat Brentford 3-1 in the Wembley final.

The Latics with the Freight Rover Trophy on their return to Wigan, where they were met by a large crowd. The players have been joined by manager Bryan Hamilton (front far right) and trainer Kenny Banks (back row far left).

4

Autowindscreen Shield

Latics won their way through to the Northern Area Final of the 1998–9 Autowindscreen Shield competition without conceding a goal. Victories over Rotherham United (Away 3–0) Scarborough (Home 3–0) Carlisle United (Away 3–0) and Rochdale (Away 2–0) set up a two-legged tie against Wrexham.

A crowd of 4,938 witnessed the first leg at Springfield Park and saw goals from Kevin Sharp and Stuart Barlow (his fourth of the competition) give Latics a 2–0 win. Still to concede a goal after five games in the competition, Latics travelled to the Racecourse Ground with high hopes of reaching the Wembley final. A goal after two minutes by Simon Haworth extended Wigan's aggregate lead and though Dave Brammer equalised for the Robins in the 37th minute, Latics' Welsh international netted his and Wigan's second goal early in the second-half. The Welsh side drew level again but Michael O'Neill scored Latics'third and winning goal two minutes from time to send them through to the final against Millwall. The 3–2 victory (5–2 on aggregate) was Wigan's eighth straight win, equalling the club record.

All the talk before the final centred on Millwall selling more than 45,000 tickets while Latics were only able to shift around 8,000. But the Latics did their talking on the pitch and won 1–0, the winning goal coming in dramatic fashion. A tense game watched by 55,349 had produced little in the way of goalmouth action and as the clock reached the 90-minute mark, extra-time seemed inevitable.

But in the third minute of stoppage time, a clearance landed at the feet of Paul Rogers on the edge of the area and he drove home a low shot for the game's only goal. While the Wigan midfielder earned the tag of match-winner, veteran Colin Greenall was named Man-of-the-Match for a superb performance at the heart of the Latics defence.

The Wigan team that day was: R. Carroll; C. Bradshaw; K. Sharp; P. McGibbon; S. Balmer; P. Rogers; A. Liddell; C. Greenall; S. Haworth; M. O'Neill; S. Barlow (D. Lee).

Wigan Athletic mascot Laura Topping with Spanish midfielder Roberto Martinez.

A section of the Wigan fans prior to the kick-off.

One or two apprehensive faces as the Latics wait to be introduced to the Guest of Honour.

That's more like it – the Latics side line-up at Wembley. From left to right – Roy Carroll; Stuart Barlow; Andy Liddell; Michael O'Neill; Paul Rogers; Pat McGibbon; Simon Haworth; Colin Greenall; Kevin Sharp; Stuart Balmer; Scott Green; David Lee; Graeme Jones; Ray Mathias; Captain Carl Bradshaw is not in the photograph.

Guest of Honour, George Best, the former Manchester United and Northern Ireland international meets 'the lads'.

Pre-match line-up with Latics' skipper Carl Bradshaw and mascot Laura Topping.

Roberto Martinez races on to a through ball as the Millwall defence claim in vain for offside.

Millwall's defence under pressure from Simon Haworth and Colin Greenall.

Michael O'Neill tries to bend his free-kick round the Lions' defensive wall.

A dejected Millwall goalkeeper Tony Roberts looks on in disbelief as Paul Rogers celebrates his late winner.

Wigan players thank their fans. In the forefront is Man-of-the-Match Colin Greenall.

The victorious Latics leave the Wembley arena flanked by former Bolton pair, David Lee and Scott Green (holding the trophy)

An ecstatic Dave Whelan joins manager Ray Mathias and goalscorer Paul Rogers in celebration of Wigan's 1–0 win over Millwall.

The Latics team celebrate after beating the Lions. The magnificent trophy (which Wigan failed to defend, losing 2–1 to Carlisle United), sits proudly in the middle of the group.

Latics' match-winner Paul Rogers and chairman Dave Whelan hold aloft the Autowindscreen Shield Trophy.

5

The Grounds

Springfield Park was opened during the reign of Queen Victoria; however, it wasn't until the formation of Wigan County in 1897 that the ground was first used for football. Prior to the foundation of Wigan County, the park had been used as a sports arena, boasting a concrete cycle track and a half-mile running track. Horse-trotting was also popular, with the horses negotiating the running track and the stables housed on the town side of the ground.

The first football match took place on 1 September 1897, Wigan County v Burton Swifts. But such was the local passion for rugby that County always struggled and gave way to Wigan United. United folded two years later, to be followed by Wigan Town in 1905. But they too survived only three years and not until November 1920 did football return in the form of Wigan Borough. The fourth Wigan club joined the Third Division (North) the following year and for a few seasons, all went well. A 2,000 seat Main Stand was built, plus a wooden shelter at the back of the Shevington End. This was complemented in the late 1920s by a cover on the Popular side.

Springfield Park's highest gate was recorded on 12 January 1929 when 30,611 attended an FA Cup tie against Sheffield Wednesday. But the effect of the Depression, rising debts and falling gates led to Borough going into liquidation in October 1931. The following May, Wigan Athletic were formed and Springfield Park purchased from its owners for £2,800.

Springfield Park barely changed until in May 1953 a fire gutted the Main Stand. The Latics fans rallied round to build a replacement stand in the summer of 1954 – aptly named the Phoenix Stand. During the 1960s, four acres of land were sold for housing behind the Popular side. A set of floodlights were switched on in October 1966 and these were upgraded following the Latics' acceptance into the Football League in 1978.

After being designated under the Safety of Sports Grounds Act in 1985, its capacity was cut from 20,000 to 10,800. In the wake of the Taylor Report, the major development came in 1994 when the Popular Stand backing on to St Andrew's Drive was re-roofed and terraced, with barriers bought second-hand from the Holte End at Villa Park.

Realizing that the Springfield Park ground offered insufficient opportunity for development, Dave Whelan's aim since buying the club in 1995 had been to relocate. Plans were drawn up to move to Robin Park before discussions were held about moving to Central Park. But after much debate and controversy, the JJB Stadium has taken shape at a cost of £28 million to provide the town of Wigan with one of the most modern sports arena in the country. Built along the same lines as Huddersfield Town's McAlpine Stadium, the ground seats 25,000 with all spectators having an unobstructed view of the playing area. All four stands are supported from above by 'banana trusses' which give the roofs their curved look.

The East Stand is the biggest, seating 8,178; while the dressing-rooms, directors' box, VIP seats, press box and conference facilities are situated opposite in the 6,022 capacity West Stand. The North and South Stands behind either goal can each hold 5,400. There are four changing rooms – home and away changing rooms and two smaller ones for reserve team fixtures.

The pitch, which measures 110m x 60m, was laid out at a cost of £750,000 and includes a Desso Fibres System. These nylon fibres bind the grass together, making it far more durable for use by both the Latics and the Wigan Warriors Rugby League side who share the ground.

Other features of the stadium include a TV studio for live broadcasts, a camera gantry, ticket office and numerous food and drink kiosks.

The Stadium has 2,500 car park spaces and two new service roads have been built.

Aerial view of Springfield Park.

Springfield Park in January 1987 when a crowd of 8,095 watched Latics' 1–0 win over First
Division Norwich City in the fourth round of the FA Cup.

Springfield Park's main offices at the rear of the Phoenix Stand.

The Phoenix Stand and the Supporters Club from the car park. One of the problems at Springfield Park was that all the entrances and exits were concentrated on this area. This caused congestion on match days and was open to the odd spot of trouble by unruly fans.

The Phoenix Stand built in 1954.

The Phoenix Stand at night. The picture was taken in December 1992 during Wigan's 1–1 draw with Bury in the second round of the FA Cup.

The Shevington End had at one time a small stand known as the cow shed. In the Seventies, the Latics planned to build a stand covering the grass bank (which was to have concrete terracing). Phase 1, the central section was built. Unfortunately, before Wigan were elected to the Football League, the stand was sold with the frame to be used as a warehouse!

The open end at Springfield Park. Notice the vast array of advertisements including the famous Uncle Joe's Mint Balls!

The St Andrew's Drive Stand, otherwise known as the 'Popular' side, during construction of the new extended cover.

The teams for the match against Blackpool on 12 October 1985 as displayed in the sponsors' lounge at Springfield Park. For the record, the Latics drew 1–1 with Cribley netting for the home side.

The Executive Lounge at Springfield Park.

The Springfield Park Home Dressing Room prior to a game during 1997.

The St Andrew's Stand crowd in the last-ever Football League game at Springfield Park, 8 May 1999. For the record, the Latics beat Chesterfield 3–1.

Andy Porter, Kevin Sharp, Ray Mathias, Neil Fitzhenry and Ian Kilford hoping to lift the roof off the new JJB Stadium.

This photograph shows the construction of Loire Drive before the JJB Stadium was started. The line of trees on the right is where the River Douglas flows by the site. Two new bridges had to be built to access the two large car parks as well as providing access for people coming from the Springfield part of Wigan.

The two homes of Wigan Athletic: Springfield Park is in the upper centre of the photograph, while work is underway on Latics' new JJB Stadium.

These three photographs show the various stages of the development of the JJB Stadium. The Main Stand, known as the West Stand, was a complex framework. It was difficult to picture what it would look like; but when it was finished, it would have seating for 6,022 supporters, hospitality suites, concourses with toilets and refreshment facilities, a bar, restaurant and offices.

The nylon-reinforced playing surface of the JJB Stadium.

6

Team Groups

1978–79   (*Back*) K. Smart; P. Houghton; N. Davids; G. Gay; J. Brown; F. Corrigan; N. Ward; J. Hinnigan; J. Wright; (*Front*) I. McNeill (Manager); A. Crompton; I. Seddon; T. Gore; I. Gillibrand; J. Wilkie; I. Purdie; K. Banks (Trainer).

1979–80   (*Back*) N. Ward; I. Purdie; D. Brownbill; J. Brown; B. Ward; K. Smart; M. Quinn; B. McDermott; (*Middle*) D. Colquhoun (Physio); J. Hinnigan; J. Wright; G. Urquhart; N. Hart; N. Davids; J. Curtis; F. Corrigan; P .Houghton; D. Fretwell; K. Banks (Trainer); (*Front*) T. Gore; A. Crompton; J. Wilkie; I. McNeill (Manager); A. Horrocks (Chairman); M. Moore; M. Wignall; A. Mayer.

1980–81   (*Back*) T. Quinn; M. Quinn; G. McAllister; L. Tierney; J. Wright; P. Hendry; D. Tait; (*Middle*) I. Gillibrand (Coach); G. Urquhart; J. Oliver; N. Davids; J. Brown; B. Ward; C. Methven; P. Houghton; F. Corrigan; K. Banks; (Trainer); (*Front*) M. Whittle; M. Wignall; J. Curtis; T. Gore; I. McNeill (Manager); D. McMullan; B. Hutchinson; D. Glenn; D. Fretwell.

1981–82   (*Back*) C. Evans; L. Bradd; N. Davids; G. Barrow; J. Brown; B. Ward; C. Methven; M. Quinn; P. Houghton; A. Cribley; (*Front*) F. Eyre (Assistant-Manager); K. Sheldon; M. Wignall; D. Glenn; L. Lloyd (Manager); S. McAdam; J. McMahon; J. Wright; K. Banks (Trainer).

1982–83   (*Back*) K. Banks (Trainer) L. Bradd; J. Rogers; G. Barrow; R. Tunks; C. Methven; P. Houghton; A. Cribley; K. Langley; H. McNally; (*Front*) J. McMahon; D. Glenn; K. Sheldon; J. Butler; L. Lloyd (Manager); P. Williams; E. O'Keefe and J. Weston; (*Seated*) Wayne Aspinall; G. Hatton; A. Phillips.

1983–84   (*Back*) S. Walsh; G. Barrow; P. Houghton; R. Tunks; K. Langley; P. Comstive; A. Cribley; J. Butler; D. Crompton (Youth Team Manager); (*Front*) K. Banks (Trainer); A. Bruce; D. Young; S. Taylor; H. McNally (Manager); C. Methven; P. Williams; D. Lowe; (*Kneeling*) Schofield; Deakin; Phillips; Wilkes; Tarpey; Barratt Mitchell; Gordon Warren Aspinal.

1984–85   (*Back*) S. Johnson; P. Comstive; K. Langley; C. Methven; B. Stewart; R. Tunks; S. Walsh; G. Barrow; M. Newell; A. Cribley; K. Banks (Trainer; *Front*) R. Redshaw; A. Bruce; J. Butler; T. Kelly; H. McNally (Manager); N. Bailey; D. Lowe; W. Aspinall; P. Cook.

1985–86   (*Back*) B. Knowles; P. Beesley; G. Bennett; P. Cook; B. Stewart; J. Butler; A. Cribley; T. Kelly; W. Aspinall; (*Middle*) R. Mathias (Coach); M. Newell; G. Barrow; S. Walsh; K. Langley; N. Bailey; R. Tunks (Coach); Bingham (Physio); (*Front*) D. Lowe; P. Jewell; C. Methven; B. Hamilton (Manager); D. Wilson; I. Griffiths; D. Wilke.

1986–87   (*Back*) R. Tunks (Assistant-manager); B. Knowles; D. Lowe; P. Beesley; J. Lowey; N. Adkins; M. Schofield; C. Thompson; J. Mitchell; P. Cook; (*Front*) D. Hamilton; G. Houston; J. Butler; R. Mathias (Manager); A. Cribley; I. Griffiths; P. Jewell.

1987–88   (*Back*) D. Philpotts (Coach); C. Thompson; M. Hilditch; B. Campbell; N. Adkins; A. Holden; P. Beesley; P. Cook; R. Tunks (Assistant Manager); (*Front*) A. Ainscow; J. Butler; P. Jewell; D. Hamilton; R. Mathias (Manager); A. Cribley; I. Griffiths; S. Storer; B. Knowles

1988–89   (*Back*) D. Philpotts (Coach); P. Beesley; A. Ainscow; P. Hughes; M. Hilditch; S. Storer; N. Adkins; S. McEwan; A. Holden; A. Cribley (Physio); (*Front*) P. Atherton; A. Tankard; D. Hamilton; A. Pilling; C. Russell; R. Mathias (Manager); D. Thompson; J. Butler; N. Rimmer; J. Crompton.

1989–90   (*Back*) Philpotts (Coach); D. Patterson; P. Beesley; J. Parkinson; P. Hughes; A. Johnson; A. Tankard; P. Atherton; T. Cavanagh (Coach); (*Middle*) D. Crompton; J. Crompton; A. Pilling; S. Senior; I. Banford; B. Hamilton (Manager); N. Adkins; N. Rimmer; D. Thompson; R. Woods; A. Cribley (Physio); (*Front*) S. Fallon; A. Ward; I. Griffiths; D. Andrews; D. Page; J. Carberry.

1990–91   (*Back*) D. Patterson; P. Daley; P. Hughes; D. Philpotts (Assistant Manager); N. Adkins; L. Rogerson; A. Johnson; (*Middle*) A. Cribley (Coach/Physio); D. Fairclough; A. Tankard; J. Parkinson; P. Atherton; D. Page; R. Woods; D. Crompton (Youth Team Coach); (*Front*) J. Masker; D. Eyre; A. Pilling; N. Rimmer; B. Hamilton (Manager); I. Griffiths; J. Carberry; R. Phoenix; J. Hunter.

1991–92   (*Back*) A. Pilling; N. Adkins; K. Langley; D. Patterson; P. Daley; G. Worthington; T. Pennock; G. Powell; (*Middle*) D. Philpotts (Coach); B. Griffiths; J. Carberry; D. Page; A. Tankard; A. Johnson; P. Atherton; J. Parkinson; S. Appleton; D. Crompton (Youth Team Coach); (*Front*) P. Gray; P. Jones; N. Rimmer; B. Hamilton (Manager); J. Smith; B. Edwardson; S. Nugent; A. Cribley (Physio).

1992–93 (*Back*) J. Roberston; J. Parkinson; A. Johnson; T. Pennock; N. Adkins; J. Doolan; S. Appleton; P. Daley; (*Middle*) D. Crompton (Youth Team Coach); N. Rimmer; A. Tankard; A. Pilling; G. Powell; G. Worthington; P. Jones; P. Gray; A. Cribley (Physio); (*Front*) B. Griffiths; S. Nugent; D. Philpotts; K. Langley; B. Hamilton (Manager); C. Sharratt; B. Roberts.

1993–94 (*Back*) M. Wright; C. Duffy; G. Strong; D. Patterson; P. Tait; J. Roberston; P. Gavin; I. Kilford; (*Middle*) D. Crompton (Youth Team Coach); H. Brooks; S. Farnworth; P. West; D. McKearney; N. Ogden; M. Statham; P. Rennie; S. Hollis; A. Cribley (Physio); (*Front*) N. Rimmer; A. Lyons; N. Morton; K. Swain (Manager); S. Gage (Chairman); J. Doolan; M. Carragher.

1994–95   (*Back*) I. Benjamin; J. Butler; N. Ogden; C. Lightfoot; S. Farnworth; D. Felgate; M. Haley; D. Miller; M. Leonard; J. Robertson; (*Middle*) J. Hinnigan (Coach); P. Tait; R. Martinez; I. Kilford; T. Kelly; P. West; J. Doolan; A. Lyons; M. Millett; D. Crompton (Youth Team Coach); A. Cribley (Physio) (*Front*) T. Black; J. Seba; N. Rimmer; G. Barrow (Manager); A. Farrell; I. Diaz; M. Carragher.

1995–96   (*Back*) A. Farrell; I. Kilford; I. Benjamin; N. Ogden; C. Greenall; M. Leonard; P. Tait; C. Lightfoot; J. Pender; (*Middle*) N. Rimmer; D. Miller; A. Lyons; A. Cribley (Physio); J. Deehan (Manager); J. Benson (Assistant Manager); T. Kelly; J. Doolan; W. Biggins; (*Front*) A. Black; J. Seba; R. Martinez; S. Farnworth; I. Diaz; K. Sharp; M. Carragher.

1996–97 (*Back*) A. Black; J. Seba; I. Kilford; P. Tait; G. Johnson; J. Pender; J. Butler; M. Carragher; K. Sharp; (*Middle*) S. Morgan; G. Jones; D. Crompton (Youth Team Coach); A. Cribley (Physio); C. Greenall; F. Lord; J. Benson; J. Doolan; W. Biggins; (*Front*) D. Lowe; R. Martinez; S. Farnworth; J. Deehan (Manager); L. Butler; G. Lancashire; I. Diaz.

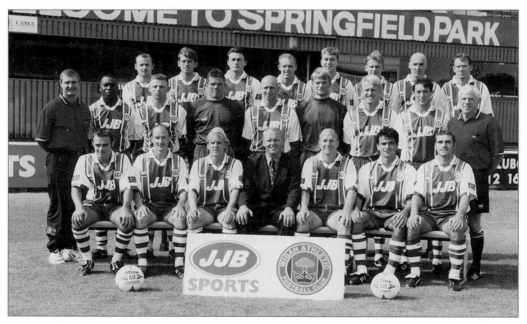

1997–98 (*Back*) A. Black; D. Lowe; C. Bishop; I. Kilford; P. McGibbon; N. Fitzhenry; G. Johnson; B. O'Connell; (*Middle*) S. Farnworth; S. Morgan; G. Jones; L. Butler; A. Saville; R. Carroll; P. Rogers; S. Green; J. Benson; (*Front*) P. Warne; D. Lee; K. Sharp; J. Deehan (Manager); C. Greenall; R. Martinez; G. Lancashire.

1998–99   (*Back*) K. Sharp; I. Kilford; L. Jenkinson; N. Fitzhenry; R. Carroll; G. Griffiths; P. McGibbon; P. Rogers; R. Martinez; (*Front*) L. Mills; G. Jones; D. Lee; C. Bradshaw; A. Porter; R. Mathias (Manager); J. Smeets; P. Warne; S. Barlow; N. Lloyd; S. Green; D. Lowe.

1999–2000   (*Back*) D. Stillie; M. O'Neill; S. Haworth; G. Griffiths; P. McGibbon; S. Balmer; R. Carroll; (*Middle*) A. Cribley; D. Crompton; I. Kilford; A. De Zeeuw; D. Lee; S. Green; A. Porter; N. Fitzhenry; J. Nicholls; K. Sharp; A. May; C. Greenall; B. O'Connell; (*Front*) D. Sheridan; S. Barlow; R. Martinez; J. Benson (Manager); A. McLaughlin; A. Liddell; C. Bradshaw.

7

Through the Seasons

Programme cover for the Latics first match in the Football League. A crowd of 5,674 saw Wigan play out a goalless draw at Hereford United. Despite playing with a five-man defence the Latics looked like an all-out attacking side. Peter Houghton rose to head home a Hinnigan free-kick but was judged to be offside. Jeff Wright almost snatched a last-minute winner with a long-range shot that Hughes in the Hereford goal just got his fingers to. The Wigan team that day was: J. Brown; T. Gore; J. Hinnigan; N. Davids; N. Ward; I. Gillibrand; F. Corrigan; J. Wright; P. Houghton; J. Wilkie; I. Purdie; (sub A.Crompton).

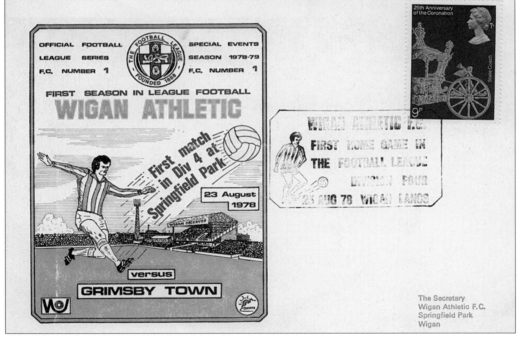

First Day cover to commemorate Wigan's first home game in the Football League against Grimsby Town, 23 August 1978. Unfortunately the 9,227 crowd that attended the game at Springfield Park saw Latics lose 3–0.

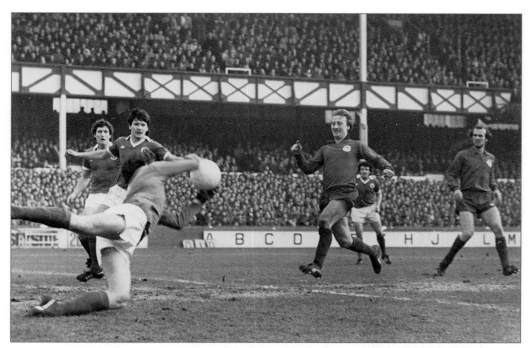

Everton goalkeeper Martin Hodge cuts out a cross intended for the on-rushing Derek Brownbill in the FA Cup fourth round tie, 26 January 1980. Also in support is centre-half Colin Methven.

Derek Brownbill in action again. The Latics' inside-forward leaves John Bailey in his tracks as he tries to connect with another cross from the left. Latics, who had beaten Chelsea in the previous round, went down 3-0 in front of a Goodison Park crowd of 51,863.

Latics players Tony Quinn, Mark Quinn and Peter Houghton watch as central defender Colin Methven and Larry Lloyd challenge for the ball in a 1–0 home defeat at the hands of Rochdale, March 1981.

Mark Wignall (No.7) and Peter Houghton challenge for the ball watched by Tony Quinn (far right) as the Latics try to get back on terms against a resolute Rochdale defence.

May 1982, Latics beat Mansfield Town 3–1 at Springfield Park to clinch promotion to the Third Division, courtesy of an Eamon O'Keefe hat-trick. Here Peter Houghton, who netted 15 goals that season, goes close with a header.

The Mansfield defence is again under pressure as Colin Methven and Les Bradd, who was the club's leading scorer with 19 goals, win the battle for aerial supremacy.

David Lowe scores Wigan's opening goal in the 2–0 win over Huddersfield Town in January 1983. He ended his first season with the club with six goals in 28 league games.

In April 1983, Latics played out a goalless home draw against Cardiff City. Against one of the few attacks by the Bluebirds, Latics' defenders Steve Walsh, Colin Methven, Jimmy Weston and Alex Cribley hold firm.

In the summer of 1983, Latics' manager Harry McNally took the squad training at Southport. Here Paul Beesley and Paul Jewell are put through their paces over the sand dunes.

Wigan winger David Lowe, who scored the game's only goal, bursts clear of the Newport County defence, April 1984, in a match watched by just 2,903.

Latics, who lost 1–0 at home to Bolton Wanderers on Boxing Day 1983, gained their revenge in the return match at Burnden Park, April 1984. Wigan won 1-0 courtesy of a Steve Johnson goal. Here Kevin Langley, watched by Graham Barrow (No. 8) goes close to netting a second goal, bringing out a fine save from Wanderers' Republic of Ireland international 'keeper, Jim McDonagh.

In December 1985, Latics beat Preston North End 2–0. The scorer of the second goal was David Lowe (not in picture) who converted a cross from John Butler, seen here celebrating with Paul Jewell and Kevin Langley.

The Famous Five – Alex Cribley, John Butler, Tony Kelly, Graham Barrow and Neil Bailey – showing where their allegiances lie.

Mike Newell scores Wigan's goal in their 1–1 draw against Brentford, January 1985, on a snow-covered Springfield Park.

The Latics' scorer almost added a second, sliding in to meet Kevin Langley's cross in the dying moments of the game but the Bees, who were beaten by Wigan in that season's Freight Rover Trophy Final, hung on for a point.

Paul Jewell challenges Chelsea 'keeper Eddie Niedzwiecki in the third round FA Cup tie at Stamford Bridge, January 1985.

Alex Bruce gets in a shot at goal. Other Latics players joining the attack are Kevin Langley and Mike Newell.

Mike Newell turns away in delight after scoring the Latics' opening goal in their 2–2 draw with Chelsea.

Latics players celebrate following Paul Jewell's equaliser. Unfortunately, despite taking the Blues back to Springfield Park, Wigan lost 5–0 in the replay with England international Kerry Dixon scoring four of the goals.

April 1985. Latics lost 1–0 at Bolton Wanderers. Here Graham Barrow challenges Wanderers' 'keeper Simon Farnworth, who later joined Wigan, playing in 151 games for the Latics.

A week after the defeat at Burnden Park, Latics entertained Burnley. Here David Lowe lets fly and the ball sails into the top corner of the net for Wigan's second goal in a 2–0 win.

David Lowe nets again, heading home Latics' second goal in a 2–0 defeat of Swansea City.

3 May 1985, the Latics beat Doncaster Rovers 5–2 with both Paul Jewell and Tony Kelly netting a brace apiece. Here Tony Kelly sends the Doncaster 'keeper the wrong way from the penalty spot for his second goal.

In the Freight Rover Trophy Northern Area Final, Latics visited Mansfield Town. Here Tony Kelly's shot is deflected into his own goal by the Stags' George Foster. The game ended all-square at 1–1 but Latics won through to the Wembley final with a 3–1 win in the penalty shoot-out.

October 1985, Latics beat Walsall 2–0 with goals from Kelly and Jewell. Here Mike Newell goes close to adding a third with a diving header.

John Butler, Roy Tunks and Neil Bailey decked out in Wigan scarfs before the Plymouth Argyle game, April 1986. Latics won 3–0 and promotion was in the air. Unfortunately, Derby County pipped the Latics by one point for the final promotion place.

The game against Plymouth Argyle was chosen to inaugurate the Friends of Football scheme. Sadly, ten Plymouth fans were charged with public order offences and another with assaulting a policeman after trouble flared just before the kick-off. Thirteen were ejected from Springfield Park after fighting broke out between fans. The FA's new Friends of Football scheme was launched in an attempt to bring back the families and pure fans. The attendance of 9,485, which included 5,000 who had travelled up from Devon, was Wigan's largest attendance of the season.

A minute's silence is held in the home match against Reading following the tragic fire at Bradford City's Valley Parade ground.

Latics celebrate after beating Wolverhampton Wanderers 5–3 in the final home game of the 1985–6 season. A few faces were to leave over the summer months. Bryan Hamilton went to manage Leicester City, taking Steve Walsh with him, while Graham Barrow and Billy Stewart joined Chester City and Colin Methven went to Blackpool.

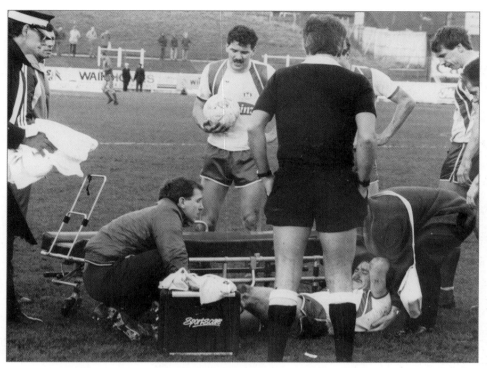

John Butler in pain following his injury in the 4–3 defeat of Bristol Rovers in October 1986.

Paul Jewell gets a shot on goal in Latics' 3–1 win over Gillingham in November 1986. Also in shot are Bobby Campbell, who netted two of Wigan's goals and Chris Thompson. Latics' other scorer was David Lowe.

Chester City players appeal that the ball has gone out of play but the referee waved play on and Bobby Campbell scored Latics' first goal in a 2–2 draw. Wigan's other scorer was Chris Thompson.

A heated moment during Wigan's fourth round FA Cup tie against Norwich City as the referee and Latics players try to separate Bobby Campbell and Canaries' 'keeper Bryn Gunn.

Norwich defenders Terry Phelan and Steve Bruce close in on Latics' striker Chris Thompson as he heads for goal. Also in the picture is Wigan's Northern Ireland international centre-forward Bobby Campbell.

A crowd of 8,095 saw the Latics beat First Division Norwich City 1–0. Here Paul Jewell scores the game's only goal.

Latics players celebrate after beating Hull City 3–0 to reach the sixth round of the FA Cup for the first time in their history.

The Latics goalscorers in the fifth round defeat of the Tigers were Bobby Campbell, Chris Thompson and Paul Jewell.

A policeman on a white horse helps to control Leeds United fans in the 12,497 crowd at Springfield Park. Though the Yorkshire club won the sixth round tie 2–0 they couldn't have complained if the Latics had won, as they displayed all the skill and poise that got them within striking distance of Wembley. However, in a game where the howling wind had the biggest say of all, Latics couldn't turn their superiority into goals.

Mark Hilditch scores the game's only goal as Latics beat Bury 1–0, April 1987.

The Wigan team take the applause from the crowd after beating York City 3–2 in the final home game of the 1986–7 season. Latics later drew 0–0 at Middlesbrough and won 3–2 at Brentford to qualify for the play-offs.

No, it's not Ladysmith Black Mambazo, it's the Wigan Athletic team of 1986–7 recording the 'hit' single 'Come on you Latics'.

The 1986–7 season saw the introduction of the play-offs, and after finishing fourth in Division Three, Latics faced Swindon Town who finished one place and two points ahead of the Springfield Park club. In the first leg at home, Wigan raced into a 2–0 lead but dreadful defending allowed the Robins to score three times in the final 18 minutes. Pictured in the return leg at the County Ground is Ian Griffiths.

Midfield terrier David Hamilton encounters the wrath of the referee as Wigan push forward in search of the goal that would level the aggregate scores.

Paul Beesley, seen here in a tussle with Swindon's Chris Kamara. Though the luckless Latics hit the woodwork, the game ended goalless and the Wiltshire club went through to the final.

Action from the club's opening game of the 1987–8 season against Gillingham. Paul Jewell's shot skims the bar. The other Latics players in the thick of the action are Bobby Campbell and Chris Thompson.

David Hamilton, who joined the club from Cardiff City and went on to score eight goals in 117 League and Cup games, gets in a shot on target in the 1–1 draw with Gillingham.

Latics' Northern Ireland international centre-forward Bobby Campbell scores the club's second goal in a League Cup first round first leg tie against Bolton Wanderers. Though the Trotters won 3–2, Campbell netted a magnificent hat-trick in the return match at Burnden Park to give Wigan a 5–4 aggregate victory.

Wigan Athletic's speedy winger Stuart Storer 'skins' the Doncaster Rovers' full-back in a 2–1 win. Latics' goals were scored by Bobby Campbell and Andy Ainscow.

John Butler (No. 2) celebrates his goal in the 1–1 draw with York City in October 1987. Also joining in the celebrations are Paul Beesley (No. 6) and Stuart Storer.

Despite Bobby Campbell, seen here scoring his ninth goal of the 1987–8 season in only his twelfth appearance, the Latics, watched by just 2,808 fans, crashed 3–1 to Fulham.

After beating Altrincham in the first round of the FA Cup, the Latics entertained Wolverhampton Wanderers in round two. Here Paul Cook, later to play for the Molineux club, puts their defence under pressure.

Wolves, who have a great FA Cup tradition, beat the Latics 3–1 with Mark Hilditch scoring the Wigan goal. However, they knew they had been in a game. Here David Hamilton is in the thick of the action.

New Year's Day 1988, two goals from Mark Hilditch helped the Latics beat Preston North End 2–0. Both of his goals were laid on by Paul Cook who sees his shot flash just wide.

Over the weekend of 16–17 April 1988, the Latics were involved in the Mercantile Credit Festival at Wembley. Here Bobby Campbell goes close in the match against Sunderland but the game ended goalless before Latics won 2–1 on penalties. In the quarter-finals, Chris Thompson scored Wigan's goal in a 1–1 draw with Sheffield Wednesday though Latics lost 3–2 on penalties when Bobby Campbell missed his attempt.

Latics are beaten 2–1 at home by Chesterfield. Paul Jewell's twenty-yard drive is well saved by the Spireites' 'keeper as Wigan go in search of an equaliser.

Bobby Campbell, who missed part of the 1987–8 season through injury, nets the Latics goal in a 1–1 draw against Brentford.

Substitute Chris Thompson, who had replaced the injured Stan McEwan, misses from the penalty spot in the final game of the 1987–8 season against Grimsby Town. The Mariners, who were completely outplayed, won 1–0.

Two goals from Craig Russell and another seen here from Mark Hilditch help Wigan beat Reading 3–0 in the second home game of the 1988–9 campaign.

A penalty from Neill Rimmer and a spectacular strike from John Butler give Wigan a 2–1 victory over Blackpool. Here the Seasiders' centre-half, former Wigan star Colin Methven, is beaten to the ball by Mark Hilditch.

Steve Senior, who scored four goals in 120 games for the Latics, nets in the 2–1 home defeat by Sheffield United, during March 1989.

Craig Ramage, who joined the Latics on loan from Derby County, netted Wigan's goal in a 1–0 defeat of Cardiff City. Here Latics' Mark Hilditch and Dave Thompson battle for the ball in the heart of the Bluebirds' defence.

When the Welsh club visited Springfield Park early the following season they came away with a point in a 1–1 draw. But Latics nearly won it in the dying moments as Dave Thompson's header grazed the crossbar.

Latics' central defensive pairing of Peter Atherton and Paul Beesley snuff out the threat of Blackpool's Dave Bamber in the opening game of the 1989-90 season as Latics played out a goalless draw in the Bloomfield Road encounter.

Celebrations all round after Phil Daley had given Latics the lead against Bournemouth. Wigan went on to win 2–0 with Darren Patterson netting the club's second goal.

Bryan Griffiths nets the Latics' last goal in a 4–1 home win over Southend United in October 1990. It was the winger's second goal of the game having earlier scored from the penalty spot.

During the 1990–1 season, Latics drew 1–1 at First Division Coventry City in a third round League Cup tie before losing 1–0 to the Sky Blues in the Springfield Park replay. Here Ray Woods, who later joined the Highfield Road club, gets in a cross during the second meeting between the sides.

Gary Worthington heads the Wigan goal in a 1–1 home draw against Bolton Wanderers. The beaten Bolton 'keeper is Dave Felgate who appeared in a handful of games for Wigan during the 1995–6 season.

Gary Powell, who scored 20 goals in 97 League and Cup games for the Latics, goes close in the 2–2 draw with Hartlepool United, September 1992. The Wigan scorers were Alan Johnson and Chris Makin, who was on loan from Oldham Athletic.

Gary Powell celebrates his goal with Steve Cooper, making his Latics debut, and Kevin Langley. Keith Branagan is the Bolton 'keeper, he was instrumental in the Wanderers winning this 1992 Boxing Day encounter 2–1.

Goals from Shaun Garnett and Gary Powell gave Wigan a 2–1 win at Leyton Orient, March 1993. Latics' defender Peter Skipper, seen here helping out in attack, had an outstanding game.

Latics lost seven of their last eight matches in 1992–3 and not surprisingly were relegated. Action here from Wigan's 4–0 home defeat at the hands of Port Vale.

In the summer of 1993, Wigan played host to Premier League Aston Villa in a pre-season friendly. Latics 'keeper Simon Farnworth makes a great save in a match the Villans won 1–0.

2 October 1993, the Latics beat Chester City 6–3. Here Alan Johnson, the scorer of the club's first goal, is carried off after damaging his knee.

Neil Morton gets in a header in the match against Lincoln City in March 1994 but to no avail. The Imps won 1–0.

Mark Leonard wins the ball to set up David Miller, the scorer of the Wigan goal in a 1–1 home draw against Torquay United.

A good end to the 1994–5 season as the Latics beat Doncaster Rovers 3–2. Here Andy Lyons who scored two of Wigan's goals (one from the penalty spot) celebrates with John Doolan.

Long-serving Neill Rimmer scores Wigan's third goal in the 3–1 defeat of Exeter City, April 1995.

The summer of 1995 saw the Latics astound the football world with the signings of three Spaniards: Isidro Diaz, Roberto Martinez and Jesus Seba. The three of them made their Football League debut at Gillingham on the opening day of the 1995–6 season with Martinez scoring the Wigan goal in a 1–1 draw.

Action from away matches against Preston North End. Latics lost this encounter towards the end of the 1994–5 season 1–0. Here Ian Kilford bursts through the North End defence but sadly nothing came of it.

Andy Mutch, who scored Latics' goal in a 1–1 draw at Deepdale, causes the Lilywhites defence problems.

The Three Amigos – the first Spaniards to play in the FA Cup. Here Jesus Seba, Roberto Martinez and Isidro Diaz hold the trophy prior to the first round match against Runcorn which the Latics drew 1–1 courtesy of a Roberto Martinez goal.

Latics lost 2–1 at home to Bury at the start of the 1995–6 season. Ian Kilford is seen scoring the Wigan goal from a very acute angle.

Isidro Diaz's shot is blocked by a Lincoln City defender. The Latics goal in this 1–1 draw against the Sincil Bank club was scored by another Spaniard, Roberto Martinez.

After beating non-League clubs Runcorn and Barrow, Latics lost 1–0 at Walsall in the third round of the FA Cup, January 1996. Leonard, Diaz and Greenall are the Latics players pressing for an equaliser.

Colin Greenall and Scott Green join the Latics attack against Wycombe Wanderers on the opening day of the 1996–7 season. Wigan won 5–2 with Brendan O'Connell scoring a hat-trick.

Wigan won the Third Division Championship in 1996–7. Captain Colin Greenall and manager John Deehan hold aloft the trophy.

Chairman Dave Whelan holds the Third Division Championship trophy.

Simon Haworth, seen here with Chief Executive and Secretary Brenda Spencer and Chairman Dave Whelan, receives his Welsh international cap from Rugby League legend, Billy Boston.

After the last league game at Springfield Park, the players celebrate reaching the play-offs following their 3–1 defeat of Chesterfield.

Further celebrations after the Chesterfield game. Sadly, Latics lost 2–1 on aggregate to Manchester City in the play-off semi-final.

The Latics line-up at Wembley for the 2000 play-off final against Gillingham. Two late goals denied John Benson's brave 10-men Wigan. Substitute Andy Thompson headed home the winner with only two minutes to go following Steve Butler's header minutes earlier. Stuart Barlow's penalty looked to have won it for the Latics after they had gone behind to a Pat McGibbon own goal. Simon Haworth replied with a glorious goal before Kevin Sharp was sent off.

Arjan De Zeeuw who joined the Latics from Barnsley in the summer of 1999 gets in a tackle during the play-off final against Gillingham.

Pat McGibbon wins the aerial duel with a Gillingham forward whilst Neil Redfern and Arjan De Zeeuw look on.

Stuart Barlow scores from the penalty spot to put Wigan 2–1 up. They were just seven minutes away from promotion to the First Division!

APPENDICES

HONOURS

Football League

Division Three Champions	1996–7
Division Four Promoted	1981–2

FA Cup

Best Season Sixth Round	1986–7

League Cup

Best Season Fourth Round	1981–2
Freight Rover Trophy Winners	1984–5
Autowindscreen Shield Winners	1998–9

LONGEST LEAGUE RUNS

Of undefeated matches	25	(8 May 1999 – 3 January 2000)
Of undefeated home matches	25	(8 April 1985 – 11 March 1986)
Of league wins	6	(26 December 1987–23 January 1988)
Of league defeats	7	(6 April 1993 – 4 May 1993)
League games without a win	14	(9 May 1989 – 17 October 1989)
Of undefeated away matches	19	(14 August 1999 – 1 April 2000)
Without a home win	6	(16 May 1989 – 14 October 1989)
Without an away win	15	(30 January 1988 – 22 October 1988)
Of home wins	8	(30 September 1978 – 3 February 1979)
Of away wins	4	(29 August 1987 – 18 September 1987)

CLUB RECORDS

Most home wins in a season	17	1981–2 1985–6 1996–7
Most home draws in a season	8	1987–8
Most home defeats in a season	11	1992–3
Most home goals in a season	54	1985–6
Most home goals conceded in a season	34	1992–3
Least home wins in a season	6	1992–3 1993–4
Least home draws in a season	3	1990–1 1995–6 1996–7 1999–00
Least home defeats in a season	1	1981–2
Least home goals scored in a season	26	1983–4 1992–3
Least home goals conceded in a season	16	1980–1
Most away wins in a season	10	1986–7
Most away draws in a season	14	1999-00
Most away goals scored in a season	36	1986–7
Most away goals conceded in a season	43	1991–2
Least away wins in a season	3	1984–5 1989–90
Least away draws in a season	4	1987–8 1994–5
Least away defeats in season	2	1999-00
Least away goals scored in a season	17	1992–3
Least away goals conceded in a season	24	1978–9 1999-00
Most wins in a season	26	1981–2 1996–7
Most draws in a season	17	1999-00
Most defeats in a season	25	1992–3
Most goals scored in a season	84	1996–7
Most goals conceded in a season	72	1992–3
Least wins in a season	10	1992–3
Least draws in a season	9	1982–3 1990–1 1996–7
Least defeats in a season	7	1981–2 1999-00
Least goals scored in a season	43	1992–3
Least goals conceded in a season	38	1999–00

FOOTBALL LEAGUE FINAL POSITIONS 1978–9 to 1999–2000

Season	P.	W	D.	L.	F.	A.	W.	D.	L.	F.	A.	Pts	Position
					DIVISION FOUR								
1978–9	46	14	5	4	40	24	7	8	8	23	24	55	6th
1979–80	46	13	5	5	42	26	8	8	7	34	35	55	6th
1980–1	46	13	4	6	29	16	5	7	11	22	39	47	11th
1981–2	46	17	5	1	47	18	9	8	6	33	28	91	3rd
					DIVISION THREE								
1982–3	46	10	4	9	35	33	5	5	13	25	39	54	18th
1983–4	46	11	5	7	26	18	5	8	10	20	38	61	15th
1984–5	46	12	6	5	36	22	3	8	12	24	42	59	16th
1985–6	46	17	4	2	54	17	6	10	7	28	31	86	4th
1986–7	46	15	5	3	47	25	10	5	8	36	34	85	4th
1987–8	46	11	8	4	36	23	9	4	10	34	38	72	7th
1988–9	46	9	5	9	28	22	5	9	9	27	31	56	17th
1989-90	46	10	6	7	29	22	3	8	12	19	42	53	18th
1990–1	46	14	3	6	40	20	6	6	11	31	34	69	10th
1991–2	46	11	6	6	33	21	4	8	11	25	43	59	15th
					DIVISION TWO (Formerly Div 3)								
1992–3	46	6	6	11	26	34	4	5	14	17	38	41	23rd
					DIVISION THREE								
1993–4	42	6	7	8	33	33	5	5	11	18	37	45	19th
1994–5	42	7	6	8	28	30	7	4	10	25	30	52	14th
1995–6	46	15	3	5	36	21	5	7	11	26	35	70	10th
1996–7	46	17	3	3	53	21	9	6	8	31	30	87	1st
					DIVISION TWO								
1997–8	46	12	5	6	41	31	5	6	12	23	35	62	11th
1998–9	46	14	5	4	44	17	8	5	10	31	31	76	6th
1999–00	46	15	3	5	37	14	7	14	2	35	24	83	4th

ATTENDANCES
Average and Highest Football League Attendances

	Average	Highest	
1978–9	6,701	9,427 v	Barnsley
1979–80	5,902	8,198 v	Portsmouth
1980–1	4,208	6,029 v	Rochdale
1981–2	5,839	9,021 v	Bournemouth
1982–3	4,439	7,724 v	Huddersfield Town
1983–4	3,898	10,045 v	Bolton Wanderers
1984–5	3,264	8,871 v	Bolton Wanderers
1985–6	4,310	9,485 v	Plymouth Argyle
1986–7	3,396	6,857 v	Blackpool
1987–8	3,737	6,949 v	Sunderland
1988–9	3,134	5,671 v	Preston North End
1989–90	2,772	6,850 v	Bolton Wanderers
1990–1	2,881	4,728 v	Preston North End
1991–2	2,847	5,956 v	Birmingham City
1992–3	2,593	5,408 v	Bolton Wanderers
1993–4	1,897	3,741 v	Preston North End
1994–5	1,748	3,618 v	Preston North End
1995–6	2,856	5,567 v	Preston North End
1996–7	3,899	7,106 v	Mansfield Town
1997–8	3,968	5,649 v	Preston North End
1998–9	4,250	6,700 v	Manchester City
1999–00	6,824	15,593 v	Preston North End

APPEARANCES

		F. Lg.	FA Cup	Lg. Cup	Total
1.	Kevin Langley	307(10)	27(1)	21	355(11)
2.	Colin Methven	295(1)	23	21	339(1)
3.	John Butler	291(11)	24(1)	18(1)	333(13)
4.	Alex Cribley	268(3)	24	20(1)	312(4)
5.	David Lowe	264(32)	20(3)	15	299(35)
6.	Roy Tunks	245	21	18	284
7.	Allen Tankard	205(4)	13	15	233(4)
8.	Neill Rimmer	184(6)	10	14	208(6)
9.	Peter Houghton	169(16)	14	19	204(17)
10.	Bryan Griffiths	176(13)	11(2)	12(2)	199(17)
11.	Graham Barrow	173(6)	13	11	197(6)

12.	Alan Johnson	163(17)	14(2)	7(2)	184(21)
13.	Nigel Adkins	155	9	15	179
14.	Colin Greenall	162	10	5(1)	177(1)
15.	Paul Beesley	153(2)	6	13	172(2)
16.	Phil Daley	152(9)	10(1)	9	171(10)
17.	Ian Kilford	145(29)	12(2)	11(1)	168(32)
18.	Peter Atherton	145(4)	7	8	160(4)
19.	Jeff Wright	139(4)	10	10	159(4)
20.	Barry Knowles	124(3)	15	11	150(3)

GOALS

		F. Lg.	FA Cup	Lg. Cup	Total
1.	David Lowe	66	7	0	73
2.	Peter Houghton	62	3	3	68
3.	Bryan Griffiths	44	6	2	52
4.	Stuart Barlow	41	3	3	47
5.	Graeme Jones	44	1	1	46
6.	Phil Daley	40	0	1	41
7.	Paul Jewell	35	5	0	40
8.	Graham Barrow	36	0	3	39
9.	Bobby Campbell	27	5	4	36
10.	Mike Newell	25	6	1	32
11.	Simon Haworth	24	4	3	31
12=	Mark Hilditch	26	2	1	29
	Colin Methven	21	5	3	29
14.	Andy Lyons	27	0	1	28
15.	Les Bradd	25	0	2	27
16.	Eamon O'Keefe	25	0	1	26
17=	Warren Aspinall	22	2	0	24
	Gary Worthington	20	1	3	24
19.	Steve Johnson	18	1	3	22
20=	Andy Pilling	20	1	0	21
	Mick Quinn	19	1	1	21

MANAGERS' FOOTBALL LEAGUE RECORDS

	P.	W.	D.	L.	F.	A.
Ian McNeill	126	55	33	38	173	151
Larry Lloyd	94	44	21	29	148	121
Harry McNally	80	25	25	30	83	102
Bryan Hamilton	229	85	63	81	314	299
Ray Mathias	184	81	46	57	283	221
Dave Philpotts	13	2	1	10	11	27
Kenny Swain	42	11	12	19	51	70
Graham Barrow	53	17	14	22	66	77
John Deehan	127	60	26	41	197	156
John Benson	46	22	17	7	72	38

EVER-PRESENTS and LEADING LEAGUE GOALSCORERS

Ever-Presents		*Leading Goalscorers*
Tommy Gore; Ian Purdie; Jeff Wright	1978–9	Peter Houghton 13
Dave Fretwell; Tommy Gore Jeff Wright	1979–80	Peter Houghton 15
Colin Methven	1980–1	Mick Quinn 14
Colin Methven	1981–2	Les Bradd 19
Roy Tunks	1982–3	Eamon O'Keefe 15
	1983–4	Steve Taylor 7
	1984–5	Steve Johnson 11
David Lowe	1985–6	Warren Aspinall 21
	1986–7	David Lowe 17
	1987–8	Bobby Campbell 11
	1988–9	Bryan Griffiths 8
	1989–90	Mark Hilditch 8
Peter Atherton	1990–1	Bryan Griffiths 12
Allen Tankard		Don Page 12
Nigel Adkins	1991–2	Gary Worthington 15
	1992–3	Bryan Griffiths 13
Simon Farnworth	1993–4	Andy Lyons 11
	1994–5	Andy Lyons 15
	1995–6	Roberto Martinez 9
Lee Butler; Colin Greenall	1996–7	Graeme Jones 31
	1997–8	David Lowe 16
	1998–9	Stuart Barlow 19
	1999–00	Stuart Barlow 22

HAT-TRICK HEROES

Player	Date	Comp	Opponents	Score
Peter Houghton	13.04.1979	F.Lg.	Port Vale	5-3
David Shearer	26.03.1980	F.Lg.	Port Vale	3–1
Mick Quinn	08.10.1980	F.Lg.	Doncaster Rovers	3–0
Peter Houghton	29.03.1981	F.Lg.	Tranmere Rovers	3–2
Les Bradd	12.03.1982	F.Lg.	Scunthorpe United	7–2
Eamon O'Keefe	10.04.1982	F.Lg.	Crewe Alexandra	3–0
Eamon O'Keefe	08.05.1982	F.Lg.	Mansfield Town	3–1
Peter Houghton	28.09.1982	F.Lg.	Doncaster Rovers	6–3
Eamon O'Keefe	09.10.1982	F.Lg.	Southend United	4–0
Mike Newell	14.09.1985	F.Lg.	Darlington	5–1
Warren Aspinall	03.05.1986	F.Lg.	Wolves	5–3
Chris Thompson	16.09.1986	F.Lg.	Walsall	5–1
David Lowe	21.12.1986	F.Lg.	Mansfield Town	5–1
Bobby Campbell	25.08.1987	Lg. Cup	Bolton Wanderers	3–1
Paul Jewell	01.03.1988	F.Lg.	Aldershot	4–0
Mark Hilditch	01.01.1990	F.Lg.	Mansfield Town	4–0
Dave Thompson	20.03.1990	F.Lg.	Shrewsbury Town	3–1
Don Page	06.11.1990	Ley Daf	Chester City	4–0
Ray Woods	23.02.1993	Autoglass	Huddersfield Town	5–2
Andy Lyons	19.11.1994	F.Lg.	Darlington	4–1
Graeme Jones	31.08.1996	F.Lg.	Chester City	4–2
Graham Lancashire	03.09.1996	Lg. Cup	Preston North End	4–4
Graeme Jones	19.10.1996	F.Lg.	Torquay United	3–2
Graeme Jones	22.02.1997	F.Lg.	Leyton Orient	5–1
Graeme Jones	25.02.1997	F.Lg.	Darlington	3–2
Brendan O'Connell	09.08.1997	F.Lg.	Wycombe Wanderers	5–2
Stuart Barlow	28.08.1999	F.Lg.	Preston North End	4–1

FOOTBALL LEAGUE OPPOSITION

Wigan Athletic have played 74 clubs in the Football League (1978–9 to 1999–00). Below is the Latics' record against each club.

	P.	W.	D.	L.	F.	A.	W.	D.	L.	F.	A.
Aldershot	12	6	0	0	13	4	2	0	4	7	9
Barnet	6	2	0	1	4	2	0	2	1	2	7
Barnsley	2	0	1	0	2	2	0	1	0	0	0
Birmingham City	6	2	1	0	5	1	0	3	0	3	3
Blackpool	20	7	3	0	23	7	3	4	3	11	14
Bolton Wanderers	18	4	2	3	10	10	3	2	4	11	12
Bournemouth	30	8	2	5	19	13	4	4	7	14	19
Bradford City	20	6	0	4	19	12	1	4	5	16	24
Brentford	22	7	4	0	20	7	5	1	5	14	16
Brighton & H.A.	6	1	1	1	5	5	0	0	3	0	3
Bristol City	16	2	3	3	11	13	1	1	6	3	15
Bristol Rovers	22	8	1	2	21	11	1	2	8	11	30
Burnley	12	3	3	0	10	3	3	2	1	6	5
Bury	26	8	1	4	16	13	3	7	3	23	22
Cambridge United	10	1	3	1	8	7	1	3	1	7	7
Cardiff City	14	4	2	1	9	3	1	3	3	8	12
Carlisle United	10	2	0	3	3	6	2	0	3	6	6
Chester City	20	8	1	1	24	11	3	3	4	8	9
Chesterfield	20	5	2	3	17	12	2	5	3	11	13
Colchester Utd	14	3	1	3	8	6	2	1	4	11	16
Crewe Alex	14	5	2	0	10	2	2	1	4	8	12
Darlington	22	7	1	3	28	13	2	4	5	12	17
Derby County	4	2	0	0	4	1	0	1	1	2	3
Doncaster Rovers	24	7	3	2	21	11	3	4	5	22	26
Exeter City	16	6	1	1	16	5	4	2	2	12	6
Fulham	24	5	3	4	15	13	1	4	7	9	21
Gillingham	26	6	3	4	24	19	3	3	7	10	20
Grimsby Town	8	1	0	3	2	6	1	0	3	7	9
Halifax Town	8	4	0	0	10	2	2	2	0	3	1
Hartlepool Utd	18	3	5	1	13	12	1	4	4	10	14
Hereford United	16	3	4	1	13	9	1	3	4	7	15
Huddersfield T.	16	3	1	4	9	11	0	3	5	5	15
Hull City	12	2	2	2	7	6	1	3	2	5	6
Leyton Orient	18	4	1	4	15	10	2	5	2	8	10
Lincoln City	22	7	1	3	15	10	4	1	6	9	14
Luton Town	6	1	1	1	3	4	1	2	0	6	2
Macclesfield	2	1	0	0	2	0	1	0	0	1	0

Manchester City	2	0	0	1	0	1	0	0	1	0	1
Mansfield Town	24	8	1	3	24	15	6	1	5	19	16
Middlesborough	2	0	0	1	0	2	0	1	0	0	0
Millwall	12	1	3	2	4	4	0	2	4	6	15
Newport County	14	1	2	4	5	8	2	1	4	13	16
Northampton Town	26	6	5	2	19	12	4	7	2	18	14
Notts County	14	5	1	1	12	4	2	3	2	9	9
Oldham Athletic	6	2	0	1	3	1	1	0	2	5	7
Oxford United	6	1	0	2	2	3	1	1	1	2	3
Peterborough U.	8	3	1	0	11	2	2	2	0	5	1
Plymouth Argyle	14	3	2	2	9	5	1	1	5	6	11
Portsmouth	6	1	0	2	3	3	0	2	1	1	2
Port Vale	18	7	0	2	18	11	1	4	4	9	14
Preston N.E.	30	5	4	6	19	18	4	5	6	22	27
Reading	22	7	4	0	21	7	4	0	7	11	17
Rochdale	16	3	2	11	4	4	1	3	1	0	9
Rotherham Utd	16	6	1	1	14	7	3	3	2	13	16
Scarborough	8	2	1	1	11	4	1	1	2	3	7
Scunthorpe Utd	20	7	2	1	18	6	5	2	3	22	17
Sheffield Utd	8	2	0	2	7	5	0	1	3	3	7
Shrewsbury Town	8	0	3	1	5	8	1	2	1	3	2
Southend United	12	4	0	2	13	5	2	0	4	6	8
Stockport County	12	4	0	2	11	8	4	1	1	8	7
Stoke City	10	2	1	2	9	6	0	1	4	3	10
Sunderland	2	0	1	0	2	2	0	0	1	1	4
Swansea City	16	5	0	3	18	11	3	1	4	13	14
Swindon Town	2	1	0	0	3	2	0	0	1	1	3
Torquay Utd	18	5	2	2	14	10	2	6	1	9	7
Tranmere Rovers	10	0	3	2	2	55	2	2	1	7	6
Walsall	24	8	1	3	25	10	4	4	4	14	18
Watford	2	1	0	0	3	2	0	0	1	1	2
West Brom Alb	4	1	0	1	1	1	0	1	1	2	6
Wimbledon	6	2	0	1	5	4	0	1	2	3	5
Wolverhampton W.	4	1	1	0	6	4	0	1	1	3	4
Wrexham	8	2	1	1	7	5	1	3	0	6	4
Wycombe Wanderers	8	2	2	0	8	4	3	0	1	6	3
York City	20	5	3	2	20	14	3	3	4	12	16

ACKNOWLEDGEMENTS

I would like to express my thanks to the following individuals and institutions who helped me in the compilation of this book.

Of great importance were Stuart Hayton (Wigan Athletic's assistant secretary) and Elaine Mitchinson who very kindly allowed me access to a wealth of photographic material possessed by the club including action shots of the recent play-off final taken by Brian Sherratt. A number of photographs have been loaned by the *Wigan Observer* and the *Lancashire Evening Post* whilst some are from my own personal collection.

Thanks also to my close friend and local referee Frank Atkins who put me in touch with Latics fans Darren Hesketh (who loaned me his collection of Wigan Athletic programmes and memorabilia) and James Kinane and his son Shaun. Also thanks to Colin Walls and his son Simon, both ardent Latics supporters.

It was hoped that the publication of this book would coincide with the Latics winning promotion to the First Division. Sadly, that is not the case but hopefully, twelve months from now. . . .